Theology of the People

The Pastoral and Theological Roots of POPE FRANCIS

JUAN CARLOS SCANNONE, SJ

Paulist Press
New York / Mahwah, NJ

Cover image vector design by saicle/Shutterstock.com
Cover and book design by Lynn Else

Originally published as *La Théologie du peuple. Racines théologiques du pape François* copyright © 2017 by Éditions Lessius. Grateful acknowledgment is made for use of previously published material, copyright © 2017 by *La Civiltà Cattolica,* and to SAGE for the English translation of chapter 1, which appeared in the February 2016 issue of *Theological Studies.*

Translated from the original Spanish by Kris Fankhouser and Carmen Fernandez-Aguinaco

Library of Congress Cataloging-in-Publication Data
Names: Scannone, Juan Carlos, author.
Title: Theology of the people : the pastoral and theological roots of Pope Francis / Juan Carlos Scannone, SJ.
Other titles: Théologie du people. English
Description: New York / Mahwah, NJ : Paulist Press, [2021] | "Originally published as *La Théologie du people. Racines théologiques du pape François* © 2017 by Éditions Lessius." | Includes bibliographical references. | Summary: "*Theology of the People* presents and studies the influence of liberation theology on Jorge Mario Bergoglio, his former teacher, who lived with him for many years and who is cited in Pope Francis's first encyclical, *Laudato Sí'*—Provided by publisher.
Identifiers: LCCN 2020037171 (print) | LCCN 2020037172 (ebook) | ISBN 9780809154753 (paperback) | ISBN 9781587688706 (ebook)
Subjects: LCSH: Francis, Pope, 1936- | Liberation theology.
Classification: LCC BX1378.7 .S29613 2021 (print) | LCC BX1378.7 (ebook) | DDC 230/.2—dc23
LC record available at https://lccn.loc.gov/2020037171
LC ebook record available at https://lccn.loc.gov/2020037172

ISBN 978-0-8091-5475-3 (paperback)
ISBN 978-1-58768-870-6 (e-book)

Published by Paulist Press
997 Macarthur Boulevard
Mahwah, New Jersey 07430
www.paulistpress.com

Printed and bound in the
United States of America

CONTENTS

Foreword v
Peter Casarella
Preface xiii
Abbreviations xvii
Editor's Note xviii

PART I: HISTORICAL APPROACH 1

1. The Argentinian Theology of the People and of Culture 3
2. Lucio Gera: A Theologian of the People and *from* the People 22

PART II: TOWARD AN INCULTURATED THEOLOGY 35

3. "People" and "Popular" in Social Reality, Ministry, and Theological Reflection 41
4. Popular Wisdom and Inculturated Theology 61
5. The Power of Popular Wisdom in the Cultural Ethos: A Theological Alternative 80
6. Popular Religiosity, Popular Wisdom, and Popular Theology.. 110

PART III: THEOLOGICAL-PASTORAL APPROACHES OF POPE FRANCIS 123

7. The Unfinished Agenda of Vatican II: *Gaudium et Spes* and Pope Francis 125

Contents

8. *Evangelii Gaudium* and the Theology of the People 144
9. Inculturation in *Evangelii Gaudium* 155
10. The Communitarian Subject of Popular Spirituality and Mysticism 168
11. Pope Francis's Four Principles for Building a People 184

Notes 203

FOREWORD

The arrival of an Argentine pope on the morning of September 23, 2015, on the South Lawn of the White House had some precedent. Francis was not the first pope to visit the White House or to speak from the South Lawn. Pope John Paul II visited President Jimmy Carter on the South Lawn in 1979, and Pope Benedict XVI's arrival in 2008 was accompanied by the soprano Kathleen Battle. But this visit was very different. Francis's visit came in the wake of a new Cuban policy that he had helped to make possible. In fact, it was no accident that he had arrived in the United States the previous afternoon from Cuba. The pope's address to Congress on the following day would be the first of its kind. At the White House he set the tone for the entire visit with these words:

> I am deeply grateful for your welcome in the name of all Americans. As the son of an immigrant family, I am happy to be a guest in this country, which was largely built by such families. I look forward to these days of encounter and dialogue, in which I hope to listen to, and share, many of the hopes and dreams of the American people.[1]

The pope did *not* introduce himself as a global ambassador. Instead he arrived in Washington, DC, with his own story of hailing from the humble ranks of immigrants. Political repression rather than economic scarcity seemed to have motivated the move of the Bergoglios from Northern Italy to the Southern Cone of Latin America. The pope's father, Mario Bergoglio, had fled the Piedmont region of Italy in 1929 to escape the fascism of Benito Mussolini. In Buenos Aires, the Bergoglios built a Catholic home that enjoyed the outreach to immigrants and labor unions undertaken in the name of Peronism. Emilce Cuda has compared the early Peronist social welfare policy to the New Deal of Franklin Delano Roosevelt. In any case, Pope Francis stood before President Obama in September 2015 and immediately allied himself with all the immigrant families who had been granted shelter in the United States or were seeking such protection. Francis hoped to strike a bond with the U.S. president that was as strong and deep as Pope John Paul II's famous bond with the anti-Communist Ronald Reagan. Bergoglio was saying that he is just as "American" as Obama, the son of a Kenyan economist, for he shared the story of being from a family of immigrants even though his American identity came from very far south of the U.S.-Mexico border. The pope's desire to share the hopes and dreams of Americans in the North echoed remarks that he had made in Havana to Cuban youth a few days earlier.

This book introduces the key ideas that led the Argentine pope to introduce himself in this way, a mode of self-presentation in the U.S. context markedly different from that of his two immediate predecessors. *Theology of the People* by Juan Carlos Scannone, SJ, is the best available resource for an English-speaking audience of the theological roots of the Latin American thinker and now Bishop of Rome, Jorge Mario Bergoglio. Other books in English have examined complementary facets of this story. Austen Ivereigh gave a masterful presentation of Bergoglio's prepontifical life.[2] Massimo Borghesi has sketched the outlines of his philosophical itinerary in an extremely elucidating and well-documented fashion.[3] Thomas Rourke offers clarity on the Argentine sources of his social and political itinerary.[4] But none of these superb books were written from *within* the Jesuit microcosm that Jorge Mario Bergoglio once led and to which he remains quite loyal. Fr. Scannone lived for several decades with Bergoglio in San Miguel, the Jesuit seminary on the outskirts of Buenos Aires. He had even taught Greek to the young seminarian. Immediately after the election of the archbishop of Buenos Aires to the see of Rome, Scannone was called to Rome to work for the Jesuit newspaper *Civiltà Cattolica* and help the pope in whatever tasks that he assigned to his former teacher. The bond between them was eminently personal, proudly *Porteño*, profoundly Ignatian, deeply intellectual, and faithfully ecclesial, and had also been forged over many years.[5] Popes seldom cite individual thinkers in their magisterial writings, but the reference in *Laudato Si'* to an essay of Scannone on the font of popular wisdom regarding generosity that can be gleaned from the poor is absolutely indicative of this special bond.[6] In other words, there are insights in these pages that were developed out of a culture of encounter between these two men that could not have been discovered, nurtured, or verified through any other form of exchange, investigation, or documentation. Scannone's *La teología del pueblo* thus gives us a front-row seat to the still unfolding historical event of the pontificate of Pope Francis.

Sadly, and to my own shock and surprise, this masterpiece of philosophical and theological learning appears in English posthumously. "Cachito," as he is known to his friends, passed on November 27, 2019, at the age of eighty-eight after unexpectedly succumbing to a stroke a few weeks earlier. The stroke had prevented him from traveling to Italy for the awarding of an honorary doctorate from the Sofia University near Florence. He died in San Miguel, also the former residence of his friend Bergoglio. My last direct contact with him was in mid-October at an inter-American theological dialogue that was organized in Rio de Janeiro by Maria Clara Bingemer and myself. In that venue he had displayed his characteristic good humor and indefatigable intellectual spryness. At one point he spontaneously interjected several well-formed paragraphs on Bernard Lonergan to help us forge a new path in the midst of an intense exchange about the intercontinental theological method that would connect Latin American liberation theology to the Catholic theology in the United States. I never expected that to be one of my last encounters. Fr. Scannone was always generous with his time and eager to contribute to both the loftiest of academic debates and the most challenging of pastoral exchanges. To the very end he remained a man of dialogue who could usually be encountered in dialogue.

English-speaking readers are still going to ask, "Who are 'the people'?" Can this category of thought of Peronist vintage be imbibed by U.S. Catholics without some alteration of the original recipe? What connotations does the concept of *pueblo* have that actually embraces the immigrant stories of U.S. Catholics and what social, political, and ecclesial meanings does it convey for those not recently arrived? Drawing upon the work of Lonergan scholar Gerald Whelan, Scannone compares the polyhedron of *Evangelii Gaudium* to the historical communitarian subject, a concept he articulates with the aid of a scholar of Lonergan.[7] Pope Francis says in *Evangelii Gaudium* that the Church listens *in a communitarian way* to the promptings of the Spirit, especially when she is gathered in a synod.[8] The Spanish edition of the apostolic exhortation abounds with references to communitarian praxis and communitarian paths of learning.[9] But the term appears just once in the English translation and then only in relationship to the sanctifying grace that accompanies the sacraments.[10]

The suppression of the communitarian "we" in the English translation calls for a new look at Scannone's writings on this matter. Scannone maintains that the communitarian celebrations of popular devotions to Jesus Christ by the poor witness to the presence of a communitarian mysticism in our very midst. This spirituality is just as rich as that of the mystics of the past like St. John of the Cross or even new female mystics like Chiara Lubich. The new sense of being a "we" that emerges in the accompaniment of the mysticism of the poor is neither a revolutionary social class as envisioned in Marxism nor the spirit of free enterprise that binds people together in a common desire for raising capital. Lonergan's contribution to this discussion is to highlight the role of a shared world of meaning and value in the midst of the fourfold process of intentionality: experience, insight, judgment, and decision. We cannot take it for granted in our North American society that, for example, the mystical worldview of *Guadalupanos* binds Mexicans and Irish Catholics or the faithful poor and the well-to-do seekers of new age wisdom on a digital platform. Pope Francis acknowledged in the address he delivered in Liberty Square in Philadelphia that the Hispanic presence is changing the very definition of religious freedom and historical progress in this country.[11] Through Scannone, Pope Francis, and Bernard Lonergan, we are challenged to forge new levels of understanding on the level of theory, practice, and creative reconfigurations of our social and ecclesial life that will enable us to develop a shared mysticism of the "we."[12] Scannone's "we" is certainly not the same as the "We, the people," of the founding documents of the United States of America. But his insights into Pope Francis's vision of both individual and community are certainly an opportunity to reexamine the authentic "we" that binds us and keeps us together as a Church, a nation, and, no less so, a people living in a context of radically plural beliefs.

By way of conclusion, I would like to return to the pope's address at the welcome ceremony on the South Lawn of the White House. True to form, the pope wanted the first encounter in the public sphere of U.S. life to transcend the customary niceties. After invoking his solidarity with immigrants to and from the entire expanse of the Americas, he noted the convergence of President Obama's clean air initiative with his call for sustainable development in *Laudato Si'* 13. He then cited a warning that had first been uttered in close proximity to the White House, a striking turn of phrase that Dr. Martin Luther King Jr. had coined on August 28, 1963, from the steps of the Lincoln Memorial while delivering his "I Have a Dream" speech:

> Our common home has been part of this group of the excluded which cries out to heaven and which today powerfully strikes our homes, our cities, and our societies. To use a telling phrase of the Reverend Martin Luther King, we can say that we have defaulted on a promissory note and now is the time to honor it.[13]

Social change is not about mapping our current aspirations for humanity onto a utopian future so that later generations can benefit from the unfolding of the inner lights of those alive today. Francis has decried that form of a neo-Pelagianism time and again.[14] On the contrary, we owe a debt to our children's children, and the penalties are accruing on account of our failure to fulfill our responsibility to future generations. Social progress is about God's solidarity with the *anawhim*, or little ones. The Baptist civil rights leader and the Argentine pope are of one mind on this point. Modes of discernment are urgently needed for an integral ecological conversion and for new models of social inclusion. The former Archbishop Bergoglio seemed joyful at the hospitality accorded to him on the South Lawn, but his words were not just about upholding a civil exchange between two heads of state. The pope used the platform of the South Lawn to remind U.S. residents of *their own version* of a prophet of the Old Testament, the preacher from Birmingham who led the march for civil rights and wove his own Christian dream out of the torn and tattered fabric of North American social memory.

Pope Francis thus has no illusions about importing an Argentine brand of the theology of the people to the United States. His own carefully chosen words belie such a simplification. With the aid of the prodigious work of Juan Carlos Scannone, we can interpret the sources that Argentine Catholics and political theorists used to build a common home for the Argentine people and for *la patria Grande* of Latin America. This offering is rich and filled with delicious morsels. But the readers in the English-speaking world will have to discover their own synthesis and their own path to a theology for the people whose identity as a people was forged "in Order to form a more perfect Union, establish Justice, insure domestic Tranquility, provide for the common defense, promote the general Welfare, and secure the Blessings of Liberty to ourselves and our Posterity."[15] The task of forging a theology of the people for the troubled but ever optimistic "we" of the North is daunting. Reading this book is no doubt a great place to start. Absorbing its wisdom will surely reap its own personal, intellectual, spiritual, sociopolitical, and, of course, ecclesial rewards. The true joy of the gospel is that we can stretch our faith-filled horizons of understanding to seek with confidence all of this urgently needed renewal, for in his mercy and through the resurrection of Christ from the dead, we have already received "a new birth into a living hope" (1 Pet 1:3).

Peter Casarella
Duke Divinity School

PREFACE

When a pope from the "ends of the earth" was elected, his simple greeting of *Buona sera!* (Good afternoon), along with his gestures, words, and attitudes, impacted the faithful people of God and beyond, starting with the people of his diocese of Rome and the countless pilgrims who had come there from all over the world.

Later, many started to wonder about the theological and *theologal* framework of a pastoral attitude that seems both deeply human and evangelical. The Colegio Máximo de San José, in San Miguel (a suburb of Buenos Aires) where I live—and where Bergoglio lived for seventeen years as student, provincial, rector, and pastor—began to receive visits from many journalists, biographers, essay writers, and thinkers who spoke many different languages and were from many different countries. They asked about the life, apostolate, and personal stories of the new pontiff, as well as the theology at the root of his reflections, teachings, decisions, and lifestyle. For the first time, many of them heard about the Argentinian theology of the people and its relationship with Latin America's better-known liberation theology and the preferential option for the poor.

Apart from some scholars, this theology—also called "theology of culture"—was unknown in Spain and Latin America, much less by the public at large, even if it had been thought out and written in Spanish. I personally became aware of this lack of knowledge, as well as the great interest that arose—and continues to arise—in some Spanish-speaking countries when I was invited to speak about the theological roots of the pope's ministry and theology. Around the time when I had an article on this topic published in *Razón y Fe* (no. 1395, January 2015), I was invited to Madrid, Granada, and Seville, where I had conferences with different groups of people, including television programs, news conferences, and interviews with various journalists.

Through some French-speaking friends, I also learned that they were unfamiliar but interested in the pope's background. This was also the case in Italy, Germany, Austria, and later the United States. It was then that they suggested I write this book, to be translated—which in fact has already been done—into French, while also publishing the original Spanish for audiences in Spain and Latin America, including Argentina. Even among ourselves, however, we still needed to better understand the deeds and writings of Pope Francis from the original sources. He not only is nourished by them but also builds his theology on them, both in his praxis and in his theoretical approaches, which are inspired without doubt by the Holy Spirit through his pontifical charism.

This book was therefore written with the purpose of gaining a deeper understanding, not only of the pope's thinking, but particularly of the actions and orientation of the Church's governance under Pope Francis, as well as his honest and open dialogue with other religious denominations, peoples, and cultures, with a particular view of fostering peace, solidarity, and justice toward the impoverished and marginalized, and toward the creation of an alternative, more equitable, and more human globalization.

Following the preface, this book begins with a historical approach (part 1). In the first chapter, the origins, characteristics, and development of the theology of the people are presented, as well as its links with other variations of liberation theology; in the second chapter, its most relevant representative, Lucio Gera (1924–2012), considered as a theologian not only *of* the people but *from* the people, is presented. The entire second part of the book is dedicated to the aforementioned theology, insofar as it is inculturated. First, there is a discussion of the meaning of the terms *people* and *popular*, both when we speak of the faithful people of God as well as the peoples of the world (chapter 3). Later, the relevance of popular wisdom for each inculturated theology is explored (chapter 4), as incarnated in any of the earth's many cultures. An example is given of the power of such wisdom in the ethos of Latin American cultures, proposing a universal approach to other cultural realms (chapter 5). Finally, the question of the theology of the people is dealt with in relation to popular piety and spirituality as well as to understanding theology as a science (chapter 6).

The third and final part develops several key points of Pope Francis's theology and pastoral approach, highlighting his rootedness in the theology of the people, as well as its relationship to Latin American social teachings. Both the theology of the people and this social teaching represent an inculturated continuation, albeit of a universal importance, of the paradigm shift and the change of theological method of the Second Vatican Council, particularly *Gaudium et Spes* (chapter 7). Later, in chapter 8, the direct link between the theology of the people and the pontiff's roadmap is developed, based on the apostolic exhortation *Evangelii Gaudium.* Lastly, Bergoglio's central topics are delved into; these are the topics that he explores in the same exhortation, such as the inculturation of the gospel (chapter 9), his understanding of the communitarian subject of popular spirituality and mysticism (chapter 10), and the four "Bergoglian" principles for building up and leading a people, meaning both the people of God and all peoples (chapter 11). Part 3 crowns what was discussed in the first two parts. It honors the subtitle of the work, as it demonstrates Francis's theological and pastoral roots in the "theology of the people," although he has elevated them to a universal level. Moreover, he advances this theology, while retaining its thought and line of action.

When I was asked for a bibliography of the theology that has influenced—and continues to influence—Bergoglio, I sent a first draft, written for a Chilean publication, of what became the first chapter of this book. I also recommended one of my own books, *Evangelización, cultura y teología,* the second volume of a trilogy dedicated to the theology and philosophy of liberation, particularly in the Argentinian versions of both movements. The second part of the book came about through a second draft—updated with more universal parameters—of the book's four most important chapters. I kept in mind as a framework for publication—in the form of a book—my lectures as guest professor of the chair of "Intercultural Theology" in the *Fachbereich* (disciplinary realm) of "Catholic Theology" at the University of Frankfurt.[1]

Finally, the second chapter of part 1 and the chapters of part 3 are a reworking of articles written, for the most part, for *La Civiltá Cattolica* or some other Roman publication, in order to make known the theological approaches of the Holy Father who has come from the peripheries. The only exception is the seventh chapter, which was written for Georgetown University's celebration of the fiftieth anniversary of Vatican II, particularly the pastoral constitution *Gaudium et Spes* and its impact on the paradigm shift and the theological methodology of Latin American theology, as well as on Bergoglio, the first pope who was ordained a priest after the Council. The entire third part explores Francis's theological and pastoral approaches, his rootedness in the Council and Latin American social teaching, and, above all, his grounding in the theology of the people, as well as his creativity, which was inspired by and taken beyond it to a new approach at the universal level. For this purpose, in several chapters (8–11), I pause to comment on Bergoglio's "roadmap" as pope, that is, his apostolic exhortation *Evangelii Gaudium,* without forgetting his second encyclical: *Laudato Si'* (henceforth, LS). In this work, Francis quotes an article of mine about a topic that is very dear to him: the "irruption of the poor" in the Church, in society, and in theology, now understood as an "experience of communitarian salvation" (LS 146). This is taking place not only in Latin America but also universally among poor nations and among the poor of all nations and constitutes a sign of our times.

ABBREVIATIONS

AD	Aparecida Document (2007)
AG	*Ad Gentes* (1965)
CELAM	Latin American Episcopal Council
COEPAL	Bishops' Pastoral Commission
EN	*Evangelii Nuntiandi* (1975)
EG	*Evangelii Gaudium* (2013)
GS	*Gaudium et Spes* (1965)
ICN	*Iglesia y comunidad nacional* (1981)
LN	*Libertatis Nuntius* (1984)
LS	*Laudato Si'* (2015)
NCNP	*Noi come cittadini. Noi come popolo* (2013)
PD	Puebla Document (1979)

EDITOR'S NOTE

Paulist Press gratefully acknowledges Peter Casarella of Duke University Divinity School for his input and careful review of the translation.

Part I

HISTORICAL APPROACH

Chapter 1

THE ARGENTINIAN THEOLOGY OF THE PEOPLE AND OF CULTURE[1]

When, during the 2013 festival of Rimini, Fr. "Pepe" (José) di Paola, an Argentinian priest of the *villas,* referred to the pastoral approach of Pope Francis as archbishop in the poorest *villas* of Buenos Aires, he recognized himself and his companions as a "son of the theology of the people" spread by Fr. Gera, adding, "In Argentina we have two very important people with whom we were formed in the theology of the people: Fathers Lucio Gera and Rafael Tello." Thus, he showed the link, at least implicit, between the *villera* ministry of then-Cardinal Bergoglio, his real preferential love for the poor and the above-mentioned theology. This is confirmed if we remember that in 2012, upon Gera's death, Bergoglio had him buried in the cathedral of Buenos Aires, as a witness at Vatican II and as *peritus* at the CELAM conferences of Medellín (1968) and Puebla (1979), and that, when the priest Enrique Bianchi, a disciple of Tello published—also in 2012—a book about Tello.[2] Bergoglio himself presented it to the public—vindication of sorts, as Tello had had difficulties with the previous archbishop, Cardinal Aramburu.

In the wide framework of Latin American theology, and particularly liberation theology, the Argentine theology of the people has a *specificity* that makes it unique. Currently its study is particularly interesting because of its impact on both the theological and pastoral approach of Pope Francis in his road map, which is the apostolic exhortation *Evangelii Gaudium*.[3]

In this first chapter, I will (1) refer to the *historical origins* of this theology in their own *context*; (2) deal with its understanding of the relationship between the *people* and the *poor*, because I consider that therein lies one of the *cores* for interpreting both the word of God and the Latin American and Argentinian historical reality; (3) deal with the *convergences and differences* from other Latin American liberation theology trends, which gave rise to healthy criticism and reciprocal enrichment; and (4) say a word about the various *generations* of the said Argentinian theology and its *current state.*

ORIGINS AND CONTEXT

Although we can speak of an Argentine theology before Vatican II,[4] I will not dwell on it but on *postconciliar* theology. However, at the time of the council, two important events took place: (1) the meeting in Rome during the council of conciliar experts from different Latin American countries, among them Lucio Gera of Argentina; (2) the meeting of theologians—importantly that of the above-mentioned experts—in the Franciscan school of Petrópolis (Brazil) in 1964. One of their objectives was the theological investigation of the issues of the Latin American Church. Among the pioneers there were the Peruvian Gustavo Gutiérrez, the Uruguayan Juan Luis Segundo, and the above-mentioned Gera.[5]

Already by 1968, before Medellín, Gutiérrez had given a lecture entitled "Toward a Theology of Liberation," thus giving a name to the theological reflection then rising in the climate of the council and applied to our own America.[6] This language and approach were taken up both at the Conference of Medellín (1968) and post-Medellín and in Argentina, particularly by Gera himself—a *peritus* at that conference—and the theologians of COEPAL (Comisión Episcopal de Pastoral—Episcopal Commission for Pastoral Work) as well as by the Movement of Priests for the Third World, born as a response to the Manifesto of Third World Bishops (August 15, 1967).

After returning home from the Second Vatican Council, the Argentine episcopate created COEPAL (1966) with the goal of creating a national pastoral plan in the spirit of the council.[7] It included several bishops (Marengo, Zaspe, and Angelelli); theologians; pastoral leaders; men and women religious; Lucio Gera and Rafael Tello (both from the School of Theology of Buenos Aires); the diocesan priests Justino O'Farrell (previously of the Congregation of Don Orione), Guillermo Saenz (from the Catholic Action Rural Movement), Gerardo Farrell (specialist in Catholic social teaching), Juan Bautista Capellaro (from the Movement for a Better World); the Jesuits Fernando Boasso and Alberto Sily (both from the Center for Social Research and Action [CIAS]); the Passionist biblical scholar Mateo Perdía; Sisters Aida Lopez, Laura Renard, and Esther Sastre; among others. It was precisely in this commission that the Argentinian theology of the people was born. Its impact was felt in the Argentinian bishops' San Miguel Declaration (1969) and document 6 on pastoral ministry from Medellín.

Although COEPAL as such ceased to exist at the beginning of 1973, several of its members continued to meet as a theological reflection group under Gera's leadership. He was also in attendance as an expert in Puebla, was a member of the pastoral-theological team of CELAM, had a strong influence on the above-mentioned Movement of Priests for the Third World, and was later part of the International Theological Commission.

Although he has done some important writings, and many of his oral interventions were recorded and later transcribed.[8]

The Argentine political context of the time included the military rule of Onganía (a dictatorship, though not as cruel as Videla's), the proscription of Peronism after its fall in 1955, the repression of the Peronist labor movement, the emergence of future guerrillas, and a new phenomenon, probably due to the above-mentioned circumstances: a number of intellectuals, teachers, and university students who supported Peronism as popular resistance to the military and as social protest, something that had not occurred during Perón's presidencies. It was then that in the University of Buenos Aires were created the so-called National Schools of Sociology, with figures like the mentioned Justino O'Farrell, Gonzalo Cárdenas, Alcira Argumedo, José Pablo Feinmann, and the philosopher Amelia Podetti, among others.

Justino O'Farrell was the link between these schools and the COEPAL, since he had a relevant role in both groups.[9] Thus distancing themselves from both liberalism and Marxism, both groups found their place in *Latin American and Argentine history* with categories such as "people," "antipeople," "peoples," "empire," "popular culture," "popular religiosity," and so on.

In the case of Gera and the COEPAL, the *people of God*—a biblical category privileged by the council to designate the Church—was first discussed, as well as the *peoples,* especially the Argentinian people. For them, what was at stake was not only the "emergence of the laity within the Church, but also *the insertion of the Church in the history of peoples*"[10] as subjects of history and of culture, recipients of evangelization and, if already evangelized, as evangelizers. I believe that they—as was the rest of the Latin American theology of the time—were influenced by the *theory of dependence,* understood not just from the economic standpoint but primarily from the *political* (imperial) domination, which includes economic, framing both into the evangelical line of integral liberation from sin, and even from its social and structural consequences.

THE PEOPLE AND THE OPTION FOR THE POOR

The People-Nation and the Place of the Poor

The category "people" is ambiguous, not because it is limited but because of its richness. It can, on the one hand, designate the people-*nation* and, on the other, popular *classes*. According to the reflection of COEPAL, it is understood above all by its first meaning, the plural unity of a common culture, rooted in a common *history*, and projected toward a shared *common good*. But it is the *poor* who, at least in Latin America, preserve the culture of their own people and their shared existence as the *structural element* of their lives,[11] whose interests coincide with a *historical plan of justice and peace* since, in our America, they live oppressed by structural injustice and institutional violence.[12]

Thus, the *preferential option for the poor*, articulated in Medellín and formally expressed in Puebla (1979), is not opposed to the option of this conference for the *evangelization of the culture and the cultures of the peoples*; rather, *in fact*, they coincide. And probably also *de jure*, since the poor—who are only *Juan Pueblo*[13] and lack the privileges of power, possession, or knowledge—are the ones who better and more authentically express that which is common to the people.

Therefore, in the "Argentine school" the people is understood first and foremost from culture, conceived of as the "common lifestyle of a people," rather than from a territory or social class. Once I asked Boasso why COEPAL had given so much relevance to the topic of culture, and he answered that it had taken it from number 53 of the Constitution *Gaudium et Spes* (henceforth, GS). Despite this, the wording of number 386 of the DP (of which Gera was one of the main authors) shows how that conciliar document was read from a Latin American and Argentine perspective, since in Puebla the words "in a people" are inserted in the nonliteral quote of the paragraphs 53a–b of GS; these words are not in the original text. Thus the conciliar, more humanistic meaning of *culture* in both paragraphs changes to what the council would later relate to its "historical and social aspect" and calls its "sociological and ethnic meaning," which the constitution only touches on in the third paragraph (GS 53c). Therefore, Puebla reads GS 53a–b from the perspective of 53c, and thus, it changes the focus of its understanding of culture. In a meeting of professors of the Schools of Theology of San Miguel and the Catholic University of Argentina (UCA) immediately after Puebla, I asked Gera if the editors had realized this change of perspective. He answered no. This was a spontaneous act, probably due to the new hermeneutical place from which the text was being interpreted (Latin America), a change of viewpoint that was not realized by the bishops, as there were no objections.

Such theology of popular ministry does not ignore the acute social *conflicts* experienced by Latin America although, in its understanding of "people," it privileges the value of *unity*. On the contrary, although class struggle is not considered a determining factor, nor is unity not understood only in its future or eschatological resolution in a *classless society*, it gives a historical place to the conflict—even of class—conceiving it from the *prior* unity of the people. In this way, institutional and structural injustice is understood as *betrayal* of their own people at the hands of the *antipeople*. The prefix "anti-" presupposes that it belongs to the people it oppresses personally and/or structurally. This theology thus recognizes both the "situation of sin" experienced by the Latin American subcontinent and the innumerable "structural sins" that form it, from which we must be liberated in order to be faithful to the plural unity of the people in the community of peoples.

However, as Luis Maldonado says, when we speak of "people" as nation and as class, there is no need to see it as a dilemma but as something that is dialectic and synthetic, because it is not a "totally equivocal but analogical term," although "if we are careless, it can give way to many misinterpretations."[14]

In my opinion, such an analogical use is based in the semantic, historical, and probably also ontological nexus between both meanings or, respectively, of the realities to which they refer. There is a *semantic* correlation because both concepts refer to a collective subject and point to what is communal and common in it. The *historical* link in Latin America consists in the fact that the poor and simple of whom *Evangelii Nuntiandi* 48 (henceforth, EN) speaks are those who better preserve among us the common historical memory and better condense the common culture that is the fruit of the foundational cultural mestizaje and of their first evangelization. Moreover, their aspirations and struggle for justice, liberation, communion, and participation are in line with the historical-cultural project of the great Latin American nation, historically influenced by Christian anthropology. Finally, the probable *ontological* link between both meanings is based in the fact that the simplicity of the simple is transparent for the communal and common and—although not exempt from alienation a priori—it more easily preserves it from being deformed by the privileges of power, money, or knowledge. In addition, the suffering of the poor tends to open them to poverty of spirit and to a recognition of their lack of self-sufficiency or ontological poverty.

The Puebla Document joins together both meanings since, on the one hand, it says popular religiosity is "the form or cultural existence that religion adopts in a particular people" (PD 444) and, on the other, adds that "this religion of the people is preferably lived out by the poor and simple" (EN 48), but it covers all social sectors and is sometimes one of the few bonds that bring men together in our politically divided nations (PD 447). Likewise, after speaking about Latin American culture born of cultural mestizaje (PD 409), and permeated by Catholic faith (PD 412 and 413), it adds, "It is a culture... preserved in a more lively way and imbuing all existence in the poorer sectors" (PD 414).

Thus, in Latin America, the preferential option for the poor includes a moment of choice for the evangelical and human values of its popular culture and religiosity—which are those of the Latin American historical culture—and the pastoral option for evangelization of culture implies at its core the preferential option for the poor.

The Religion of the People

All that has been said up to now impacts the consideration of *popular religiosity*. On the one hand, *religion* is considered (or, respectively, the negative attitude toward religion)—following Paul Tillich—as the *core* of a people's culture, and, on the other, it refers—with Paul VI—to the piety of the poor and simple (EN 48). But here the contrast is only apparent if we consider that at least *in fact* in Latin America, and probably also *by law*, these are the ones who better preserve the common culture and its values and religious symbols, which in their own right tend to be shared by all, thus being in our countries the seed—even in those who are not poor—of a conversion to the poor in order to achieve their liberation and, hence, the liberation of all. Therefore, the religion of the people—if authentically evangelized—far from being considered an "opiate," has not only an evangelizing potential but also one of human liberation, as has been demonstrated and continues to be demonstrated by a popular reading of the Bible.

Hence, Puebla has been considered as a true *continuation* of Medellín, although it has enriched the preferential option for the poor—even understood structurally—in its recourse to *history*, its approach of *evangelization of the culture*, and its theological and pastoral esteem of *popular piety*, taking the two last topics of the post-synodal exhortation EN (1975). Apparently, it can be proven that, in turn, the Synod of 1974 addressed these last two topics under the influence of the "Argentine theology of the people," thanks both to the interventions of Latin American bishops during the synod and through the person Eduardo (later Cardinal) Pironio. Thus, Paul VI gathered these contributions in his post-synodal exhortation, which, in turn, was applied by Puebla (1979) to all America and enriched with new contributions, among which is, as we said, Gera's in the chapter "Evangelization of Culture" as well as that of the Chilean Joaquin Alliende of the Schönstatt in "Popular Religiosity."[15]

One of the most important novelties is to be found, in my opinion, in the relevance given by Puebla—in the line of Argentine theology, although not exclusively—to the category "popular wisdom" in the two above-mentioned sections of the document (respectively, PD 413, 448), in both cases connecting it to the religion of the people and to a wisdom knowledge that does not replace science but rather existentially places it in context, complements it, and confirms it. Later, the Argentine theological trend will consider it key for bridging popular piety with an *inculturated* theology in Latin America.[16]

A TREND WITHIN LIBERATION THEOLOGY?

In this section I will adopt a more testimonial style, since I will try to relate some personal and ecclesial experiences that are, I believe, part of the history of theology in our continent.

In 1982 I distinguished four trends within Latin American liberation theology. Among them I placed the "Argentine theology of the people"—so named by Juan Luis Segundo in his critique and adopted by Sebastian Politi. Gutiérrez characterizes it as a "trend with particular traits within liberation theology"; recognizing it as a variation of this, Roberto Oliveros saw it as a variation and named it pejoratively "populist theology."[17] Later, this formulation—by no means the only possible one—was adopted by the then-secretary of CELAM, Cardinal Antonio Quarracino, when in 1984 he presented the first Instruction of the Congregation for the Doctrine of Faith about liberation theology, *Libertatis Nuntius* (henceforth, LN), and it was accepted by theologians such as Joao Batista Libânio as well as those in opposition such as Alberto Methol Ferré and Cardinal Moreira Neves.[18]

Among the "particular traits" mentioned by Gutiérrez, besides those of a *thematic* nature indicated above (such as the importance given to culture and popular religiosity), there are others of a *methodological* nature, related to the former, namely: its use of a *historical-cultural analysis*, particularly favoring the socio-structural one without neglecting the other; its use—as a means to know and transform reality—of *syntactic and hermeneutic* sciences, such as history, culture, and religion, thus completing the use of more *analytical and structural* sciences; the above-mentioned rootedness of such scientific mediations in a wisdom knowledge and in a discernment through affective connaturality, which in turn confirms them; a critical separation from the Marxist method of social analysis and from the action strategies and conceptual categories associated with it.

I believe that the contributions of this trend enriched liberation theology as a whole, as other trends helped Argentine theology to avoid falling into a certain *culturalism or populist romanticism*, recognizing not only the conflict but also the fact of class struggle, even without considering it a "determining principle" (LN X, 2). On the other hand, although there were enemies of liberation theology who tried to use some aspects of it in opposition to others, I believe that in the long run they did not achieve their aims, but instead there was a cross-fertilization among them, respecting social and geo-cultural contexts. In this sense we can recognize that in the different lines of the theology of liberation there are not only "context theologies" but also a Latin American *inculturation* of theology.

The instructions of the Congregation for the Doctrine of the Faith of 1984 and 1986—properly understood—helped to prevent extreme positions that were not followed by most liberation theologians. On the contrary, John Paul II himself, in his message of April 9, 1986, to the bishops of Brazil, gave this theological line an ecclesial recognition, not only as something "opportune, but also useful and necessary," as well as the initiator of a "new stage" in the socio-theological reflection of the Church.[19]

The second meeting of El Escorial (1992)—twenty years after the first, in which I had also participated[20]—was for me tangible proof of such fruitful cross-fertilization between the main trend of liberation theology and mainly Argentine theology. At the same meeting an important role was assigned to issues of culture, to a new sociocultural vision, popular wisdom, and so on, for instance in keynotes such as those of Pedro Trigo, Diego Irarrázaval, Antonio González, Victor Codina, and others.[21]

After one of those interventions, the Italian editor Rosino Gibellini approached me and asked me whether I was happy with the general approach toward the Argentinian school he had noticed.

Some years later, in September 1996, the leadership of CELAM, with participation of authorities from the Congregation for the Doctrine of the Faith (among them then-Cardinal Ratzinger and Archbishop Bertone), a relatively small group of Latin American theologians and experts gathered in Schönstatt (Germany) to reflect on the "future of theology in Latin America," asking them to develop four topics, namely: *Liberation Theology, Social Teaching of the Church, Communitarianism,* and the *Theology of Culture*.[22] I, who had also participated in that meeting, asked the organizers why these topics had been chosen. The answer was that they were considered the *most relevant* (or *among* the most relevant) for a Latin American theology of the third millennium. The first was entrusted to Gustavo Gutiérrez, and the fourth—because of Gera's health—to his disciple Carlos Galli, with the mandate that he reflect the theology of his teacher. That is, he was given a decisive role for the theological future of Latin America, both in the main trend of liberation theology and in the Argentine trend. After Gutiérrez's brilliant exposition, Ratzinger explicitly praised his Christ-centeredness and his generosity.

In November of that same year, the School of Theology of the Catholic University of Louvain, Flemish language section, convened another meeting around the issue of an eventual *paradigm shift* in liberation theology "from a *socio-economic* paradigm to one that was *cultural*."[23] Thus there was an attempt to go to the core of an eventual change of axis between the various approaches of this theology. For this reason, I took advantage of a meeting with Gutiérrez in Schönstatt to ask him what he thought about this. He answered that the issue of culture had been present from the beginning and that there had not been a paradigm shift but a change of *emphasis*. This was the majority response of the participants in the Louvain meeting: the pressing social and economic concern for liberation not only continued but had widened and deepened. In my opinion, there was a cross-fertilization of various approaches, for the greater good of the Latin American people and its liberation and for the growth of theology in our America.

DIFFERENT GENERATIONS AND THE SITUATION OF THE THEOLOGY OF THE PEOPLE IN ARGENTINA TODAY

From the First Generation to the Present

In his foreword to my book *Evangelización, cultura y teología,* Carlos Galli distinguished three—even four—generations of this theological current, placing Gera and the other experts of COEPAL in the first one, me in the second, and himself and his colleagues in the third. Later, Marcelo González would place Gerardo Farrell, because of his age and theological writings, as well as Pablo Sudar, in the second, and Galli, together with himself, in the third.[24] We must not forget that Orlando Yorio also belonged to the second generation; as a Jesuit, he was outstanding because of his theological reading of the signs of the times in the history of the Argentinian people, including the conflict between subversion and repression, which he himself suffered with a period of "disappearance," or clandestine imprisonment, torture, and exile. Later, as a diocesan priest, he became the main theological and spiritual animator of the Seminarios Populares de Formación Teológica until his death in 1999.[25]

On the other hand, those who later jointly published the book *A mitad del camino. Una generación de teólogas y teólogos argentinos*[26] are part of the next generation, although not all of them are representative of the theology of the people. Among them are the already mentioned Galli and Gonzalez, as well as Víctor Manuel Fernández (currently an archbishop and rector of UCA)—who, with Galli, played an important role in drafting the Aparecida Document—as did Marcelo Trejo, Guillermo Rosolino, and others. The last three are part of a growing number of theologians from the interior of the country. I believe this generation shows a greater theological pluralism and diversity than does COEPAL, more in accordance with the new, more pluralistic times, in the Church and among the Argentinian people. The fourth generation would be formed by younger or more recent representatives; many of them wrote or are writing theses about their predecessors and follow their approaches in singular, sometimes regionally influenced ways originating from—but not exclusively—the School of Theology of UCA.[27]

Finally, to characterize the current situation of this theological trend, I will deal only with some of the last and most significant contributions, namely: an important ecclesiological contribution (4.2) and some new reflections on the people and their culture (4.3) as well as popular piety current in Argentina and Latin America (4.4).

"The People of God in the Peoples of the World"

This is the title of Carlos Galli's doctoral dissertation, directed by Gera, and published only partially in 1994.[28] This work not only synthesizes and systematizes—in its first section—everything that has been contributed to the topic by contemporary European and Latin American theology (preconciliar, conciliar, and postconciliar), from the 1930s to the end of the 1980s, but it also accomplishes—in its second speculative section—a significant "systematic understanding of Catholicity, incarnation and interchange between the People of God and the peoples of the world." In the opinion of many, this is a true milestone in an inculturated ecclesiology that reflects upon itself theologically, as well as an important contribution to the ecclesiology of the people of God in general, based on the premises of the Argentinian theology of the people.

To understand Galli's systematic ecclesiological reflection, we can be aided by looking at the second section. In the first place it studies, still separately, the people of God and the peoples, dealing first with the people of God (insofar as *people* of God, people *of* God, and people of *God*) and then the peoples of the world. In the second part, he deepens the relationship, although in one direction, approaching first the people of God *for* the peoples insofar as a universal and missionary people of God. Then, in a third stage, he presents in a deeper way the *interrelationship,* from the theological priority of the people of God, considering the people of God *in* the peoples; the incarnation (in general) of the people of God, its incarnation *in* the peoples; as well as the people of God as a historical subject *between* the peoples and the union *among* the people of God and the world of the peoples. Finally, the fourth part takes a more direct approach to such interrelationship, looking particularly at the second relationship, that is, the one from the peoples, since the people of God is thought to start from the peoples. To do this, he uses the category of interchange, focusing first on the interchange between the people of God and the peoples, concluding finally with a wholistic understanding: the people of God; *people* "of" *peoples.* Thus, from an inculturated reading of "Pentecost: A Spirit and Many Tongues," he reinterprets the expression *laós ex ethnôn,* culminating in a new comprehensive ecclesiological formulation. As I said, this allows one to discover—according to the Latin American and Argentine ecclesial experience and according to the spirit of the theology of the people—the ecclesiological relevance, and not merely the historical one, of cultures in the "wonderful *exchange*" of inculturation. Thus, the Catholicity of the people of God is understood in a new way as an "*incarnation* of the People of God in the peoples."

However, the path of the main thread of the second section cannot encompass the ecclesiological richness of the work, at both the historical and speculative levels. This is not the place to comment in detail. Suffice it to say that what underlies it is not mere erudition, but a systematic understanding, from the theology of the people, of the various ecclesiological contributions of the contemporary theology of the people of God and the speculative work of contemplating the various relationships between the people of God and the peoples. He does this by using the central categories of *Catholicity, mission, incarnation,* and *exchange,* reflecting on the meaning of the conjunctions and the prepositions (*and, of, for, in, among, from*), using the category of *subject* (e.g., the people of God and the peoples as collective *subjects* who intercommunicate their goods), turning to various theological and philosophical frameworks in order to think—among other problems—about the oppositions of *contradiction* and *relationship* (inspired by both St. Thomas and Hegel), and so on. Therefore, I believe it is one of the most valuable contributions of the "Argentine school" to a contemporary Latin American theology, even to theology in general.[29]

New Reflections on the People and Its Culture

Like most liberation theology, the Argentinian school uses the "see, judge, act," method, using the interdisciplinary mediation of human and social sciences for its faith vision. Thus, theological reflection about the people and corresponding pastoral and social action today cannot be the same as in the 1960s or 1970s but must take into account emerging factors in society and culture, both in globalized cultures as in Latin America and Argentina.

Probably as a reaction against the competitive individualism and the social fragmentation caused by it, there is emerging in the world and in our continent a civil society different from the market and the state.[30] Its beginning certainly had to do with the struggle for the civil rights of people of color in the United States; the Solidarność in Poland; the revolt against Marcos in the Philippines; movements such as pacifism, ecology, feminism, and so on; and its continuation with new social actions in Latin America: such as the mothers and grandmothers of the Plaza de Mayo and other multiclass groups; the marches of silence in Catamarca in the face of the unpunished murder of María Soledad; the movements of the "landless" in Brazil, of ethnic groups in Bolivia, Ecuador, and southern Chile; as well as various volunteer groups and NGOs of all kinds against impunity, for justice, for green spaces, and so on, that, even if varied, coordinate in networks (of health, solidarity, factory workers, and others). They struggle and work for interests that, even if their own, nonetheless are "universalizable" according to Adela Cortina's expression—such as justice, life, work, respect for creation, rejection of impunity, and so on. Frequently, popular ministry accompanies this central role of the self-organized people, particularly that of the poor and of those who support them. I don't claim that the above-mentioned individualism and fragmentation have been overcome, but "where sin abounded, grace overflowed," so this positive is also happening, countering the negative. It is a true sign of the times that moves one to hope against all hope.

One of the forms the new emergence of civil society in Latin America has taken is *neocommunitarism*, particularly at the *grassroots*, at all levels: religious, cultural, economic, social, and even political. Corresponding to this renewed social fabric, a new *cultural mestizaje of visions* is taking place in *collective visioning*, of which Pedro Trigo of greater Caracas or Jorge Seibold of greater Buenos Aires speak.[31] Thus it is that in the peripheries of large Latin American cities a new *vital synthesis* between the values of popular cultures and particularly the *suburban* and others proper to modernity and postmodernity is being attempted. Thanks to the "new poor"—that is, the impoverished middle class—and academics, professionals, pastoral ministers who opted for the poor, another important phenomenon is taking place: a sociocultural *mediation* between the popular wisdom of the people and the contributions of *modern science and technology*. One example among many is the alliance—thanks to the service of volunteers and particularly Christian ones—working with scavengers from south of Buenos Aires and scientists from the Universidad Tecnológica Nacional in order to achieve recycling by the scavengers themselves with technical advice from the university.

In the third part of this work, I will once again take up the topic of popular movements on different continents, and the importance given to them by Pope Francis for the future of humanity.

A New Vital Synthesis in the Religion of the People

If, as I said in the previous paragraph, there are new factors in the culture of the Argentinian people (and Latin American peoples), both in its collective vision and in the corresponding social fabric, this transformation is shown more in *popular piety,* despite ambiguities and the need for discernment. I refer to the popular religiosity of basic Christian communities, Bible groups, charismatic prayer groups, as well as mass expressions, such as youth pilgrimages to Luján, the ministry at shrines such as that of St. Cajetan—patron of bread and of work—in Buenos Aires, in this same city, the devotion to Our Lady Untier of Knots, including the popular religiosity of non-Catholic communities, such as Pentecostals or those originating from Afro-American religions coming to Argentina from Brazil.

Latin American popular religiosity was able to *resist* the influence of both the Enlightenment and secularism, although it opened itself to the *plurality* of religious expression and confessions. Several studies point to the coexistence—more or less in synthesis—of the three mentioned above, namely: (1) the tradition of popular Catholicism of Iberian and indigenous roots (more or less mixed, with predominance of one or another) and, depending on the region or country, also of African American and immigrant roots, particularly Italian and/or German (there are some who claim that the non-Catholic cults move within the cultural *matrix* of popular Catholicism[32]); (2) the modern vision, fostered by the states, the market, and the public school but also—in its religious forms—by numerous pastoral ministers; and (3) the *postmodern,* frequently filtered through mass media and religious pluralism.[33]

Thus the meaning of transcendence and closeness to God, celebration and generosity, devotions to the saints and the dead, and the *traditional* "wisdom" are joined by *modern* elements, such as the greater adult responsibility of the laity (which extends from the religious to the historical and social realms); the search for *effective* mediations; the appreciation of the peoples' new free religious organizations; the popular interpretation of the *written* word of God (not only orally transmitted); new, more *participatory* styles of the exercise of authority in the churches, and so on. To all this *postmodern* components are added, such as a greater *feminine role,* reflectively self-conscious (and sometimes *combative*) in the churches; flexible forms of organization as a *network* rather than a pyramid; the importance given to experience and to the *felt* personal religious witness; the revaluation of *mystical, magical, and miraculous* (e.g., healings) events; the new rootedness in *immediate* relationships of groups in the framework of a coldly functional society. All in all, there remain certain ambiguous or negative elements of postmodernity, such as porousness, *self-enterprise,* and religious syncretism.[34]

Recently in Aparecida (2006), the Church was able to discern in Latin American popular religiosity—uninfluenced by Argentine theology—examples of true *spirituality* and *popular mysticism.*[35] Gustavo Gutiérrez had already pointed it out when he said, "Drink from your own well," focusing on the communitarian and collective spiritual experience of the theological virtues among the poor (particularly among those that Ignacio Ellacuría called the "poor in spirit"); more recently, Jorge Seibold indicates it by introducing the category "popular mysticism."[36] Taking them into account today is a new challenge for the theology and ministry of Latin American popular religiosity. Moreover, I believe that a new Latin American reading of the *phenomenology of self-giving,* its *method,* and the concept of "saturated phenomenon" of Jean-Luc Marion can not only help to deepen the understanding and faith experience of such new religious phenomena but can also bring strength to their evangelizing potential and, therefore, their liberating potential in all dimensions of culture, moving toward a society that is more just, human, and united in solidarity.[37]

Thus, even in Latin American popular media (including Argentinian), the *hermeneutical cycle* of illumination of their new sociocultural as well as religious experiences for the light of the word of God is reproduced for a renewed reading of the signs of the times in their history, not least those above mentioned of new communitarianism, new cultural mestizaje, and popular spirituality; and in a second phase of the same circle, the renewed reading of the word and the faith of the church "from these particular experiences... since they evidence of certain aspects of the word of God whose total richness has not yet been perceived." But, "so that this reflection may be truly a reading of Scripture and not just a projection of a meaning on the word of God that is not contained in it...one must be attentive to interpret the experience from which...it is started in the light of the experience of the church herself."[38] According to the Argentinian Bible scholar Horacio Simián Yofre, this semantic correspondence is achieved when there is an analogy of pragmatic attitudes between the text itself and its interpreters in the new situation and experience.[39]

CONCLUSION

Therefore, the Argentine theology of the people—a trend with its own traits within liberation theology (Gustavo Gutiérrez)—has contributed, from its inculturated and contextual perspective to the brief but already rich Latin American theological tradition. It is to be hoped that, with the renewal of its generations, we may continue to contribute maturity and growth, for the good of our peoples and in particular those who are poor and excluded, and for the coming of the reign of God among us. Today it is having a universal impact because it is one of the theological roots of the pastoral and government style of Pope Francis.

Chapter 2

LUCIO GERA

A Theologian of the People and from *the People*[1]

After a general presentation of the "theology of the people" in the first chapter, this one will be devoted to illustrating some of the key characteristics of this theology and its main representative: Lucio Gera. Until quite recently, he was little known outside of Argentina and practically unknown outside of Latin America, although some of his works had been translated into Italian. The preface of this translation, by L. Bianchi, introduces the author, saying, "The Latin American theologian Luci Gera, the son of Venetian immigrants, is known in Argentina as one of the most valuable representatives of the 'theology of the people' or the theology expressed 'from the people.'"[2]

This is precisely the reason for the current interest in him and his theology, since several of the theological-pastoral approaches of Pope Francis—not the least of which is his apostolic exhortation *Evangelii Gaudium* (henceforth, EG)—are not easily understood at a basic level without the context of the theology of the people and of culture[3] and therefore without a more or less direct reference to Gera.

In this chapter, I will not attempt to provide a synthesis of all his theology. Instead, I will touch on two of its core points—those that the aforementioned Italian translation took into account because of their particular relevance at the end of the 1970s, although I will not limit myself to these two texts. In the first part, I will focus on the first of them, since, as I have come to understand, it presents quite well the fundamental core of this theologian's thinking, namely, his concept of "people" and its relationship to the people of God, as well as the theological appreciation of popular religion, particularly in Latin America. The second part addresses another core ecclesiological point: the relationship between evangelization and liberation in the mission of the Church, which is intimately connected with the preferential option for the poor.[4] I believe that this exposition, even if it is a partial one, will touch on not only the central viewpoints of Gera's theology but also many of the theological-pastoral tenets of Pope Francis.

THE PEOPLES OF THE EARTH, THE PEOPLE OF GOD, AND POPULAR PIETY

In Latin America, the years between the conferences of Medellín and Puebla were extraordinarily rich in creativity and theological controversies. The post-synodal exhortation *Evangelii Nuntiandi* (1975) had introduced a new topic in the universal teaching, that of popular religiosity, so that the Latin American Episcopal Council (CELAM) entrusted the Chilean pastoralist Joaquin Alliende with organizing a meeting to discuss it. In this context, Gera presented his contribution that I will examine, which, in my opinion, represents a signpost, not only for the public exposition of his thinking, but also of the theology of the people.

The introduction takes as its point of departure themes that were very close to Gera's heart. On the one hand, it involves the pastoral capacity to discover, here and now, the demands of *new* responses by people in the face of new challenges at a specific moment in their history; on the other hand, it involves the appreciation of people's knowledge of their own situation, by way of emotional identification, that is, for the "affective connaturality given by love,"[5] a way that is complementary to the use of typologies in the human sciences.

People: In What Sense?

Evidently, we are speaking of a collective subject, a community, a plurality unified by a common element that determines it and gives it form. Depending on how this is conceived, we will be speaking of a people-nation or of the sectors of a nation that are denominated as popular.

The People-Nation

This first concept of people—preferred by Gera—is not approached as a territory or a race but rather as that which is unified by the same culture or by a common lifestyle, which is made concrete by a particular political will and decision to unite, self-determine, and self-organize in order to achieve the common good. It is therefore born of a common culture and of historical conditions that offer a possibility of political solidarity to a given community. For my part, I add that, among the same people, there might be different and even opposing understandings of the common good, but together the "will and action" for its achievement prevails.[6]

Gera connects his understanding of culture to the cultural *ethos,* or the way in which a people organizes its collective conscience and, above all, its value system. Let us recall that Ricœur, referring to national cultures,[7] states that they possess an ethical-mythical core: ethical because they imply values, and mythical because they are expressed, above all, in a symbolic way.

Gera then considers whether there is a single or many cultures in Latin America. He takes an intermediate position, recognizing the mestizo culture and its unifying and dominant nature, to which an enlightenment culture of a secular bent has been contradictorily opposed from the time of the Bourbons. Galli, a disciple of Gera, prefers, rather, to speak of a "plural unity,"[8] which is analogous in the various Latin American cultures.

The Popular Sectors

There is another understanding of people, akin to the category of social *class*, which designates mainly, or rather exclusively, the poor and working-class sector of the people-nation, setting it in opposition to the nonpopular or antipopular sectors. For Gera, this exclusive sense seems to be too rigid and ahistorical, since he notices throughout history and today's present reality among the nations of the world a gradation of nuances of belonging to the people or to the antipeople. The latter is formed in the *historical measure*, in which others are oppressed or excluded from the common good, or in which the common culture is rejected. Thus, although the elites are frequently antipopular, they are not so inevitably, because each case depends on their social, ethical, and historical place (personal and structural). This does not deny that certain groups will objectively have the inclination of belonging to the "people," such as the poor, because their lack of power and possession facilitates the consciousness of needing others and, therefore, solidarity. Hence, belonging to the people is an ethical and historical reality that demands moral attitudes, a value system, and their corresponding structures.

The Church and the Peoples

Evangelization of Cultures

Taking a new step, Gera explains that the pastoral ministry of the Church is addressed not only to individuals but to peoples as well, with the goal of evangelizing their cultures, as fostered by EN 20; however, as the Body of Christ, it preferentially takes the poor into account, as they are more forsaken. Thus, by referring to peoples and their cultures, it focuses on all dimensions, even the structural ones, of their life and living together, in which the gospel should be incarnated, namely, the religious, cultural in a restricted sense, social, political, and economic dimensions, and so forth.

For their part, the hierarchy of the Church lends the people of God incarnated in peoples and their cultures the service of discernment of the authenticity of its faith and of its sense of inculturated faith, as well as reading the signs of the times in their yearnings and aspirations, so that its ministry may not only be directed toward the people but also begin with the people itself, as the document of the Argentinian bishops on popular ministry has asked for (San Miguel, 1969, applying Medellín to Argentina). Gera had a relevant role in the redaction of this document.

The Religion of the People

We denominate our relationship of communion with the sacred, with the divine, with God, as "religion." It is accompanied by both symbolic and narrative representations and affective attitudes of respect and attraction to the holy mystery that Rudolf Otto describes as *tremendum et fascinans*. They correspond to a system of exterior mediations such as cultural rituals, words (books, dogmas, formulas, prayers, and so on), that is, the religious existential inner life is objectivized, intercommunicated, and institutionalized in religious communities.

For Gera, just as for Paul Tillich, the basic thing of each culture is found in religion (or irreligion) because it is related to the *ultimate meaning* of life and of relationship, which permeates the penultimate and antepenultimate senses. For the same reason, it relates to the human experience of *limitation* (death, sin, failure, ontological contingency, and so on) lived as a limit and even *beyond* the limit.

On the other hand, our author rejects both the secularist interpretation of religion, which he considers to be alienating because it would deny the autonomy of human reason and freedom, and its *sacralized* understanding, which denies such legitimate autonomy and tends to sacralize it, that is, to make its mediations fixed and absolute.

Regarding Latin American religiosity, he characterizes it typologically according to two universal criteria referred to as the representations of the divine and the corresponding attitudes. One of these types places the emphasis on the power of God and is preferably expressed in petitionary prayer and worship; the other views Christ as a model and teacher of wisdom, and the response is an ethical one: discipleship.

The faith that is incarnated in a people is, for this very reason, inculturated in its religiosity, reaching the ethical, symbolic, and religious core of its culture. According to Gera, this happened historically in Latin America's culture in its most characteristic form. We could say that this is the "principal analogue" within the plural unity (analogical) that is recognized by Galli. In it, there are not only seeds but also fruits of the word of God, thanks to the sowing of the first evangelization and its lights, despite its shadows. Hence, on the one hand, there is the importance that a poetic and artistic mediation acquires in it and, on the other hand, its radical opposition to secularism and to de-symbolization.

Finally, Gera develops five criteria of discernment for Christian faith in popular religion: (1) a personal relationship with God, Christ, and Mary; (2) the consciousness of belonging; (3) the feeling of fraternity and solidarity with others; (4) a relationship with the deceased; and (5) a relationship with worship and the sacraments, beginning with the appreciation of baptism. For Gera, as has been previously stated, the religion of the people in Latin America in its principal form is popular Catholicism (cf. PD 444).

EVANGELIZATION, DEPENDENCE, LIBERATION

Being Christian in a Situation of Dependence and Liberation

The text that I commented on in the first part (PRP) advises the ministry of the Church to begin with the people and their situation before God, according to a faithful reading of the signs of the times. Then, ISD looks into the situation of the Latin American people at this time, and it concludes that it is becoming aware of the dependence on and the consequent yearning for liberation, which was placing the Church's whole previous pastoral ministry in crisis mode.[9] Thus, following Medellín,

Gera poses the question, "What does being a Christian today in Latin America mean?" by addressing both laypeople and their pastors. On the one hand, the situation of dependence-liberation must *historically* change the way of living out the faith and practicing pastoral ministry in Latin America today. On the other hand, however, if such reality is lived out *in and within* the faith, the answer—both practiced and pastoral—acquires a Christian *specificity*. For Gera, in my opinion, just as for Pope Francis today, it is important to discern not only the here and now from the gospel but also the evangelical nature of the option that is taken as a consequence.

In order to demonstrate the experience of dependence, the author not only turns to the human sciences but also, as he did in PRP, avails himself of the wisdom and charismatic knowledge "by connaturality," which is proper of the politician and of the prophet, and through both methods, he interprets the symptoms affecting the majority of Latin America's people, namely, poverty, infant mortality, low wages, loss of civil rights, underdevelopment, and marginalization in a conflictive situation of imperialism.

At the same time, he recorded that the memory of liberating events has already taken place throughout history, as well as a creative and hopeful imagination of projects that make a future of peace and justice truly possible. Finally, he asks to what extent the Church could *objectively* contribute from the gospel to the Latin American process of liberation, immediately posing a series of questions. Standing out among them are those regarding the relationship between the sacred and the secular, above all, by considering this in its political dimension.

The second chapter of ISD rejects the extremes of secularization and sacralization, following the lead of Vatican II, Medellín, and the theology of liberation, because the issue is not about *reducing* evangelization to human liberation, or vice versa, nor is it a mere "addition" that only juxtaposes them, but of the *single* mission of the Church, namely, evangelization, which *objectively* includes liberation. For Gera, the mutual implication between faith and the historical process (in the Latin American sense, one of liberation) is based on a trinitarian understanding on the fatherhood of one God, Creator and Savior of all, in the recapitulation of everything in and through Christ, and in the unification of the entire human being and all of humanity through the work and grace of the Holy Spirit.

The article ends by criticizing the opposition between the word (of God) and the sacrament and therefore rejects both a radical theology of secularization and a "sacralizing" mentality, instead fostering a liberating evangelization that articulates both (word and sacrament) without separating them. Here again, Gera does not place them in contrast but rather binds the dimensions (divine and human) of the incarnation and, consequently, of the Church's mission.

Evangelization and Liberation

From Medellín to Puebla: The Importance of Evangelii Nuntiandi

After Puebla, the author takes up again, now in a deeper and more mature form, the same ecclesiological theme of the single mission of the Church. I present it here because it complements the previous point and, in my opinion, is one of his most lucid writings that can help us understand the theological roots of the pastoral ministry of Pope Francis.

Gera wrote (he did not express orally) this important work ("Evangelization and Human Development") for the second volume of the series compiled by Peter Hünermann and me, with the valuable collaboration of Margit Eckholt, titled *America Latina y la doctrina social de la Iglesia. Diálogo latinoamericano-alemán* (Buenos Aires: Paulinas, 1992–93), during the preparation of the Conference of Santo Domingo (1992) when John Paul II was already speaking of a *new* evangelization, a topic that was emerging in Latin America.

Thus, Gera observes that at Medellín and afterward the topic of evangelization was increasingly more relevant as a fundamental pastoral topic (it is even more so today with Pope Francis) and that its concept and contents are being expanded, that is, it now includes *constitutively* human promotion and liberation, with the concomitant effect of *specification* of both from the gospel. These are ideas Gera already had, as I mentioned earlier in this chapter, but he now records that the magisterium is gradually assuming them explicitly. I do not think this would have happened without the intervention of Latin American theology, including Gera's quiet and modest contribution, above all, regarding the aforementioned Christian specificity.

For this reason, he studies both points, first in Medellín (1968), then in Puebla (1979), and with John Paul II on his way to Santo Domingo (1992). In Medellín, he demonstrates that there are texts still using the term *evangelization* in a restricted sense to the first announcement or in the case of those who are baptized without catechesis, although other texts, in contrast, are already pointing toward a *dynamic unity* between evangelization and human promotion, justice, and liberation.

An important signpost along this journey was the 1971 Synod about justice in the world, which stated that the struggle for justice is a *constitutive dimension* of the proclamation of the gospel. The Synod of 1974 about evangelization interpreted that as an *integral* part of its understanding and concluded with the masterful work on the subject, the post-synodal exhortation *Evangelii Nuntiandi.* According to Gera, the synodal intervention of Pironio helped to emphasize the Christian nature of liberation, even the human one. I dare say that, behind Pironio, we can see his friend Gera.

Puebla took another step forward, adopting the broad concept of evangelization of EN (which will bear fruit later in EG). Moreover, it explicitly recognized the evangelical and ecclesial quality of its pastoral options, first in the preferential option for the poor and for their liberation. According to Gera, one of the historical reasons contributing to this was the fact that Latin American Catholic popular religiosity, even though it must constantly be evangelized, is in itself an evangelizer, so that the people evangelize themselves in the new context of growing religious pluralism. Another reason for this is the relevance granted to culture, including the evangelization of modern culture and its legitimate secularizing dynamism, lest it may be perverted into secularism.[10]

The study pauses at the evolution of the search for an adequate language, which avoids both separation and mere juxtaposition of evangelization and promotion (liberation, development, the struggle for justice) and reductionism to one or the other. In the beginning, an integrative language was used, using the epithets *integral, full, complete,* or rather a hierarchical one, as when we speak of "a liberation subordinate to evangelization." However, Gera prefers dynamic formulas that are in tension, such as "liberating evangelization," responding to a more adequate theological approach. Because the theological dimension of faith, hope, and charity also demands and seeks fulfillment in the secular dimension of history, granting its transformative action, its own specificity, in turn, respects and brings to fullness the autonomy of the human dimension.

Hence, according to Gera, Medellín and Puebla coincide on this point, coming from different viewpoints. For the former, the criterion of an adult and mature faith is its commitment to liberation, while for the latter the criterion to discern the liberation inspired and practiced evangelically is provided by faith.

Toward Santo Domingo: John Paul II and the New Evangelization

It is not Gera's intention to explain all of John Paul II's teachings on the relationship between evangelization and liberation, but rather to focus on three of his interventions regarding the new evangelization, referring specifically to Latin America, namely (in the order in which they are discussed), the Homily in Santo Domingo, October 11, 1984; Speech to CELAM, on the following day; and Speech of the XIX Ordinary Assembly of CELAM in Port-au-Prince, March 9, 1983.[11]

Although it was not within the field of the author's vision, it seems important to me in this context to cite explicitly how the pope, from his first encyclical onward, has responded to the central question concerning

Gera in this article, resolving what type *constitutive* of evangelization is human promotion: only *integrating*, or also *essential*, because if it is essential, there is no evangelization without it. *Redemptoris Hominis* 15 states,

> The Church considers an *essential*, unbreakably united element of her mission this solicitude for man, for his humanity, for the future of men on earth and therefore also for the course set for the whole of development and progress.[12]

Immediately, the pope provides the christological foundation of this ecclesiological claim, adding, "And it finds the principle of this solicitude in Christ himself, as the Gospels state."

Thus, Gera reads and analyzes the three chosen texts in tandem, responding to the three topics articulated in the pope's thought: (1) "evangelization-human promotion," approached on the basis of the difference and the unity between the two; (2) "first evangelization–new evangelization," understanding the newness within continuity; and (3) the relationship between the people of Latin America taken in its totality as well as the ecclesial institution that is at its pastoral service.

It is for this reason, according to the same theologian, that John Paul II presented the unity in the distinction between new evangelization and human liberation as the "double dimension of the gospel" (Homily in Santo Domingo, 3), indicating two priorities for Latin America, articulated together: one of them being faith and the other being the option for the poor. Gera shows how the pope conceives the *new* evangelization: *not* as re-evangelization (as if the first had not been valid), but rather as "new in its methods, ardor, and expression," due to the need for a continuous proclamation of the gospel. In addition, the pontiff does not forget the shadows of the founding evangelization, which is accompanied by historical sins against the native peoples, but neither does he ignore the lights—which are more important than the shadows—at the beginning of the faith and of the Church in the New World, where not only were, and are, the seeds of the Word planted, but also where it yielded fruit that must be multiplied and mature further. Gera had already dealt with this in ISD.

Thus, the holy father was frankly judging the religious situation of the people of Latin America as positive, hungry not only for bread but also, and especially, for the word of God, while, at the same time, threatened by secularism, indifference, and sectarianism. Hence, there is a need for greater attention to the people on the part of the ecclesial institution, the importance of the growth in number and quality of its pastors (which are far too few), and the urgency of a new evangelization.

Later, both Aparecida and Pope Francis would require the Church to undergo a true *pastoral conversion,* overcome *obsolete structures,* and adopt a permanent state of mission, which consists in a new and renewed evangelization that demands a struggle for justice and love in all relationships between human beings and with nature, in building—already here on earth, but not *yet* definitive—the kingdom of God.

Finally, in the section titled "Recapitulation and Open Questions," the author concludes that, between Medellín and Santo Domingo, the Church was increasingly focusing on its *evangelizing* mission, while avoiding the pitfalls of dualism and reductionism. It also overcame the false dichotomy between evangelization and human liberation, since the latter arises as an *intrinsic* demand of faith itself, which operates out of charity.

Another important conclusion is the recognition that in Latin America Christianity, in its Catholic expression, is the faith of the majority, despite the fact that there are some native peoples who have not yet been evangelized, that there is a growing religious pluralism, and that there is the phenomenon of atheism and agnosticism. Despite all this, there is still an open question about the need for a wholistic vision and a mature and well-founded judgment of the pastoral teaching on popular Catholicism in Latin America, based on concrete traits and theological criteria. This is not because its fundamentally Christian nature is in doubt, but because the people of Latin America were (and continue to be) faced with a historical challenge, which was noted by

John Paul II at that time: the challenge of certain internal weaknesses as well as the external threats mentioned above. Hence, we have the insistence on the new evangelization that John Paul II first considered for Latin America and then extended to the universal Church. Hence, we also have the importance of Gera's contribution to universal theology and to all the particular churches in view of a new evangelization of their respective cultures.

In regard to the immaturity of popular cultures today, Pope Francis sees the remedy within themselves, because "popular piety itself can be the starting point for healing and liberation from these deficiencies" (EG 69), particularly if it is taken into account that "the people evangelizes itself" (EG 122, quoting PD 264) when they have been evangelized, and also that "underlying popular piety, as a fruit of the inculturated Gospel, is an active evangelizing power which we must not underestimate: to do so would be to fail to recognize the work of the Holy Spirit... especially at a time when we are looking to the new evangelization" (EG 126).

For my part, I consider that the evangelizing and liberating potential of the popular spirituality of the poor not only extends to themselves and their culture but also radiates to everyone, in the service of the new evangelization of the entire world, both of individuals and of cultures and their structures.

Part II

TOWARD AN INCULTURATED THEOLOGY

The two chapters of the first part of this work delved historically and thematically in the theology of the people (chapter 1), explained the fundamental characteristics of its most important author, Lucio Gera (chapter 2), and pointed out some of its accomplishments, such as in ecclesiology for which we summarized the partially published thesis of Carlos María Galli. Galli is one of the most representative and fruitful disciples of Gera and his successor as chair of ecclesiology at the Pontificia Universidad Católica de Argentina. In 2015, he was appointed to the International Theological Commission, to which his teacher had also belonged.

This work does not attempt to give a complete view of the aforementioned theology. First, it has not finished its systematic development of all the functional specializations and theological disciplines; second and more important, it would be too pretentious. It only attempts to offer, from the perspective of the theology of the people, some reflections—particularly epistemological and methodological—about a key issue: the inculturation of theology itself.[1]

This attempt might perform a true service to the universal Church and theology, which has already begun, in a way, through the work of Pope Francis. He takes seriously the option for the poor as a theological category (EG 198) and therefore recognizes expressions of popular piety as a theological locus (EG 126), as I consider, for an *inculturated* theology at the service of the inculturation of faith, given "the importance of evangelization understood as inculturation" (EG 122).

Hence, this book is born of the conviction that these three affirmations—the option for the poor as a theological category, popular piety as a *locus theologicus,* and their interaction with each other and with the inculturation of theology—are universally valid, not only for Latin America, but for the whole Church and for each particular church, especially when thinking theologically about the new evangelization (EG 126).

Although he had no personal experience of Latin America, Karl Rahner had an acute sense of theological reality. Thus, he had already perceived two characteristic areas of Latin American life and particular reflections as important contributions to the Church and Latin American theology. Those are *a liberating theology* and a *religion of the people.* That is why he compiled and edited a book about each of these subjects.[2] The two are connected, respectively, to the option for the poor and popular piety. These are the two foundational characteristics of the theology of the people and, in my opinion, are also part of the fresh air from the south irrupting in the Church, thanks to a pope who came "from the ends of the earth." From both we can derive an inculturated theology, which in its context contributes not only content but also method to the universal theology and Church.

Although these two theological issues have been discussed in Europe since El Escorial (1972), the first (liberation) was increasingly well known, thanks to global diffusion of the main currents of liberation theology and the passionate discussions about it, as well as the ecumenical dialogue among Third World theologians, including Africans and Asians, who were also concerned about the second, religion and culture.

Hence, the reevaluation of popular piety, which had not been dealt with at the council, was proposed at the level of the universal Church by the "bishops of Africa, Asia, and above all, Latin America"[3] in the 1974 Synod on evangelization. I previously spoke of the role taken by Eduardo Pironio—later a cardinal—in the reception of this issue by Paul VI and in his post-synodal exhortation *Evangelii Nuntiandi.* This had an impact on Latin American pastoral practice and theology through the Conference of Puebla, whose objective was to apply this exhortation. Gera was an important expert in its preparation and in the redaction of the document on the evangelization of culture, since a true popular pastoral ministry and theology based on the praxis of the peoples should listen to the people and begin with them and their human and evangelical values, among whom popular piety occupies a central role. It was no accident that Gera's Italian translator had already designated him not only a "theologian *of* the people" but "*from* the people."

Thus, the religion of the people, rather than being viewed merely as one pastoral and theological topic among others, was reaffirmed as a *hermeneutical locus* both for the reinterpretation of the history of the Latin American evangelization for theological reflection and pastoral action and as the *matrix* of theology.[4]

Thus, I approach popular piety as the hermeneutical locus of an *inculturated* theology, that is, as a place of reflection, interpretation, and critical knowledge of the Christian message, because it is the privileged place of its experience, its practice, and its wisdom. Thus, I will attempt to respond to the legitimate desire for the inculturation of theology.

Previously, I stressed the nature of this *hermeneutical locus* of popular religiosity and piety. After Aparecida and EG, however, we must advance even more beyond the ground already covered. While Vatican II (1962–65) does not deal with this topic, the Conference of Medellín (1968) speaks of popular religiosity and, in contrast with Puebla, connects it to the ministry of the masses and to natural religiosity. Puebla

(1979) instead interprets it more positively, not only as a seed, but also as fruit of the Word, without denying its deficiencies. *Evangelii Nuntiandi* (1975) had already introduced a positive vocabulary, calling it "religion of the people" and "popular piety." Later, the Aparecida Document (2007; henceforth, AD) enriches it, mentioning "popular spirituality" (AD 259, 263) and even "popular mysticism" (AD 263).

In EG, Pope Francis takes several decisive steps in the same line of the theology of the people and Aparecida, but he extends it. This must be taken into consideration, above all, because he elevates the discussion from the Latin American regional level to a universal level, as Paul VI had already done, and with a positive approach. It interprets popular *mysticism* not only in its religious elements, as AD did, but extends it to the *whole* of life and of Christian shared life, since "the genius of each people receives in its own way the entire Gospel and embodies it in expressions of prayer, fraternity, justice, struggle and celebration" (EG 237). Finally, and particularly, he encounters in such expressions a hermeneutical place for theology, a true *theological locus*, a declarative source of revelation in its inculturated reception of a particular culture, and, consequently, the place of a genuine *inculturated* theology that, because it is theology, has universal validity. It can serve as universal inspiration for various inculturated theologies in other cultures.

It is a theological locus in the strict sense, a source of knowledge of revelation for theology, not a *constitutive* locus such as Scripture or tradition, but a *declarative* one.[5] In spite of this, at present there has been reflection about the interaction of the ten places that Melchor Cano had explicated, and the fact that he placed "the authority of the Church" as the first of the declarative ones and in intimate and direct relationship with the constitutive ones has been valued. Thus, Marie-Dominique Chenu and René Laurentin consider as *locus theologicus* "the life of the Church," and, following them, Gustavo Gutiérrez, "the life, preaching, and historical commitment of the Church,"[6] and Hans J. Pottmeyer, the saints.[7] For Hans Urs von Balthasar, "the presence is given [*Vergegenwärtigung*: making oneself present] of the theological existence of Christ in the existence of his faithful and saints [who] seek this realization of the event of revelation."[8] In addition, for Peter Hünermann, the addressees are a *constitutive* part of the same trinitarian event,[9] in which an important role is played not only by Jesus Christ but by the Holy Spirit. The *loci* are, according to Max Seckler, the "bearers of the witness of revelation, and instances of witnessing of the same":[10] as disciples, the addressees are also witnesses, missionary disciples, and in this double nature they also constitute not only a theological but a hermeneutical place.

This illuminates and enriches the aforementioned statement of the pope regarding popular piety, an essential part of the life of the Church, in evangelized people who, through it, continue to evangelize themselves. Revelation is an event whose centrality belongs to the Holy Spirit, although it needs missionary disciples—as addressees and witnesses—as a constitutive part of it. Although this event is above all theologal and theological, however, it is also historical and cultural, given the incarnational nature of Christian revelation. Thus, I think that popular piety is a source of knowledge not only *of the faith* but of an *inculturated faith*, without diminishing its transcultural and universal value.

Pope Francis goes further, since when he affirms, "Expressions of popular piety have much to teach us; for those who are capable of reading them, they are a *locus theologicus* which demands our attention," he immediately adds, "especially at a time when we are looking to the new evangelization" (EG 126). For my part, I interpret this last phrase as referring particularly to Europe, which is experiencing a powerful secularization, comparable to a "fourth dark night" or "cultural dark night" (Chiara Lubich).[11] It therefore needs a new evangelization, but this requires conversion. It is precisely mercy and conversion toward the poor, excluded, refugees, Christian or not, who teach religiosity, that will return to Europe the ultimate meaning of life and religion, if they only open their hearts to mercy.

Ignacio Ellacuría indicates another important point relating the theological locus in itself in a wide sense[12] as a hermeneutical locus; for instance, the option for the poor makes theological loci—and even Scripture—"yield more of themselves,"[13] starting from where it is experienced and read. Thus, the two meanings of the expression "theological locus" not only are not mutually exclusive but also empower each other. This is popular piety in both senses.

Henceforth, I will show that *popular wisdom* can be a bridge between the religion of the people and the inculturation of theology in a particular culture, according to the following categories: religion of the people, popular wisdom, and inculturated theology. I will deal with this in chapter 6, referring not only to Latin America, where this approach originated, but also to the issue of its universal power. In chapter 5, I will use Latin America as an example, looking up to its analogical application in the various inculturated cultures and in context, which today already present themselves "in each great sociocultural arena."[14] Before that, however, it is necessary to better define the concept of "people," since it is implied in *of* the people (a genitive that is at the same time objective and subjective), or in the adjective *popular*, and indirectly in the concept "culture" as belonging to each people. So, before delving fully into inculturation and inculturated theology, I will devote the third chapter to the understanding of "people" both at the civil level and at the level of people of God, as conceived by the theology of the people.

Chapter 3

"PEOPLE" AND "POPULAR" IN SOCIAL REALITY, MINISTRY, AND THEOLOGICAL REFLECTION

Gustavo Gutiérrez, one of the main representatives of the theology of liberation, characterizes the "irruption of the poor in the Latin American history" as their coming to "the forefront both in society as in the Church and, through this means, to the theological reflection accompanying these realities."[1] In this way, Gutiérrez directly points out the close relationship present among social realities (the poor and its irruption in society), the pastoral praxis of the Church, and theology. This took place in Latin America and should also happen in each "major socio-cultural area" (AG 22), above all, in a "Church which is poor and for the poor" (EN 198).

Such a connection is not surprising, as pastoral charity seeks to respond efficaciously to the human and Christian situation of the people, particularly of the poor. For its part, theology interprets and discerns in the light of the word of God the historical situation as both the pastoral and social praxis responding to it. Theology is the "second act" (reflective and critical in the light of revelation) of the "first act," which consists in the spiritual experience incarnated in the faithful, not least that of the poor, in search of both their eschatological and historical liberation.[2]

This is not to deny either the distinction of real dimensions unified in theological, ethical, and historical praxis without being confused, or of epistemological levels in critical reflection, respectively that of theology, philosophy, and the human sciences, but to orient the consideration of the practical and theoretical.

This chapter tries to contribute to the understanding of this interaction between social reality, ministry, and theology. It will not approach it in an abstract manner, but concretely: the determination of the meaning of *people* and *popular* in the area of popular religiosity and ministry as these are experienced, theologically reflected on, and oriented to pastoral practice according to the theology of the people, particularly, but not only, in Argentina. In this way, I will complete what has been said about this theology in part 1, wishing to contribute to a better understanding of the theology underlying the pastoral approach of Pope Francis.

I will not, however, fail to allude to the praxis and understanding of "people" and "popular" in other social and pastoral experiences and in other Latin American theological conceptualizations distinct from the theology of the people, since in both cases we are dealing with the irruption of the Latin American people, poor and faithful, in society, in ministry, and in theology, though interpreted differently in each case. Such a consideration may help to universalize analogically these interpretations and refer them to the lived experiences of other particular churches of other continents.

Now, because social reality is complex, a mere global intuition is not enough to understand its structure and the processes that generate and transform it. Hence the need, both for ministry and for theology, historical and social reflection, of going through analytical mediation,[3] that is, the analysis provided by the human sciences of society, history, culture, and religion.

Although this is necessary, however, it is not enough because the pastor and the theologian also need—as human beings and as Christians—an ethical and wisdom-based judgment about the society in which they live, in which the believer is also born from this vision of faith and of the "innate capacity of affective understanding given by love."[4] This pastoral judgment does not exclude analytical mediation and could guide it, while assuming a certain degree of reality analysis, even though it is unscientific. Perhaps this is what has been called a "pastoral vision of reality"—an expression adopted by Puebla in the title of the first part of the PD.

Therefore, from now on when I deal with the understanding of "people" and "popular" in what some call the Argentinian school of "popular pastoral"[5] ministry, I will distinguish four instances: (1) the social realities in themselves; (2) their interpretation by the various human sciences (history, sociology, and cultural anthropology); (3) pastoral experiences responding to such realities that assume (at least partially or tacitly) such interpretations; and (4) the theological reflection that accompanies them. Such a differentiation becomes necessary for the clarification and exposition of the topic, but I am aware that the interaction among these four instances was not only given in the generation of the "Argentinian school" itself but underlies my own understanding of it and the realities that it tries to respond to. On the other hand, it would be naively positivist to think that we could separate the facts from their interpretation at the various levels of knowledge, even though they, of course, transcend them and set the guidelines to judge their validity.

THE SOCIAL REALITY OF ARGENTINIAN POPULAR CATHOLICISM AND ITS REAPPRAISAL

A massive social reality in Argentina, as in all Latin America, is popular religiosity, which, among us, is fundamentally popular

Catholicism. Although it is concentrated in the humblest sectors of the population, both urban and rural, articulating their culture, it is shared among almost all, particularly those of the middle class. First, it is characterized by its historical origins in the cultural Hispanic–Indigenous American mix,[6] the trunk on which contributions of later immigration easily inserted themselves. It is characterized by its capacity for resistance and cultural assimilation; it endured in spite of the scarcity of the clergy caused by the downfall of colonial rule and the struggles for independence and the attacks of official anticlericalism, particularly toward the end of the nineteenth century. In assimilating the contributions of popular Catholicism of immigrants (especially that of Italians and Spaniards), in two generations it took away a lot of certain anticlericalism that often accompanied it. Moreover, in spite of the progress of urbanization and industrialization, popular Catholicism not only did not weaken but apparently still finds urban forms of expression, as shown by the growth of mass Marian pilgrimages, even of the young, to Luján; the spread of typically urban shrines, such as St. Cajetan (patron saint of workers); the rapid spread of new popular devotions, such as Our Lady Untier of Knots;[7] and the basically Christian consciousness of the working class and the organized labor movement. (This had been started by anarchist immigrants, but at the time of its "expression," it took on a national character of its own, influenced by the first social encyclicals.)

Another social phenomenon, secondary but important for understanding the context of the popular pastoral ministry in Argentina, was the revaluation of popular culture by Argentinian intellectuals, including the clergy.[8] Of course, the "popular" in itself had already irrupted in Argentinian history, both in the formation of the culture proper to its mixed-race character and in political or military popular movements, before emancipation but especially during and after it (from the *artiguismo* and the guerrillas of Güemes during the struggle for independence, until the "populist" *irigoyenismo* and Peronism in the last hundred years).[9] However, the "popular" was insufficiently valued by Argentinian intellectuals, or by those with liberal convictions (oriented culturally toward the French Enlightenment and economically toward

Anglo-Saxon capitalism), or by those of a conservative bent (and, since 1930, also the nationalist right) who were nostalgic for pre-Bourbon Spain. Nor would it have been appreciated by the intellectuals of the left, who were strongly elitist and biased toward Europe. In all these cases, the culture and religion of the people were either despised as "barbarian" and reactionary, or they were considered in a paternalistic way as deficient forms of Western culture and religion, judging them tainted by superstition.

Instead, during the time of the military governments and the political proscriptions following the fall of Perón (from 1955 to 1973), in some Argentinian intellectual circles there was a revaluation of their own people and culture, one whose central elements is popular Catholicism. They were led to this not only by their opposition to new structures of economic, political, and cultural dependence but also by the experience of resistance of the Argentinian people and their worker organizations against that dependence and against the military regime.

On the other hand, in Catholic intellectual environments and in the clergy, there was an even more relevant influence, of which I will speak later, namely, the reception of Vatican II (1962–65) by the Argentinian Church and the second general conference of the Latin American bishops in Medellín (1968).

THE CONTRIBUTION OF THE HUMAN SCIENCES

The very style of my exposition reflects the influence that historical research and reflection had over this new consciousness, both pastoral and theological, of the reality and value of popular expressions. Already in the 1930s, there had been in Argentinian historical science so-called "historical revisionism" of a nationalist bent (although still not popular) that, sometimes unilaterally, had subjected the interpretation of Argentinian history, built and taught by the liberal historiography (illuminist and pro-British), to a critical revision, reclaiming the Spanish colonization, particularly in the time of the Habsburgs. Later, a more scientific and nuanced post-revisionism continued this work, which helped in understanding the formation of the Argentinian people and to detect a line of historical continuity among various national and popular movements in different periods, including Peronism. The new historical consciousness of intellectuals such as Vicente Sierra, José María Rosa, Juan José Hernández Arregui, or Abelardo Ramos contributed from quite different and even opposing positions, but all nationalistic. The revaluation of the people and its history led in many cases to a revaluation of their culture and religiosity.

In this climate, the social sciences reacted against the modernizing sociology represented in 1950s Argentina by Gino Germani.[10] This placed the traditional society (sacred) in opposition to the modern (secular), neglecting the cultural element in its social analysis. This was just a step away from considering Argentinian popular Catholicism as a static element proper to a traditional agrarian society.

In the mid-1980s, there was a reaction throughout Latin America against the modernizing "scientific sociology," in the name of a "critical sociology" committed to structural change. For this to occur, a dependent capitalist modernization was not the solution for the Latin America under development but rather its structural cause. While elsewhere the "theory of dependence" had a Marxist bias, however, in Argentina the orientation was nationalistic, although popular and anticapitalist. This was the time of the so called "national chairs" at the University of Buenos Aires, which in their analysis privileged historical categories, influenced by post-revisionism, such as that of "people" over those of the sociology of modernization, or the Marxist ones. As we said in the first chapter, Justino O'Farrell served as a bridge between those chairs and the Bishops' Committee for Ministry, where the theology of the people was born and who applied this notion primarily to the people of God and in the second place to its relationships to peoples and cultures.

It was in this context and that of the post–Vatican II era that the Argentinian postconciliar religious sociology approached the issue of popular Catholicism. First, the reaction against the sociology of secularization moved within its categories and used the opposition of "mass religion" and "elitist religion," as well as the hypothesis of the "popularization" of a universal religion and its further massification, with the consequent loss of power in the face of the attacks of secularization. However, by then, authors such as Aldo Büntig revalued, although still within theoretical frameworks, Argentinian popular Catholicism, not only as a generalized phenomenon to be taken into account at the social and pastoral levels, but also as the inculturation of a universal religion and as the eventual bearer of evangelical values and, in relationship to it, as a possible factor of historical liberation.[11]

Such an approach facilitated a further evolution. Disciples of Büntig, as well as others, took a critical look at the same theoretical frameworks of his religious sociology, inspiring themselves on perspectives taken from historical science, cultural anthropology, and, above all, pastoral praxis and reflection.[12] The latter had deemed such theoretical proposals inadequate for the reality at hand. Thus, sociology influenced the pastoral and theological both through action and by reaction and, in turn, was influenced by these in order to elaborate new hypotheses and theoretical frameworks of religious sociology.

This is how this sociology, based on the Argentinian and Latin American experience, began to question the identification between modernization and secularization, affirming the possible "coexistence of urbanization, industrialization, and bureaucratic organization with the maintenance of a cultural pattern of popular religiosity in urban contexts."[13]

A similar ebb and flow of influences in historical science, ministry, and politics seems to have also taken place in the case of *Argentinian cultural anthropology*, which, perhaps more decisively than sociology, has been researching popular Catholicism from a new approach: the world of symbols, narrations, and devotions of popular culture, whose understanding of life and death is profoundly religious.[14]

The cultural and intellectual environment we have described, although by no means encompassing the whole Argentinian academic world, dedicated to the human sciences, is nonetheless sufficiently significant and interrelated to social, political, and religious facts to which I have alluded before, as well as to the theological and pastoral reflection that I will soon discuss.

THE PRAXIS OF POPULAR PASTORAL MINISTRY

One of the most important pastoral fruits of the council in Argentina was doubtless the emergence of popular ministry. I will deal with this now, leaving for the next section the consideration of the pastoral-theological reflection done from and about it, although both were given in a kind of dialectic unity of theory and praxis. Both elements are important to understand more deeply the theological and pastoral approaches of Pope Francis.

The council's shift toward humanity in its historic-salvific reality caused in Argentina, as in many regions of the world, a pastoral shift to the concrete person, their social situation (often of poverty and structural injustice), their culture, and religiosity. All this prepared the stage in which the new leaven of Medellín (1968) found fruitful ground in which to develop. Together with traditional ministry and a certain modernizing, somewhat irrelevant pastoral outlook, a new line gradually took strength, which self-defined as "popular ministry."[15]

The fervor caused among us after Medellín by the Movement of Priests for the Third World, the *villas* priests (called this because they worked in *villas* [slums] of misery), the transfer of works and schools of the religious from aristocratic neighborhoods to popular suburbs, and so on was an index of pastoral vitality and at the same time of the search, sometimes difficult, for ecclesial discernment.

In the first phase (around 1970), this shift by many pastors toward the impoverished, oppressed, and faithful people was partly channeled to social protest and to the prophetic denunciation of injustice and structural dependence, sometimes taking a strong political tonality: it was the moment to own and embody the challenge of the poor. However, because turning to the poor was, in the majority of cases, real and not merely rhetorical, the poor and faithful people themselves once again began to show their piety to the pastoral agents, with their knowledge of how to give space to the political aspects but also transcending them while keeping their religious identity; their historical memory, which is wise and astute both because of its rootedness in tradition and because of its lived experience of achievements and failures; its sense of time and expectations without yielding, but without impatience (such as what the guerrilla movements were proposing at the time); its sense of work, which knows how to shape at a slow but sure pace a resistant reality; and the sense of fiesta in which the "not yet" recognizes and celebrates the "already" of salvation, of fraternal communion and liberation. I consider that without these bases, it is not easy to ascertain many of Bergoglio's pastoral attitudes.

Thus, pastoral agents slowly understood that people repudiate not only injustice but also terrorist and repressive violence; they recognize their feeling, at the same time popular (of the dignity of the poor and of work, of solidarity and struggle for justice) and national (with a treasuring of social friendship in the search for the common good), and they mistrust both liberal capitalism and the doctrine of national security (having suffered in their own flesh the consequences of both), as well as Marxism, which they perceived as opposed to their cultural, religious, and national values.

Such a school of contact with the people, together with theological reflection—above all, ecclesiological—and the doctrinal orientations of the Church, helped Argentinian popular pastoral ministry, without losing its evangelical critical and prophetic spirit, to become truly pastoral and popular, freeing itself from the risks of Enlightenment elitism (both liberal and Marxist) and the danger, which was real, of being swayed by a dialectic of class struggle transferred to the inside of the Church.

The people who, in spite of many deficiencies, in a large measure already enjoyed consciousness and social and political organization, but who at the same time had been able to preserve (although sometimes transforming them) many of its religious values and traditional devotions, retaught many pastoral agents the value of devotion and of devotions and became an antidote against the spirit of secularization to which perhaps some of the most committed postconciliar Catholics were inclined. It is true that at this time a grave vocational crisis of priests and religious took place, but one of the factors facilitating the overcoming of this was revaluing not only popular piety but piety itself, through the closer contact of the religious with simple people and allowing themselves to be taught by the people. I consider that this whole history explains many attitudes and thoughts of Pope Francis, which can be elevated to the universal pastoral level, insofar as they are deeply evangelical and culturally situated.

Such a renewed encounter with the religious aspects helped pastoral agents (particularly priests and religious) to relocate themselves close to the people, in their capacity as shepherds, but without losing the social and prophetic dimension they had just acquired, so that, indirectly, such a relocation was, I believe, an important factor in the later vocational resurgence in Argentina.

Such experiences and the accompanying theological reflections (of which I will later speak) served as the basis for important contributions of Argentinian popular ministry to the Document of Puebla (1979), particularly in reference to the chapters on "The Evangelization of Culture" and "Evangelization and Popular Religiosity," trying to reflect on a ministry not only for the people but *from* the people.

An important fruit of such a new encounter of the shepherds, not only with the people, but with themselves as shepherds, was also the rising of new forms of evangelization of popular religiosity and of evangelization through it, as "evangelizing" and socially liberating as were, for instance, the new ministry of shrines and pilgrimages, the self-social promotion of the *villeros*, the rising of religious and social leaders (including priestly vocations) from the popular sectors, the apostolate in the barrios and, in some dioceses, of small Christian communities, and so on.[16]

Overcoming the crisis of the beginning of the 1970s, the learning from the people, the discernment that took place, and the subsequent pastoral refocusing helped Argentinian popular ministry to stand with the people, without going to any extremes in the difficult years that followed: the worsening of subversive terrorism, the repression carried out by the same inhuman methods of terrorist violence (especially since 1975), the war in the Falkland Islands (1982), the hard return to democracy in 1983, the period of "Menemist"[17] neoliberalism, the unprecedented socioeconomic crisis (2001), and the rebuilding that started with Néstor Kirchner[18] but is not finished and is still in question today.

THE THEOLOGY OF POPULAR MINISTRY

The perspective from which I am writing, and many of the assessments and value judgments made thus far, were taken to the level of theological reflection by what we can call "the theology of popular ministry," whose main representative is, no doubt, as I have repeatedly expressed, Lucio Gera. Gustavo Gutiérrez recognizes this theological line as a "trend with its own traits within the theology of liberation";[19] many times this is presented as its "national or popular" or "populist" version (according to whether it is accepted or criticized), although some prefer not to call it "theology of liberation," because of the most common use of the term.

I will first deal with pastoral-theological reflections of this trend regarding the understanding of *people* and *popular* when speaking of religiosity, culture, or popular wisdom. Later, I will say something about their impact not only in the understanding of civil society, but also of the people of God. Both concepts attempt to have a universal value (respectively, philosophical and theological), although the core is an analogical and inculturated universality.

With this new development, I complete what was said in the first part of this work, whose focus was about all historical, without ignoring systematic, characteristics. I believe this will also help us to better understand the terminology of Pope Francis when he likes to refer to the Church as the "faithful people of God."

The Understanding of "People" and "Popular"

Based on the Argentinian historical, political, and pastoral experience, such a theology understands the people as a communitarian subject of a history and a culture.[20] It is the subject of history because it is so of common historical experiences, of a collective consciousness of mutual belonging, and of a historical project of the common good (not necessarily explicit). When we say "subject of a culture," this is understood as a common lifestyle, that is, a way of relating to each other, to nature, and to the ultimate meaning of life (which our people recognizes in God, Father of our Lord Jesus Christ).[21]

Hence, this meaning of *people* is close to that of *nation*, but this is understood not from the state or the territory but from the culture and the ethical-historical decision of those who participate in a same history and culture, for the same common good. For more than one reason, at least in Latin America, it is the poor and working classes, rightly called *populares*, who constituted the backbone of the people-nation, since, on the one hand, they were the ones who resisted the domination culturally and better preserved the human and Christian values of the culture born of the original cultural mestizaje. On the other hand, the common good, particularly in a situation of deep injustice and structural dependence, includes justice, effective solidarity, and national and social liberation—values to which those who suffer the lack of the first or the second and whose only strength resides on the second are more sensitive. Thus, for this theological line, the determination of who "people" are or who have become an "antipeople" is not given by mere citizenship or residence, or by a socio-structural class analysis, but by an ethical-historical discernment. "Antipeople" refers to those who are opposed to the common good, both ethical-historical (justice, inclusive of structural justice) and ethical-cultural (the cultural identity of the nation). Those who oppose the common good, oppressing persons, social classes, races, or cultures, insofar as they do it and to the extent that they do it, exclude themselves from the ethical-historical "us" of the people. This implies the need for an ethical-spiritual discernment in each historical situation.

Likewise, this type of reflection, because it is opposed to the theology of secularization, is characterized by an understanding of the close bonds uniting religion and, in our case, the Christian faith with the different dimensions of culture, even political culture (without diminishing its autonomy), because the ultimate meaning of life and of culture is played out in the religious or irreligious attitude. This indirectly impacts, through the mediation of the ethical-historical element, all the spheres of life and of common life, not only at the level of values and personal and collective practices, but also in the sphere of the institutions and structures that made them effective—by an analogical transference of perspectives—on the theories that reflect, critique, and guide such practices.

Hence, this approach strongly values Latin American and Argentinian popular Catholicism as the cultural form that faith and a Christian understanding of the human person and life assumed in our own culture. Although it emphasizes the religious and pastoral moment of popular religiosity, it doesn't forget its cultural moment and political aspects. Because it is historical, it is not static but dynamic and always open to the new. Besides, as above all it deals with the meaning of the ultimate and of the human, it does not identify with what is professedly Catholic but is shared by other Christian confessions and other "Abrahamic" religions and even by many humanistic nonbelievers.

Such a theological trend, without ignoring what is valid in the socio-structural analysis, also uses and privileges the mediation of the historical and cultural analysis (which is proper of more synthetic sciences, such as history or anthropology), as well as poetic and symbolic and explicitly religious categories, both for interpretation and for the theological discernment of popular religiosity and culture, and of the social and historical situation, indirectly by semantic transposition, as for its theological reflection.

An Inculturated Theological Reflection

It is characteristic of this trend to attempt to articulate the wisdom of the people of God inculturated in our popular culture into a theological discourse.[22] In Latin America, the people of God in fact takes flesh in peoples who from their own culture understand sapientially the faith, which, as has been said, had a decisive influence, in turn, on the formation of their culture. The idea is, then, "to gather in a theological concept" that popular wisdom in order to understand faith in an inculturated way, also at the level of theology as a science. Of course, as is the case with a strictly philosophical conceptual mediation,[23] such categories taken from the history, culture, praxis of the people, or their interpretation by the human sciences must be critically purified from faith itself as they are placed at the service of its understanding, enfleshed in an inculturated way in popular wisdom. The sciences, including philosophy, serve then as mediation for a theological articulation of popular wisdom, without exhausting them in concept.

A case of such inculturated theology is presented by ecclesiological reflection. As the Document of Puebla says, the council took place during a special time for Latin American peoples: "years of problems, of anguished search for their own identity, marked by the awakening of popular masses and by attempts to Latin American integration….This has prepared the environment in the Catholic people to easily be open to a Church who also presents itself as 'people'" (PD 233). In Argentina, the experience of being a people and the accompanying categorization helped to avoid in postconciliar Argentinian ecclesiology placing "communion" and "institution" in contrast to one another. By way of contrast, responding to the "vital synthesis" between the two, and following Puebla's highlighting of the lived experience of Christian popular wisdom (PD 448), they would understand them in their unity.

It is thus that the ecclesiology of authors such as Lucio Gera could overcome the legalism of certain preconciliar ecclesiology without falling into the other extremes: that of some postconciliar ecclesiologies centered on the small community (network of communities in a secular diaspora) or in a rather classist understanding of "people" (with the tendency to oppose "popular Church" to "institutional Church," or to transfer the class struggle to the inside of the Church). The concept of "people" elaborated from the Argentinian popular experience joins the emphasis on the bases of communion and participation to a deep sense of the institutional organic structure.

This concept of "people," therefore, proved apt both for theological reflection on popular religiosity and ministry, and for serving as an inculturated categorization in order to understand the teachings of the council about the people of God. In the first case, this category (taken from historical experience and its interpretation by the human sciences) works as an analytic mediation for a theological reading of the social and socio-pastoral reality. In the second case, however, it is an indirect contribution of such experiences and conceptualization to the understanding of the revelation about the people of God, through an analogical transposition, at the same time faithful to revelation and rooted in history and culture.

In this context, the Church-world relationship was theologically interpreted, as discussed in GS, above all as a relationship between the people of God and peoples with their own history and culture. It is thus that an interest for the history of evangelization of Latin America was awakened as well for the issues of evangelization of culture. This latter approach served to understand in a new way the conciliar affirmation of the autonomy of the temporal realities, thus avoiding not only the aftertaste of Christendom but also the secularist danger of attempting to carry out social, political, and cultural life without the influence of the gospel. In the first chapter of the present work I briefly presented the wide and mature ecclesiology of Galli, who considered the approaches I just indicated, in the line of the theology of the people.

Difference and Convergence with Other Latin American Conceptualizations

This is not the place to compare in detail the social pastoral experience and the Argentinian (although not exclusively Argentinian) categorizations with those that have taken place in other parts of Latin America and that led to another analytic understanding of "people" and theological understanding of "people of God" as "popular Church."[24] I can only sketch out a relationship of convergence and divergence that is given between both interpretations.

Both socio-analytical concepts of "people" are historical and refer to the historical identity of a collective subject. This is distinguished from the mass by consciousness and organization, and it integrates various powers and social groups around a common project. Its axis is made up—in both understandings—by the poor and the oppressed, in contrast with the elites who enjoy unjust privileges. Hence, both respond—at the analytic level—to the preferential option for the poor and the struggle for justice toward a new society in which the present supremacy of capital over work is overcome.

Where, then, lies the difference? The position described above, without denying the oppositions and even contradictions of class, and recognizing the historical and ethical-political fact of the "antipeople," is going to look at the historical-cultural unity of the nation around a popular and national project for the common good. The other type of conceptualization will place the accent not only on the nation but on class, so that the concept of "people" tends to be identified with the classes (races, cultures) who are oppressed, in dialectic opposition to those considered the oppressor.

The second concept has an analytical reach that is theoretically clearer and more distinct, since it dissects sociostructurally the people into its components, according to their conflicts of material or ideological interests, which not infrequently are antagonistic. In contrast, the first concept is more historical and syntactic because in its critical discernment of what people is here and now, or of the authentically popular, it joins together the socio-structural analysis to the historical-cultural and historical-political ones, as well as ethical-historical criteria, namely, the realization of the common good and justice.

The risk of this last conceptualization is its possible "populist manipulation" that may use it as a mask for a project of a national but not popular development, under the hegemony of the national bourgeoisie, breaking apart from the effective participation and the historical centrality of the majority. The danger of the other conceptualization is, on the contrary, the ultimate classist ideological manipulation, from a perspective that reduces society and history to the dialectic class struggle, leaving aside the ethical, historical, cultural, and political unity of the nation.

In recent times, another Argentinian, Ernesto Laclau, reclaimed the populist reason with a concept of "people," which is very different from that of the theology of the people, privileging permanent conflict, the "Gramscian" notion of hegemony, and division of society as strategy of power over the unity of the people-nation.[25] Although its conception is different from that of Gera and his colleagues and disciples, there could be an approximation between both positions if each would fill the significant vacuum of Laclau with their own proper and different content; then the unity of a people could be achieved—and if this fact would be conceived—against Laclau, *analogically*. For instance, the meaning of *justice* is the same, although not univocally equal, but analogically, according to what type of injustice (economic, political, racial, gender, religious discrimination) they are fighting and what type of justice is claimed. From now on, I will not consider this "Laclauian" concept of people in order to think theologically about the people of God.

The different analytical conceptualization could have an incidence, by analogical transposition, in the understanding that, from a faith perspective, we have of the "people of God." In the two cases indicated (before the diversion about Laclau), the following were accentuated: the preferential place that, by a free election of God, the poor occupy in it (a way of being Church that fosters the effective communion and participation of the laity) and the oppressed poor, for example, women (in the way of living historically their being people of God); the need for an inculturation in the pastoral, theological, and legal modalities of the Church in popular culture, although in continuity with tradition; a new pastoral style and exercise of the authority in the Church in accordance with this historical and inculturated way of living, understanding oneself, and organizing as people of God, in fidelity to revelation; an awareness raising also of the ethical-political and sociohistorical realities of popular ministry, without ignoring their religious specificity and the autonomy of the temporal; and so on.

In both approaches, however there are also certain divergences of perspective and ecclesiological accents, with important pastoral and doctrinal consequences. For, if some elements of the Marxist tradition are used for the socio-analytical understanding of people, and then the same concept is used to think theologically of the people of God, the following risks are run: (1) understanding the need to be people in such a way in order to be people of God (i.e., the need and priority, at least chronologically, of a material sociohistorical and practical social structure for the constitution of the people of God), which remains clear to many that this, as such, does not come from down up, but "from above" by a free gift of the Lord; and (2) translating oppositions of class to the historical relationship between hierarchy and laity (particularly the poor) in the Church, understanding it as dialectical conflict of (religious) power among those who hold the means of symbolic production and those who are deprived of them.[26]

These risks are not present in the other sociological understanding of people that, as has already been said, unites the ideas of communion, participation, and differentiated organization. For this is more easily "analogizable" by thinking of the people of God—in the light of revelation—as being at once fraternal and hierarchically structured. As an inculturated and historical way of doing it, however, this emphasizes and revalues aspects of revelation that are historically more relevant, such as the place of the poor in the people of God, the experience of authority as a service, and the affirmation of an effective practice of participation of all as the social "base," which "gives body" to the gift of God who convokes and constitutes his people.

In my estimation, the image of a *polyhedron,* presented by Pope Francis to represent both the people of God and each people and the universal interaction among the peoples (EG 236), responds to the understanding exposed above as it implies a unity superior to differences that, however, it assumes and respects in their undeniable differentiation. Its model is the Trinity as communion.

In regard to the participation mentioned above, let us take into account that the Argentinian sociological understanding of "people" does not distinguish it from the mass through a type of consciousness, organization, and effective participation manifestly self-conscious (mistaking the real self-consciousness and the explicit *reflective* self-consciousness in an "enlightenment" way). Thus, when it uses the concept *pueblo* to understand the people of God in faith or to discern theologically the evangelic and liberating value of popular Catholicism, it does not ignore the *wisdom* consciousness of collective identity given by faith itself, although this may not be sufficiently reflected on; the unity in a *project* that gives the hope of the kingdom, even if all their consequences, even the historical ones may not be explicit; and the *effective participation* born of charity, even if it may not be explicit and reflectively organized. Obviously, popular ministry must foster such articulations, but not without recognizing the existence of a practical and social (and in this sense "socio-material") support, so that the people of God be appropriately and really people and not only by a metaphor, being such a people by analogy (in the technical sense of the word).[27]

What has been said thus far can help us understand, in a concrete way, the Argentinian case and how social realities, their analysis and interpretation by the human sciences, ministry, and theology, are articulated.[28] First of all, through a theological and pastoral reading of the historical and social reality, the human sciences operate by providing theology with an analytic mediation in order to interpret and discern reality (e.g., Argentinian popular religion) in the light of the word of God. Once again, the categorization taken from social realities (e.g., "people") can be used, through an analogical transference, to understand newly, in a historical and inculturated form, the same revelation (e.g., the Church as people of God). In both cases, however, faith provides the ultimate theological and pastoral criteria because it is theology itself that must discern, in the light of revelation, the mediations that helped it as an instrument, for a theological reading of social realities and for the reading of faith itself and for a pastoral and social praxis inspired in the gospel.

Chapter 4

POPULAR WISDOM AND INCULTURATED THEOLOGY

In its decree *Ad Gentes,* the Second Vatican Council, recalling the economy of incarnation, refers to young churches—and in some way to all churches—and affirms that it is necessary for each great sociocultural territory to promote theological research that might undertake a new investigation of its own reality, in the light of the tradition of the universal Church as well as the words and deeds revealed by God that are consigned in Sacred Scripture and explained by the fathers and the Church's magisterium. In this way, we will see more clearly the ways that faith can reach the mind, taking into account the philosophy or wisdom of the peoples, and how customs, the meaning of life, and the social order can be combined with the understanding of divine revelation (AG 22).

Note that this involves "each great sociocultural territory" (for instance, sub-Saharan Africa, India, China, Latin America, and so on), the method ("by what paths"), and the theology (the latter two, at least at the level of wisdom, if not science), since the text calls for "faith to reach the mind." "The philosophy or wisdom of the peoples" is placed in parallel, so that this is given the comprehensive mediating function for this intelligence, which for St. Thomas, for example, is the domain of philosophy (Aristotelian). Even if not all peoples developed their own philosophy at the same scientific level as the Greeks did with Plato and Aristotle, there is not a people that lacks a popular wisdom, concentrated above all in the ultimate meaning of life. With Ricœur we could say that popular wisdom is distilled in the ethical-mythical core of its culture.

As it was stated in the first part of the book, the theology of the people—called by others the "theology of culture"—favors historical-cultural analysis, without ignoring the socio-structural one, in order to interpret and critically discern the particular situation of a specific people and of the community of nations, in a particular time of history, and in the light of the word of God. Such procedure culminates when popular wisdom serves as a mediation to inculturate theology, with theology both as wisdom and as a science.

Such theological trends apply, above all, to the peoples of Latin America, and not least to Argentina, but it claims that "these paths to reach the intelligence of faith" can be undertaken beginning with the wisdom of each and every one of the peoples and that, in fact, they have been undertaken throughout history, although very seldom with explicit awareness. It does not claim to be the only way to inculturate and contextualize theology, but it is a valid way to achieve it.

In the next section, I will take the following steps: first, I will demonstrate how popular wisdom in Latin America, explicitly recognized in Puebla, in fact served to propose an inculturated theology and took its role seriously as a hermeneutical locus and also as a theological focus. I will then demonstrate that, although placed in a certain context, this theology not only has a universal value, but its journey of inculturation is analogically "universalizable," so that faith reaches the intelligence (knowledge and scientific), incarnating itself also in other cultures. Later, I will approach the issue of whether the people, the subject of wisdom, is also the subject of theology. I will theoretically draw the epistemological consequences of the argument, and I will demonstrate them in a practical way in a brief theological text of my own.

PUEBLA AND POPULAR WISDOM

One of the central topics of the Conference of Puebla was the evangelization of culture, as outlined by Paul VI in the exhortation *Evangelii Nuntiandi*. In this document, the Latin American bishops recognize that the culture of the peoples of Latin America has been historically evangelized in its fundamental core of values, attitudes, beliefs, and symbols, as manifested, for example, by popular religiosity.

In this context, the bishops introduce the topic of popular wisdom, relating it to the event of the evangelization of Latin American culture from its origins, such as its manifestation in religiosity. In Latin American popular wisdom, the "contemplative traits" are intimately linked to the "deep sense of transcendence and, at the same time, the closeness of God" (PD 413), which is proper to the religiosity of the people. In addition, such wisdom "inspires the concrete way in which our men [and women] experience their relationship with nature and with other men [and women]" (PD 413). Later, in the chapter devoted to popular religiosity, they also affirm that

> the religiosity of the people, at its core, is a deposit of values, responding with Christian wisdom to the great questions of existence. Popular Catholic wisdom has a capacity for vital synthesis: it creatively contains within itself both the human and the divine—Christ and Mary, spirit and body, communion and institution, individuals and community, faith and homeland, intelligence and affectivity. This wisdom is a Christian humanism that radically affirms the dignity of every person as a child of God, establishes a fundamental fraternity, teaches us to have an encounter with nature and understand its work, and provides reasons for joy and humor, even in the midst of a very harsh life. For the people, this wisdom is also the beginning of [a process of] discernment, an evangelical instinct by which it spontaneously gathers other elements to itself, both when the gospel is present in the Church and

> when it is absent or suffocated by other interests. (John Paul II, Inaugural Speech, III, AAS LXXI, 203; PD 448)

TOWARD AN INCULTURATED THEOLOGY

As a service to the evangelization of culture and, in turn, the fruit of it, there is an inculturated and "in context" theology that Vatican II (AG 22) desires for each great sociocultural realm (and therefore for Latin America as well), as I have already stated. The council itself points the way when it speaks about considering not only philosophy but also the *wisdom* of the peoples (no. 22). People like those in Latin America, who have not elaborated—at least until recently—a philosophy rooted in their own culture, and reflectively expressed it at the universal level, have recourse to a popular wisdom that could be a mediation for the inculturated understanding of faith since it, as Puebla says, guides the *particular way* in which our people experience and understand their relationship with God, nature, and one another. This is much more feasible when the wisdom of the very life of a people has been evangelized, so that it is a *Christian* wisdom constituted basically for that people as a response to the "great questions of existence"; it is for them a "Christian humanism"; it has a capacity of "vital synthesis," integrating apparent dualisms, and serves as "evangelical instinct" for discernment. All this is applied to the wisdom that constitutes the core of Latin American popular piety, and it also implies a concrete manner of intelligence of the senses, a way that we could denominate prephilosophical[1] but that implicitly contains a philosophy of life.

Thus, popular wisdom can be the mediation for an inculturated theology because it implies a *logos*, or prereflective intelligence, of the meaning of the world, of humanity, and of God, which could provide for the intelligence of faith a mediating function similar to the one fulfilled by a systematically elaborated theology. Moreover, when the issue is the Christian wisdom of the faithful people, inculturated in people like those in Latin America, whose cultural core has already been evangelized, this sapiential *logos* is not only a prephilosophical one, but also pretheological, since the influx of faith is already at work in the understanding of the meaning that is implied by it, once this has been incarnated and inculturated in a "sapiential realm."

For his part, Karl Rahner responds positively to the question of a certain preeminence of popular religion over theology, affirming that it does not consist in the faith of the people being necessarily free from depravation, but rather in its greater *proximity* to the original source of authentic religiosity and faith. This source is constituted by God's free self-communication, which he offers to all. Popular religion owes this greater proximity, according to Rahner, to the fact that it has not yet gone through the network of categories and theological systematizations that would constrain it, but that, without such hindrance, it assumes and fulfills, together with the profound dynamics of grace, all the human elements with their many possibilities as well.[2]

Therefore, recognizing the truth in Rahner's affirmation, we must add that, if we explain popular religion's moment of *wisdom*, we are introducing in said assumption a principle of evaluation and discernment of the human and of the naturally religious, which, in fact, comes with deviations and false interpretations. This is even more certain if we deal with a *Christian* wisdom, as Puebla states. Clearly, theological critical reflection will help us to distinguish true wisdom and Christian popular piety from those that are false or lack authenticity. However, as John Paul II says in the aforementioned quote, such wisdom is an "evangelical instinct" of critical discernment, not just at the reflective level but, according to my interpretation, *per connaturalitatem*, since the pope affirms that it operates "spontaneously" as a "principle of discernment" (PD 448).

INCULTURATED BUT UNIVERSAL THEOLOGY

I will first consider how such a theology can be *universal* while being *situated* and what the mediations are that must be considered methodologically for such a historical-cultural rootedness of the universal.

A Situated Theological Universality

A characteristic trait of theology is its universality, not only as a science, but also as to how the revelation that it studies transcends every concrete historical and geocultural reality and addresses all human beings, peoples, and times. How can it be universal if it is rooted in the popular wisdom *of* a *specific* people, in their culture and religiosity? Or how can it be so without *cutting off* such roots, so that one can no longer speak of inculturation?

Popular wisdom, even if it is proper to a specific people and better illustrated in the poor and the simple, insofar as it is *human* wisdom and sense of life, nevertheless has a universal validity. Of course, we are not talking about an abstract level, or even *the* universal concrete (in a Hegelian manner), but rather a universal that is *situated* historically, geoculturally, and socioculturally, whose conceptualization can only be *analogical*, though no less universal.[3]

What is communitarian and common to *every* human being, as well as what is communitarian and common to a particular people, is more clearly reflected in the poor and simple people (particularly in the poor and simple of poor nations). In them, the human universal is better demonstrated. But this poverty is not so much socioeconomic as ontological (the lack of self-sufficiency and human contingency), which is easily experienced and recognized in physical poverty. Therefore, the criterion to determine this is ontological—not an idealistic ontology, but one incarnated in the social reality. This incarnation, however, is not the ultimate criterion of ontological poverty, although it is its real symbol.[4] Moreover, for a vision of faith, the last criterion is not even at the ontological level but rather at the evangelical one. It is through the poor Christ and the gospel of the Beatitudes that a genuine evangelical poverty is discovered, and in it, as in its internal moment, the true ontological poverty opens to God and human universality. It is not surprising, then, that a true humanism, in accordance with the gospel, is contained in the Christian wisdom of the poor and simple.

Cultural and Theological Rootedness

How could it be possible for theological conceptualizations to be universal without losing their historical and cultural rootedness? To answer this question, we must consider that popular wisdom is first thematized and expressed in forms of language and praxis that are not self-reflective but that imply a certain reflectivity and intelligent articulation. Such wisdom is expressed, above all, through symbols (religious, poetic, political) of every people and their popular songs, proverbs, narratives (myths, sagas, legends), as well as in their historical ways of political and cultural action (e.g., customs, norms, ways of coexistence), religious tradition (rites and devotions), and so on, though all of them are transcended. In them, historical memory, the experience of life and meaning, and the hopes and aspirations of a people are condensed. There, we see in *a single glance* the human-universal and what is proper and original about it, although not necessarily exclusive of that people. I do not conceive of these forms as fixed or petrified (we would once again fall into abstraction), but in the dynamism of their actualization, which transcends them and even modifies them in faithfulness to the same life and history. To paraphrase Ricœur, I would say that they demonstrate such wisdom insofar as they renounce *being* idols in order to be its *symbols*.

If a reflective conceptualization, without leaving behind the universal level of the concept, has its starting point and "gathers in concept" (collectively, not reductively) the "metaphoric truth" of the symbol without attempting to reduce it to its preconcepts,[5] the analogical categorization arising from it will be at once both universal and historically and culturally rooted.[6] In this way, it becomes apt for an intelligence of faith to be inculturated in popular wisdom.

As I said earlier, the *logos* is prephilosophical (and eventually pretheological), insofar as it is universal. This does not imply, however, that it should be considered *protophilosophical*, so that previously elaborated philosophical conceptualizations are projected onto the sapiential and prereflective levels, with which the *specific* contribution of popular wisdom and the weight of tradition of inculturation that comes out of it would disappear. On the contrary, a fruitful hermeneutical circle can be achieved only if it can be found in its "originality."

Juan Luis Segundo, although extremely critical of what he denominates the "theology of the people," recognizes that "from a methodological viewpoint... [it] appears as leading to a hermeneutical circle destined to enrich it and to keep it alive. Indeed, one of the more fruitful methodological suspicions lies in the comparison between a culture logically and conceptually structured on the one hand, and popular wisdom, on the other hand, serving as its imaginative and ritual content, i.e., the internal logic of its strangest attitudes."[7] This requires a task of philosophical reflection at the service of theology—one that takes popular wisdom seriously as a hermeneutical locus, that is, without abandoning the speculative space and, at that level, thinks through the truth of the symbol and of its popular practice. I consider that the symbol being alluded to can be fruitful not only among peoples who do not have a theoretically elaborated philosophy but also among those who have been losing their rootedness in themselves and their wisdom of life.

The "How" and "What" of an Inculturated Theology

The rootedness of theological reflection in the wisdom of the people will not influence so much its "what" (content) as its "from where" and its "how." The "what" of the intelligence of faith is given through revelation. But the "from where" is heard, understood, interpreted, thought out, and necessarily influences that intelligence, although it is in turn illumined, healed, and transformed by faith. So then, the distinct "from where," or hermeneutical, perspective and therefore the cultural solidness of a theology will be demonstrated not so much by its contents but by "how" it is categorized, "how" its understanding is structured, systematized, and interrelated, and in the context of the human situation. The issue is not mainly the judgment of truth and the corresponding doctrines, but the insight and meaning of the same, and of the hermeneutical paradigm corresponding to this understanding.[8]

Nevertheless, it is impossible to distinguish form and content adequately. Just as the word of God is offered in Scripture that is already conceptualized and articulated (although not at the scientific level), so theology must duly take into account this determined form and its historical tradition, as well as the *way* that a people lives, understands, and thinks through the faith, and will *also* be demonstrated at the level of content, at least with a different *emphasis* on the elements of the Christian message, within the parameters of what is permissible. If it is true, for example, as John Paul II affirmed and Puebla reiterated, that Marian piety is part of the Latin American cultural identity and that Marian symbols—such as Guadalupe—express this identity and the cultural mestizaje that founded it, a Latin American theology will have to emphasize, in systematizing its intelligence of faith, the central role of Mary in the economy of salvation, although all Catholic theology must also accept it unreservedly. However, the cultural solidity is demonstrated not at the level of content but only on the accents that positively correspond to the sapiential preunderstanding that a culture has of humanity or of God (and, if it has been evangelized, it is one of faith). On the other hand, sometimes an inculturated theology must accentuate in the gospel message that which responds to what is subject to criticism or is deficient in said preunderstanding, or it remains as an open question. The last criterion of the theological hermeneutical circle is not, nor can it be, popular wisdom, but rather Christ, the Wisdom of God, who reveals the Father as well as humanity.

THE SUBJECT OF POPULAR WISDOM AND THEOLOGY

The subject of popular wisdom is the communitarian "we": the people, whether we speak of a particular historical people or of the people of God inculturated in a specific culture, which through its Christian wisdom "knows" about God and the truths of faith and life. Regardless of our approach (both are complementary when we speak of the evangelization of a culture), this is a collective subject, a "we."[9]

Can we affirm the same thing when we deal not only with wisdom and practical knowledge, but also theoretical and scientific knowledge? Is the historical-cultural people a subject of philosophical conceptualization that could be assumed as an internal moment for an inculturated theology? To answer that question, it is necessary to distinguish the levels in the task of "theologization" of popular wisdom.

The term *people* refers to an organic community that, because it is *organic,* contains within it a differentiation of tasks and functions specifically distinct (and, theologically speaking, of charisms), but, because it is *community,* these functions in themselves are not an exclusive and exclusionary privilege, but a community service that can and ought to be shared actively in some manner by all the members of the community, in a kind of *communicatio idiomatum,*[10] or communication of roles, without losing the specificity of each one.

Among the people of God, there are also roles and charisms that are specifically distinct, one of which is that of the theologian. However, the function of the theologian is not only at the service of the whole community but is in some way shared by the entire community, including the poor and simple faithful people in their "sense of faith." It is precisely there that the incarnation of faith in a culture is found in a more synthesizing manner of all existence if it has been evangelized at its cultural core.

This sense of inculturated faith not only implies in the faithful people an athematic sapiential knowledge and its prereflective thematization in symbols and determined ways of praxis; it is also thematized and logically and conceptually articulated, reaching a certain level of reflection, categorization, argumentation, systematization, and critical discernment, even if not scientific, that is congruent with such feeling and knowledge.

Of course, the professional theologian must methodically, systematically, and critically extend these structured lines of the discourse of faith that begin with the inculturated feeling of the people of God; he or she should do it without breaking or skewing them, but rather respecting them, even purifying them according to the hermeneutical circle about which we are speaking. Neither an intelligent understanding of the word of God, nor a reflection of faith, nor the logically structured articulation of such intelligence and reflection, nor critical discernment are exclusive to the theologian; they also belong to the believer and to the believing community. The methodical, scientific, and theoretical service of the theologian must therefore respect not only the word of God itself, but also the inculturated way in which it is understood by the faithful people's sense of faith, although, of course, part of that service is the critique of pseudoinculturations that might deform the gospel message. Hence, theology as a science must, in turn, be critiqued by its reception and not by the faithful people and their "evangelical instinct" or by the shepherds, the authentic interpreters of the revelation and the sense of faith of the believing community, both at the local and universal levels. The theologian's theology could again and again revitalize the intelligence of faith and the praxis of charity by the faithful people and could perhaps even be assumed by the magisterium or, on the contrary, could be left aside in the long term as a mere theoretical elucubration. And this could be due to two reasons: either because it is not faithful to the faith itself or because it does not respond to the cultural *way in which* the faithful people experience it and think about it.

Hence, it is necessary for the theologian not only to be close to the faith of the people, but also to be close to their culture, their piety, and their sapiential feeling, so that his or her theological service can be done "from within" the inculturated ecclesial "we" in which, above all, the poor and simple have been able to incarnate the faith in popular culture. Thus, for many theologians, a cultural conversion will be necessary.

What Clodovis Boff says in his work "The Pastoral Agent and the People"[11] could be applied to the relationship between the theologian and the people. The model for thinking about the relationship between both is not given by counter-positions such as "knowledge-ignorance," "popular knowledge–scientific knowledge," or "implicit knowledge (previous and inferior)–explicit knowledge (later and superior)," but by the model of the exchange of knowledge that is specific, distinct, irreducible, and valid in their kind, that is, the exchange between the wisdom of life and objective science, in the unity of knowledge.

The previous reflections give us the necessary elements to respond to the questions we had earlier. Theology, even as a science, has an undeniable communitarian character, first, due to its ecclesial nature. Moreover, in the second place, it has it if it is an inculturated theology, since the subject of culture and of the wisdom of life is, at its core, the people.

Therefore, at the level of people of God as such, theology has a collective subject: the community of believers (whose scientific interpreter is the theologian, essentially referring to the faithful people of whom he or she is part, and to its authentic interpreters). So, if we consider the organic nature of this communitarian subject, we will be able to affirm that, in some way, it also pertains to theology as a science.

Additionally, in the case of unique peoples that the universal people of God penetrate, we can also affirm that philosophy, which is an internal moment of an inculturated theology, also has in some way a collective historical-cultural subject (Rodolfo Kusch). The theologian, as he or she "philosophizes" in an *inculturated* way, as an internal moment of his or her own speculative theological task, is therefore an interpreter of popular wisdom—at the scientific level—but within his or her own people and as an organic part of it.

Let this suffice for now, and we will take up this subject again in chapter 6.

SOME EPISTEMOLOGICAL CONSEQUENCES

First of all, it is important to point out, as fruit of the interaction between theology and popular wisdom, the theological and theological-pastoral revaluation of culture, piety, and popular wisdom, among whose fruits is the hermeneutics I am presenting. By the end of the 1970s, both the document of the Interdepartmental Encounter of CELAM on "popular religiosity" and the Puebla Document were moving, at least implicitly, in an epistemological direction that was permeated by such revaluation. In regard to the former, Joaquín Alliende detailed at the time the new *epistemology* at play, for, although the document accepts the contribution of the *human sciences* to the theological appreciation of popular religiosity, it also recognizes the limitation of this instrument and turns likewise to the mediation of categories that are *intrinsic* to the Christian faith (which is also religion) and to religiosity itself. It privileges the historical self-understanding of the people of Latin America as the people of God and introduces the "*poetic* category" as necessary mediating instruments for a theological understanding of the people and their religion.[12]

This is not a matter of a populist romanticism that ignores the critical contribution of the sciences; rather, it recognizes that the sciences must, in turn, be critiqued in their anthropological assumptions, both from the perspective of faith and the human understanding that is implied and from popular wisdom itself. Moreover, there is a consciousness of the importance of the mediation of practical knowledge, such as the religious, poetic, and political, as well as reflective nonscientific interpretations (pastoral, political, literary, or artistic) of the same, in which the *people recognizes itself*. Naturally, among those types of knowledge and their nonscientific interpretations on the one hand, and the critical contributions of human and social sciences on the other, there is also a fruitful hermeneutical circle, prior to its assumption by philosophical reflection and/or the intelligence of faith.

However, such a task of hermeneutical discernment will not be fully possible if we remove it from its *historical* dimension. It is in the historical process where the popular and human authenticity of certain symbols and praise, as well as their interpretations, is demonstrated, as they are being placed in the historical line of a genuine human self-realization of the people (in justice, fraternity, peace, and openness to transcendence), according to a true wisdom of life, or, on the contrary, in the long term, they demonstrate over the course of history their lack of authenticity.

Of course, the ultimate hermeneutical criterion here of discerning from the theological viewpoint the *truly* human tradition of a people, as well as the genuine tradition of the people of God inculturated in it, arises out of a human understanding that is implied in faith and of faith itself, but these are mediated by the historical self-understanding of peoples or, respectively, of the people of God (in a hermeneutical interaction with historical science). Among these various levels of discernments there is, likewise, the hermeneutical circle.

In the epistemological lines indicated above, we note a movement distinct from the one that has occurred in wide circles of European theology: in these the critical and scientific elements are valued and sometimes a theory of science that does not take into account its specificity as applied to theology; in those lines, the irreducible value of theory is recognized and the indispensable contributions of scientific critique are assumed, but likewise the importance of symbolic, practical, historical, and sapiential knowledge in the field of theology is rediscovered.[13] Moreover, it is from this wisdom that scientific critique itself is criticized in its tenets, and both are critiqued and localized from a faith perspective.

In the same line of epistemological renewal, a new emphasis is placed on the *sensus fidei* of the faithful people as criterion and *locus theologicus,* as has been previously stated, and importance is given to knowledge "not only by a scientific way, but rather by the connatural capacity of affective understanding" that the people of God has about nations and the general movement of culture (PD 397). This also corresponds to the "vital synthesis" between "intelligence and affection" (PD 448) that Puebla recognized in Latin American popular wisdom, as well as in its culture (sealed in particular by the heart and intuition), which is expressed "not so much in the categories and mental organization of the sciences, as in their artistic expressions, in piety made life and in the spaces of common life in solidarity" (PD 414).[14] It is precisely these categories that Alliende speaks about that intend to bring to the scientific level of theological reflection the knowledge implied therein, always respecting its sapiential character. Let us note as well that all these considerations presuppose a collective subject of knowledge.

In the next chapter, I will illustrate much of what I have already said about popular wisdom as a mediation for an inculturated theology. I thought it important first to give the reader a concrete example of where they come into play in theological practice—not simply a few of the theoretical elements listed above. Thus, in the next section, I will reproduce a brief theological reflection about an Argentinian rite that summarizes the valuable contributions of popular wisdom: the *Tinkunaco*.

EL NIÑO JESÚS ALCALDE: A "POLITICAL THEOLOGY" IN SYMBOLS

What I will only be able to suggest here about the Argentinian religious feast of the *Tinkunaco* may be further developed and explained in greater detail, in the light of Scripture and with the guide of history, anthropology, and the social sciences. I consider, however, that my brief description of this rite and the suggestions for reflection that I will add to the description should be enough to indicate, with a concrete example, a *possible* way forward in thinking about theological inculturation.[15]

Each year, on December 31 at noon, the town of La Rioja, a province in the Argentinian Northeast, celebrates the popular feast of the *Tinkunaco*,[16] a Quechua word meaning "encounter." It is truly a symbolic and ritual celebration of the encounter and reconciliation between two peoples, two races, and two cultures, namely, the Spanish and the indigenous peoples, who today constitute a single mixed-race population that is the common fruit of both. With Puebla, we may also address the "cultural and racial mixing" (PD 409), which is a product not only of the dialectic of the conquest—lord and servant—but also of the dialogical aspect of encounter: male and female.[17]

The symbol for such an encounter is found in two images: St. Nicholas (the patron of La Rioja) and El Niño Jesús Alcalde (the Child Jesus symbolically recognized as the city's mayor), or rather the two processions that carry them. The first of these starts at the cathedral, and the second from the Church of St. Francis. Both come together from different directions in front of the Government House (formerly, in front of the church) on the last day of the year, which traditionally was the installation day for new mayors during colonial times.

The procession carrying the statue of St. Nicholas is presided by the *alferez* (a lieutenant, who during colonial times would bear the royal banner). The members of the pious union accompanying the statue on horseback wear a purple sash across their chest (the episcopal color of St. Nicholas) and hold in their hands a staff that has a colored flag wrapped around it. All these symbols represent, along with the lieutenant, the Spanish.

The other procession, bearing the Child Jesus dressed as a mayor (with the typical feathered hat and the staff), is preceded by an "Inca," who symbolizes the indigenous people. Thus, those who accompany the statue have white marks on their foreheads and a kind of scapular made with little mirrors on their breasts and backs. An arch adorned with ribbons is held above the head of the Inca, as he dances in pace with a drum, while the song of *Tinkunaco* is sung in honor of the Holy Child and his Mother, in Quechua (which none of the participants now speak or understand). During the encounter itself, under the burning midday sun of the Riojan summer (we are in the southern hemisphere), there is absolute silence. Then all those present genuflect three times before the Child, thus recognizing him as the mayor of the city, the province, and the world. Even St. Nicholas, through the genuflection of those who bring him, adores the Child supported by those who represent the Indians, who remain standing.

An old legend tells the origin of the rite. According to the story,[18] in colonial times there was an indigenous revolt due to the injustices committed by the Spanish mayor against them, when they were not yet Christian. They threatened to destroy La Rioja. While the Spanish prayed and did penance to beg God for the salvation of the city, St. Francis Solano, a Franciscan missionary, went unarmed—perhaps with his famous violin—to the rebels to pacify them. In response to his preaching, thousands of them accepted baptism. The condition for reconciliation was the removal of the unjust mayor. Since then, all Riojan people, Spanish and indigenous, have recognized the Child Jesus as the mayor of the city, so that justice would prevail in La Rioja. Even today, the governor of the province—that is, the highest civil authority—recognizes the sovereign authority of the Child Mayor and gives him the keys to the city and, through this act, acknowledges that he governs in the Child Mayor's name and recognizes that he must do so in a spirit of peace and justice, particularly toward the most vulnerable.

The rite and the legend symbolize the origins of the Riojan people and make them aware again of their nature as a fruit of the encounter of two peoples, races, and cultures in a rich mixture. These symbols, in their graphic power, question injustice and inequality, but they do not exacerbate the conflict; rather, with their symbolic potential, they promote reconciliation based in justice, righteousness, and encounter.

Both the rite and the legend also tacitly demand, through their symbolism, a just and social peace, in which the poor and oppressed are given preference as they congregate around the Child Mayor. In addition, the *Tinkunaco* symbolically professes that any political authority comes from God and must be exercised for the common good, with a special care for those who are victims of injustice.

Christ is Lord and Mayor, but that Lord is a Child, who preferentially loves the little ones who have him as both patron and symbol. He is the pacifier who accomplishes reconciliation among those who recognize his rightful and meek authority. Hence, the *Tinkunaco* can be considered as a "political theology" structured in symbols, rite, and legend, which is celebrated annually in order to bring it to mind, represent it ritually, and thus proclaim it.

If, as Ricœur says,[19] symbols communicate not only meaning but also truth, insofar as they discover and metaphorically expose the most essential reality and the most proper real possibilities, then *Tinkunaco* is the ritual expression of the deepest historical reality of the Riojan people (and perhaps, by extension, of the peoples of Latin America), as it is perceived by popular wisdom. At the same time, it is a living symbol, both of their deep yearning for justice and peace and of the real possibilities contained in them to carry out effectively the ongoing encounter between God and human beings. Moreover, it is a graphically portrayed protest against any eventual injustice or breakdown of reconciliation.

Each time that it is repeated, the annual rite represents a new call to carry out, in a historical praxis, its real possibilities, thus responding to the origin and the most intimate historical essence of the people, who are the fruit of the encounter and mestizaje, despite the accompanying conflict.

Of course, symbols, because of their ambiguity due to their "polysignificance," can also be manipulated to cover up oppression, thus limiting justice, conversion, and reconciliation merely to the symbolic and cultic levels, without any effective ethical, political, or social impact. But in this way, the internal dynamism proper to them would be held back, and the truth they expose and metaphorically announce would be betrayed.

By contrast, a true theology of liberation, of the people, and of culture could illumine, with the word of God, human and Christian popular wisdom, portrayed symbolically in order to interpret them theologically and place them effectively in practice. Thus, those symbols and their human interpretation may serve as instrument of an inculturated understanding of the word of God itself and its proclamation of reconciliation, peace, and justice in Christ.

Important guidelines for a theological and pastoral interpretation of the *Tinkunaco* in the key of liberation and light of the gospel can be found in the pastoral letters, preaching, and actions of one of the most outstanding Riojan shepherds: Monsignor Enrique Angelelli, who, as bishop of La Rioja, was assassinated by the army due to his defense of justice and human rights (1996).[20] After the judges and the democratic system acknowledged the crime, which was disguised as an accident, his process of beatification was initiated (2016).

Therefore, the *Tinkunaco* is a ritual fruit of the evangelization of culture, portrayed in symbols of popular piety. Human and Christian wisdom expressed through them may serve as mediation for an inculturated political theology that considers the religious symbols of the people and may illumine, discern, and interpret them in the light of the word of God.

Chapter 5

THE POWER OF POPULAR WISDOM IN THE CULTURAL ETHOS

A Theological Alternative

This book first presented the theology of the people as a "trend with its own characteristics within the theology of liberation" and its main representative, Lucio Gera. It then explained how this theology understands the categories "people" and "popular" and the place that popular wisdom plays and its incarnation in the culture. In this case, we are speaking about the culture(s) of Latin America, but it is also presented as a universal model for the whole inculturation of theology.

At the end of the last chapter, we examined epistemological considerations in this respect and offered a brief practical example. This chapter aims to demonstrate that example in greater detail, both for the peoples whose wisdom of life has received the impact of the gospel as well as for those who have not yet received it or have lost it, but who cannot avoid the question about its ultimate meaning and, therefore, about the wisdom of life.

Thus, a kind of model for all inculturation of theology is proposed, employing the wisdom of each people, as proposed by AG 22. It is proposed even for peoples not explicitly evangelized, particularly for Latin America, and especially for Argentina and any other culture that has been penetrated by the gospel and its theological wisdom. In every case, this will be a contextualized and inculturated theology, with a universal influence.

I will particularly keep in mind what the Argentinian theology of the people has elaborated in order to detail the *perspective* and *assumptions* of any theology done from a specific sociocultural environment. Guidelines and clues for later interdisciplinary and theological work will be delineated, which I cannot complete here.

In the case of the theology of the people, this approach was based, in my opinion, on a double line of assumptions: (1) those referring to the *theoretical interpretation of the national history of a people*—in our case, Argentina—and of the *cultural* ethos formed through it (an interpretation that could, in turn, serve as the basis for a theological hermeneutics of the same); and (2) those that have a more *direct theological nature* and refer to the relationship between *faith, culture, and theology,* applied to any inculturated theology. In the first part of this chapter, I will refer specifically to my own country, although many of the statements are valid for all Latin America and could extend to other peoples. In the second part, I will try to unpack the inculturation of theology, thus completing what was stated in the previous chapter.

THE POWER OF CHRISTIAN WISDOM IN A CULTURAL ETHOS

First, I will explain the first type of assumption: (1) that the people is the *collective subject* of a national history and of the cultural *ethos* that has formed it; (2) that cultural *ethos* implies, as its ethical-anthropolitical core, a *sense of life and death,* which is a knowledge of humanity in its essential relationships and, ultimately, a knowledge of God; and (3) that sense of life is given, for historical reasons particular to the Argentinian people (and in many other peoples), as the meaning of life (*sentido de la vida*) implied by Christian faith.

In the second exposition, I will deal with the first two points separately. I will deal with the third in conjunction with the second because it will provide the perspective of its analysis. Of course, I will not analyze *all* the traits of our cultural *ethos,* but only those that respond to the Christian meaning of life. I do not mean to say that such traits are due *exclusively* to evangelization, or that they are *exclusive* to our culture, even if they are proper to it. On the contrary, this lack of exclusivity will allow an easier *universalization* of our experience in universal categories, but *historically and geoculturally* contextualized.

Before explaining these interpretative assumptions of Argentinian history and culture, I would like to acknowledge that they are influenced (1) by a historical vision proper to so-called historical revisionism and, in particular, of *post-revisionism;*[1] (2) by certain *political interpretations* of our reality, such as those of some of our federal leaders, especially José Gervasio de Artigas (1764–1850); (3) by certain *poetic understandings* of the same, such as those whose highest expression is the *national Argentinian poem Martín Fierro;* and (4) by the *theological-pastoral interpretation* of the country reflected both in the document of the Argentinian bishops on popular pastoral ministry (*Declaración de San Miguel,* 1969, VI), as well as the theological and pastoral movement in which it was expressed and through which it found its strength. As was previously mentioned, both are in continuity with the historical vision of Puebla concerning evangelization in Latin America (cf. PD 314 and 408–19) and the document in which the Argentinian bishops interpret their country's history, *Iglesia y comunidad nacional* (1981, see especially 4–37, 11–137; henceforth, ICN), which took up what Puebla affirmed, referring it to Argentina and specifying its particularities in greater detail.

I also recognize that all these interpretations particularly take into account the power of the Christian faith in our cultural *ethos,* since they have been influenced by them and, in being used for theological and pastoral reflection, *theologically* reinforce such historical power. This is one more example of fruitful interaction between faith and culture: the first influences the various levels of cultural objectivation, including, among others, the theoretical-scientific interpretations of history, political visions, literary expressions, while these, in turn, influence the understanding of faith and the pastoral and theological judgment about historical and cultural reality in the light of faith.

In addition, I would like to emphasize that, as I take up these interpretations, I am not looking so much at the interpreters as at the people who are being interpreted and, in some way, how they interpret themselves through them. I give special relevance to the historical, political, literary, and pastoral hermeneutics in which *the people have recognized themselves.*[2]

If this recognition were merely occasional, passing, or coincidental, however, it would remain tremendously ambiguous. Ambiguity is eliminated because among the various salient points in which the people have recognized themselves (whether at the political, literary, or pastoral level) a *historical line* is gradually drawn, giving all of them a *concrete orientation and meaning*. I am speaking of a historical line with a human and humanizing popular and national sense. It is not continuous, but it shows successive steps of growth in consciousness and popular organization, within certain parameters of discovery and a realization of greater dignity for the human being as well as greater justice and solidarity. Thus, the criteria for choosing the popular expressions and interpretations that I am analyzing were not only historical but also ethical-anthropological and evangelical, since some of them were chosen because they represent milestones in the historical line of experience of human and Christian values indicated above (justice, dignity, solidarity, and so on). I consider this method applicable to the history and culture of other peoples, and, for this reason, it is analogically "universalizable."

Additionally, in the case of such a historical line, there is an ebb and flow, not among synchronous levels of hermeneutics (historical, political, literary, philosophical, theological), but also among historical moments.

These historically influence one another according to a prospective cause-effect relationship. Moreover, the newness of the later moments has a retrospective effect on the interpretation of previous moments. From a new degree of consciousness and realization of the people, the previous events of one's own history are reinterpreted. Hence, in the current situation, after cultural phenomena, such as historical revisionism, on the one hand, and political movements such as "irigoyenism," or Peronism, on the other, or the current Argentinian democratic consensus, it is possible to reread the previous historical experiences or their expressions in order to discover their *pool of meaning*. It is necessary to interpret not just anecdotal information but meaningful events as well.[3] Very often, they do not coincide.

The People, as Fruit of a Historical and Cultural Mestizaje

Above all, let us remember in what sense the category "people" is understood here, as I indicated in chapter 3. Above all, it is used with a historical-cultural meaning, as people-nation, though, in this context, in close relationship to its concentration in poor sectors. It is understood as a historical category because it is only in a specific historical setting that a *people* is defined in relation to a memory, a praxis, and a common historical destiny, as well as a *cultural* category, because it refers to the creation, defense, and liberation of a cultural *ethos*, or a human lifestyle as a community, that is, its way of living in the world and relating to nature, to other human beings, to other peoples, and to God. For both reasons, it is also principally, but not exclusively, a political category, because it designates a historical community, praxis, and destiny (common good), which is capable of constituting itself as a state but whose common history, praxis, and destiny encompass all realms of culture, not only the political in the strictest sense, but also the economic, cultural (in the restricted understanding of the term), religious, and so on.

The cultural *ethos*, among the peoples of Latin America, which identifies us as people-nation, is the fruit of a cultural mestizaje because, in fact, unity (mestizaje) overpowered conflict, even if such unity was imposed by conquest. In fact, it also prevailed, for example, in Argentina, over the mere transplantation by immigration.

I consider that the category "mestizaje" is full of meaning and serves admirably to interpret our history and culture, although such mestizaje has not always been racially understood in various regions of Argentina, Uruguay, and so on. In this concept-symbol, the two dialectics of which Alberto Methol Ferré speaks, following Gaston Fessard, come together. First, the dialectic *male-female* bears fruit in history: this historical novelty is very much ours as a "new people" (according to the typology of the Brazilian anthropologist Darcy Ribeiro) and distinguishes us from other peoples who are searching for their own mythical origins. This opens us to the reality of a historical, not mythical, time. In addition, mestizaje was also the product of another dialectic: that of *master-slave*. But, as master-male and slave-female, the intersection of both dialectics founded the real possibility of the prevalence of *national unity* and of the *fraternity* proper to a people,[4] overcoming conflict and domination, despite the tremendous and undeniable reality within that same people, which has unfortunately been prolonged in new forms of oppression.

We can note that both characteristics—the sense of historical novelty and the prevalence of unity over conflict (without covering it up)—are traits that correspond to a Christian meaning of life.[5] Let us also note that the concept of people as a collective subject of history does not surprise those who know the biblical story of God's people, both in the Old and the New Testaments (without denying the essential differences given among these three: "people," "Israel–people of God," and "Church–People of God").

Unity also prevailed in the integration that occurred in Río de la Plata, as well as other regions, of the contributions of immigrants to the people born of the first cultural mestizaje. I therefore disagree with Darcy Ribeiro, for whom the Rioplatense are "transplanted peoples" as is, for example, the population of Australia. Ribeiro accepts that, until the massive immigration beginning in 1860, we were a "new people" (emerging from mestizo proto-ethnicities), which, for him, also include Chile, Paraguay, and Brazil. Immigration would have broken the historical continuity of one people. This book affirms the opposite point of view, although it recognizes that the liberal governments of the time intended to radically change the ethnicity and culture of the country (see ICN, 20) through immigration (of desired Anglo-Saxons). They did not achieve it, however, not only because the immigrants, mostly poor Latinos (Italian and Spanish), were fully integrated within two or three generations, but particularly because the Creole culture wielded such power that, through its own transformation and growth, it managed to fruitfully assimilate the new without losing its own identity.[6]

This is how the Argentinian bishops, after affirming that "America...was not a mere cultural repetition of Spain or pre-Colombian cultures. It was born and formed a new people" (ICN, 7), added, "From the wide spectrum of that cultural unity were born the Argentinian nation and other sister nations. The Argentinian people is born in the fraternal space of Latin American solidarity that cannot be erased from historical memory" (ICN, 8). Later they added, "The immigrants, predominantly of Latin and Catholic origin, that arrived in a country, affirmed [its culture] in its more genuine roots and allowed the immigrants and their children an integration that will lead them to actively contribute to the formation of a country of Argentinians with all the traits proper to us" (ICN, 20). Of this integration Puebla had already said, "During the last two centuries there came new waves of immigration, particularly in the Southern Cone, which contribute their own modalities, basically integrating themselves into the cultural ground" (DP 411). Hence, according to the Argentinian bishops, this new racial and cultural contribution, although "it distinguishes us from the countries with predominantly pre-Colombian populations, it does not separate us from them because above all we are united by the same faith, the same history, and a common language" (ICN, 28).

Therefore, in spite of internal tensions and the structure of regional dependence, whether *salteños, correntinos,* or *litoraleños,*[7] we are part of *one and the same* country; subjectively and objectively, we continue the *same* national history as our ancestors, and we have a *common* destiny. A political movement such as radicalism reflected, in its origins, the assumption of problems and national memory by the numerous children of immigrants together with others who were not. Later, Peronism expressed the unity of ideals (political sovereignty, economic independence, social justice) that was shared both by the "Cabecitas negras" and by the descendants of "gringos" or "Galicians."[8] Both movements are conscious of being the heirs of a national and popular tradition emerging before the massive immigration phenomenon. In another cultural sphere, that is, the religious, we can note how popular Creole-based devotions (Our Lady of Luján, Our Lady of the Valley, and so on) or those introduced by immigrants (such as St. Cajetan) unite Argentinians of various origins in the same popular faith and religiosity, as is now taking place with the new veneration to Our Lady Untier of Knots, introduced from Germany by Pope Francis. And so, the testimonies could be multiplied that a historical continuity prevails, even through a dialectic of conflict and tension, despite rupture and transplantation.

The People as a Collective Subject of History and Culture

The people born out of this cultural mestizaje is the collective subject of a historical memory, or a national consciousness, of a historical project (or sometimes the implicit concept of common destiny) and of an organization of mutual coexistence.

This way of living and interpreting the people as a collective subject has very deep historical roots. On the one hand, it dates to the tradition of the indigenous peoples, organized collectively, as the Andean and Guarani communities. On the other hand, it goes back to the mode of colonization that Spain brought to these lands, following the methods of the Spanish Reconquest.

Vicente Sierra says that during the war of the Spanish Reconquest, Moors and Christians at first attempted to destroy each other. But then they understood that in order to accomplish the Reconquest it wasn't enough to fight; it was necessary to *populate* (thus reinforcing the dialectic of male-female, even if in the context of struggle for liberation). These peoples, these settlements, were border populations. They emerged in the struggle to defend both their homeland and their faith, with profound feelings of national and religious unity. These towns were organized under a leader (*caudillo*), but in this case the Visigothic tradition was fulfilled: "King, if he is just."[9] That is, the mystique of the people's unity was experienced in the context of social justice and national liberation. Out of this arose the valuation of the rights of the people, the organization of councils, and the phenomenon of the common soldiers. Later, in absolutist Spain, particularly under the Bourbons, the democratic sense was blurred, but out of that history arose the Spanish idiosyncrasy that came to America and that our ancestors inherited. If we fail to take this into account, we cannot understand the history of councils, federalism, and popular movements. Thus, the categories of analysis that were born not out of this experience but from distinct historical experiences, such as the economic rise of the bourgeoisie as a class in the cities of the Hanseatic League or in northern Italy, are not adequate to understand the reality that is the byproduct of this history.[10] Therefore, the category "people" must prevail in the interpretation of our reality, without denying the analytic value of the category "class," which by the same token cannot be understood in the Marxist way of thinking. The value of the category "nation" is not denied, but if it is not made fertile by that of the "people," it could easily become the instrument of nationalist authoritarians who are both anti-populist and antidemocratic.

The category "people," understood as such, is key to interpreting a phenomenon that also verifies it: "Artiguism." I address it now as one of the salient points of our history in which the people recognized themselves in a popular leader. The same thing could be said of others—from Irala and Hernandarias during colonial times, through Güemes or Rosas in the era of national independence, up to Irigoyen and Perón in the twentieth century—without attempting to idealize them or failing to discern them critically, including the values that the people recognized in them and the ethical and political flaws that they possessed.

It was in "Artiguism" as a national movement that the May 1810 Revolution, the origin of our political independence, was shown to be a popular movement.[11] The people are the protagonists of this struggle, which later continued with José de San Martín and the army of the Andes, the Montoneras of Martín Güemes, who defended the northern border against the Spaniards who had regained their military strength once Ferdinand VII returned to the throne after defeating Napoleon.

The people as a collective subject is a recurring theme for Artigas. In his letters and resolutions, he constantly speaks of the "general will," the "will of the peoples," "the heart of the people," and "the authority of the people," while designating himself as their leader and interpreter. These are not mere words; he had a deep respect for the "general will" as expressed, for example, in the popular assemblies that he consulted and to which he submitted his own authority.[12] This will of free peoples was the federal national historical project, in contrast with the elitist, centralized, and unifying project of Buenos Aires. The Uruguayan historian Óscar Bruschera sees in Artiguism "the only Ibero-American example of an institutional process emerging from its own pluralistic being, through the channel of liberation and popular election, not only abiding in, but promoted and sponsored by the *caudillo,* who is the incarnation and representation of an egalitarian democracy that seeks the guarantees of the law and trusts in them."[13] This same historian points out that Artiguism, besides being genuinely national and integrationist (the "community on the move" of the eastern exodus integrated vertically all strata of society under the leadership of a *caudillo*), also implied the establishment of an egalitarian republic based on the justifiable relationship between stewardship of the land and the regulation of trade, which radically threatened the unjust economic and political privileges of the ruling class—another example of unity in the struggle for national liberation that gives justice a preeminent place.[14] "The general will of free peoples" is a collective will of national unity and of social justice.

I have taken Artigas as an example because he helps us to understand both the Hispanic and the Amerindian roots of the category "people" as a collective subject, as well as the later recurrence and evolution in other popular movements that pepper our history. This revered figure can help to interpret other minor federal *caudillos* and to discern in them what is true and what is false. We must also investigate the influence on Artigas of the Jesuit heritage of the Guaraní reductions and the paternal relationship with the Indian Andresito.

I do not intend to study national history analytically. I will simply mention one of the last political expressions of this converging and growing line of interpretations of the reality of the category "people," which in turn helped it to become a reality. Here, I refer to Peronism. I consider it not so much an organization or political movement but rather a cultural phenomenon with profound social repercussions, encompassing even non-Peronists. Eva Perón expressed the understanding of what "people" is in the following terms: "The masses have no collective consciousness, social consciousness; the peoples are, by contrast, masses who have acquired a social consciousness. It is as if peoples had a soul and, therefore, they feel and think, that is, they have a social personality and organization."[15]

Before going forward, I would like to indicate that this collective personality of the peoples has manifested itself at levels other than the political. At the religious level, there is the collective phenomenon of popular religiosity with its symbols and rituals; on this topic, we can cite the aforementioned book of Fernando Boasso.[16]

At the literary level, *Martín Fierro* stands out as a poetic expression of that collective consciousness, from which one can discern earlier popular literature and see later literature. It is a collective expression of the people for two reasons: First, the figure of Fierro—the hero, wise man, and prototype—is the distillation and symbol of the gaucho and, through him, the whole nation and its national being.[17] Second, the Argentinian people (especially the gauchos) *appropriated the poem* and recognized themselves in it. The reception of this work from its publication is proof of this. So much so that, as Hernández himself says, the audience had already titled it "before the author had thought of writing it."[18] Thus, the people came to exchange the names of the author and the character as if it were an anonymous poem. The character himself, Martín Fierro, became the symbolic expression of the national myth of the gaucho.[19]

These brief references demonstrate that it would be possible to elaborate a philosophy (and a theology) of Argentinian history, taking as the core of its intelligibility the category "people" as a collective subject. I also think this is possible in the history of many other countries with longer and richer stories than our own.

Our Cultural Ethos and the Christian Sense of Life

I will now take up the second and third historical assumptions listed at the beginning of this chapter. Every cultural ethos implies at its core a wisdom, a sense of life, of humanity, and of God, which is concretized in the experience of historical and cultural objectifications. The praxis of the peoples—of individuals—has as its parameters of meaning a global understanding of existence. This understanding is known "thematically" by peoples, and they assume it every time they live and objectify it in their ways of relating to nature, to other people, and to God, which are proper to them. In this ethical-anthropological core of the cultural praxis of a people, the influence of faith on culture, as well as through it, is present at all cultural levels. This is because faith does not provide thematic cultural models that are proper to it as such (*Christian* art, politics, science, philosophy). It does not juxtapose itself to the cultures it encounters, but rather tends to inform them and transform them from within, from the ethical-anthropological core proper to it. Faith also implies a sense of humanity, an "understanding of humanity and society" that functions as a parameter of meaning. Through it, cultures can be influenced and hearts converted to the gospel in order to move to cultural creations that are respectful of their temporal autonomy without being identified with faith.

The sense of being a person (*el sentido del hombre*) that lies at the root of the cultural praxis of our people has been evangelized,[20] although we do not deny that this evangelization must be deepened and completed. To give a name to the understanding of the person discovered in the cultural manifestations of the Argentinian people and in their aspirations, one can call it a "social humanism open to transcendence." Of course, this abstract name hardly does justice to the richness of its reality.

Let us keep in mind that this humanism is the result of the intersection of two dialectics mentioned above that merge in our cultural mestizaje. Hence, it follows that two apparently contradictory tendencies exist: on the one hand, a special sense of unity and integration; on the other, a marked respect and defense of the differences and of the dignity of each member of this unity. Therefore, this is about a humanism, a social humanism, that is open to transcendence. As previously stated, the model is the polyhedron (see EG 236), and it is better applied to the dialectic of binary oppositions of Romano Guardini[21] than Hegelian or Marxist ones.

Therefore, there are apparently contradictory traits: (1) in the relationship between the ideal of justice (in favor of and in defense of the most oppressed) and that of national unity; (2) in the tension between the individual (person, people) and community (of persons, of peoples); and (3) in the integrating power of the antagonistic values of our cultural ethos.

A Humanism of Justice on the Horizon of Unity

The sense of justice and human dignity is characteristic of the value-awareness of our people, not merely as one more universal value that any culture seeks, but rather as a core value among other values, which therefore gives a characteristic shape to its cultural ethos. Not accidentally, when Perón wanted to express his national doctrine, he called it "justicialism." Here, we are not interested in demonstrating whether or not he achieved his goal but rather that he thought that, in this way, he was interpreting the deepest popular desire and that for the most part the Argentinian people recognized themselves in the ideal of social justice (powerfully influenced at the theoretical level by the Church's social teachings).

Our Hispanic historical roots are not alien to this primordial value of justice; we have already pointed out the tradition of "king, if he is just." This corresponds to the Christian sense of our own dignity, so typical of the Spanish nobility (the nobility even of those who were not noblemen, such as the Mayor of Zalamea or the farmers of Fuenteovejuna).[22] The ideal of justice belongs to a people who know what it means to suffer injustice and to fight against it.[23] Hence, our bishops—the interpreters at the pastoral level of the national being—have rightly said that justice is the "fundamental principle of the nation" and that our common destiny is expressed in it, which "also springs forth from the seed of the gospel word, sown from the origin of nationality."[24]

I will not speak here of the popular justice project in conflict with the successive designs of domination and dependence, which can be found at every moment of our history. I will only list some significant typical examples, which are representative of this journey as it is manifested at various cultural levels.

At the political level, I indicate popular expressions of a key and foundational moment, emancipation, by mentioning some characteristic documents. In them, one can see what I have indicated above: that the sense of justice has as its principal goal those who are most vulnerable, but this takes place in the wider context of the common national good.

For Artigas, the idea of the "peoples invested with dignity" is key. To this sense of dignity correspond the provisions of the 1815 Reglamento Provisorio, which refer to the distribution of land made with the desire to "populate" and "work" the border territories in order to defend them against the Portuguese invasion. In this distribution, "the most vulnerable will be the most privileged." Therefore, these will include the Blacks, *zambos,*[25] Indians, Creoles, and the poor. He adds, however, a condition that points to the common good: "if by their work and nobility they tend to their happiness and that of the Province."[26]

Let us point out Artigas's continuous care for the Indians—counted among the most abandoned—who sought self-governance in their towns, following the tradition of the Jesuit reductions "so they will experience practical happiness and will come out of the state of devastation to which they are enslaved by misfortune," and thus have the primary right as the first inhabitants of these lands.[27]

The same ideal of social justice experienced through a spirituality of national liberation defense can be seen in the so-called "jurisdiction of the gauchos." Güemes defended the northern border (as Artigas had the eastern), while San Martín would attack the center of Spanish power in Lima. Traveling through the province of Salta, he discovered the sharp social contrast that reflected a remarkably diverse national sense. He observed the "luxury in which many merchants and not a few landowners live" and that "this luxury and waste is in painful contrast with the life led by many good citizens, integrated in the army and wearing tattered clothes." He added, "I conclude that those who have and discard don't give to the homeland, nor do they serve it; on the contrary, those who don't have suffer, because they have given everything for the homeland, so that it can be free." He based this conclusion on the ideas of a kind of land reform. Here, social justice is accomplished, without denying the contrast and conflict, for the common good: "They give all for their homeland, that it may be free."[28]

The same characteristics of yearning for justice and of consciousness of human dignity are expressed, at the poetic level, in our national poem. All of *Martín Fierro* is a denunciation of the injustice suffered by the gaucho (and the people symbolized by him); his journey of struggle and suffering is a search for authentic liberation; and the advice in which he summarizes the wisdom of life thus acquired condenses the "ethics of the national being and philosophy of life,"[29] which are radically Christian. I will not repeat here what I have already mentioned above and elsewhere.[30] I will only touch on two undeveloped points. Fierro, despite strongly denouncing the injustice of "those who rule," does not for a moment cease to feel Argentinian (*Vuelta*,[31] 3869–70), to recognize the province of Buenos Aires as a mother, even if he complains about it (*Vuelta*, 3715–20), and to accuse the unjust for their lack of patriotism (*Vuelta*, 3723–24). Therefore, although the poem—in his own words—"strikes" without pity at those responsible for social injustice, it does not wish "evil for anyone, but for the good of all" (*Vuelta*, 4893–99).

The other point that I would like to make is the following. The poem unites something that dignifies the gaucho as a man, the capacity to sing (with word and poetry, which creates community) with his Christian being. He says, "With the guitar in my hand ... no one sets his foot on me" (*Vuelta*, 55, 57), and he affirms, "Because with the waters of baptism, I received the ability to sing" (*Vuelta*, 22–25). I can glimpse in this the profound intention of the people when they join in human civility and the *civitas Dei* by asking for baptism for their children. Already at the beginning, the dignity of the free person that the Indians had lost in the conquest is recovered—at least as a right in the eyes of their conquerors—through the baptism that makes them God's children and brothers and sisters to one another. This is another example of the crossing of dialectics.[32]

Here, we have passed to another cultural level: the religious. The special dignity of the most humble and oppressed, from a Christian viewpoint, appears symbolically in Latin American stories about Mary. Eduardo Hoornaert demonstrated this in his structural analysis and hermeneutic of the Guadalupe tradition. In it, Mary's preference for the Indians is demonstrated by choosing Juan Diego and the area where he lived for her shrine, instead of the place where the authorities and the Spanish lived. These, represented by the bishop, must convert, accept the message of the Virgin transmitted through a poor and humble Indian, and go to the place chosen by Mary where the Indians lived. Both she and the shrine are a sign of unity in the same faith (between races, cultures, and social classes), but in recognition of the divine preference for the most vulnerable and in conversion to them and the place where they live (the physical place is a symbol of their cultural, social, and theological locus).

Something similar could be said about Argentinian Marian stories and their rich symbolism: Our Lady of the Valley, who was encountered and celebrated mainly by Indian believers and who escaped at night from the most honored place where the Spanish had placed her to return to the Indians; or Our Lady of Luján, in whose story the African slave Manuel has a prominent place because, as a servant of Mary, he is freed and can no longer be enslaved. These are profound symbols of the Christian dignity of those who are most forsaken, in the unity of all who recognize their dignity.[33]

Communitarian Humanism

Our humanism is not individualistic, like that of the Renaissance or in the liberal sense. This is proven by the reality and idea of people as a collective subject, which we have already discussed.

At the level of political philosophy, this experience was articulated under the category of "organized community." This avoids the pitfalls of both abstract individualism and "insectification" of the person in community.[34] It therefore corresponds to the Pauline concept of "body" and the Johannine one of "communion."

This same communitarian sense lies behind the federal concept of the "League of Free Peoples" (Artigas), which was opposed to the unitarian project. This was because it did not respect that freedom through the imposition of centralization by Buenos Aires, which intended to break the homeland into regions that it could dominate. Thus, the motto of British imperialism, "divide and conquer," could be applied. The federal idea, however, based on the freedom of each people, remained open to the greater community, the "Greater Homeland," and saw Latin America as the homeland of brotherly peoples. There has been no popular leader in our history who was not considered "American"—such as San Martín or Bolívar—whose strategy of liberation did not keep in mind Latin American geopolitics. This feeling came not only from the political or military leaders but also from the popular masses, which was demonstrated, for example, in the nineteenth century by the gauchos' instinctive rejection of the war with Paraguay. They had the intuition that such a conflict would destroy their brotherhood and strengthen English imperialism, which sought to fracture the "Greater Homeland."

The systematization of this conviction at the level of philosophical reflection on universal history appears in Perón's thought. For him, history is, on the one hand, the history of the peoples' struggle against imperialism: we could add that the master-slave dialectic can be seen (although not understood in a Hegelian sense). On the other hand, and perhaps at a deeper level of understanding, history is also the evolutionary way toward progressively greater human and geocultural integrations: from the family, tribe, and clan, through nations and continents, toward universal unity (not carried out by imperialism). In this second vision, we could say with Gaston Fessard, the male-female dialectic prevails (in its derivations: fatherhood, motherhood, people, nation, homeland, Greater Homeland, universal fraternity). Perón considered his era to be one of continentalism.[35]

The Integration of Antagonistic Values

A similar dialectic, one of the struggles of integration, has been occurring in our history regarding cultural values. Here, we are speaking of values characterizing two political and anthropological projects that describe the *Sarmientine* opposition: "civilization and barbarism." At the strictly cultural level, this is the opposition between "enlightened culture" and "popular culture." It was this cultural antagonism that Martín Fierro was referring to when he said:

> Your Professors are no good here, experience is all that counts.
> Here, those people who know everything would see how little they know—
> because this has another key to it, and a gaucho knows what it is. (Ida 1457–58)[36]

Popular culture, however, has such an integrating power (originating from the fruit of the integration or cultural mestizaje) that it assumed, and continues to assume, what is valid in another antagonistic historical project, even in the midst of contradictions and struggles against that project of cultural dependence taken in its entirety. This is not a synthesis of commitment or syncretism, therefore, but rather the "salvation" (or redemption) of what is valid in a project through another, which, being more just and more human and by better responding to the identity of the people, has the power to assimilate values of the antagonistic project, thus transforming them by changing their context.[37] In this way, a higher synthesis is achieved.

Martín Fierro also bears witness to this, not only because Hernández was a writer who knew how to place his "letters" at the service of an often-illiterate popular culture, but also because the poem rescues for the gaucho values such as "school" and "rights," represented by the "professors" that it castigates. These values, that is, progress, instruction, and the Constitution, had been used to belittle and persecute the gaucho. Instead, Hernández rescues them in his defense:

> He's a poor orphan, and he's the one who gets crushed by destiny—
> because no one makes it their business to stand up for his kind—
> but the gauchos ought to have houses and a school and a church and their rights. (*Vuelta*, 4823–28)

This dynamism of cultural conflict, and of an integration more profound than conflict, is characteristic of our history. Even before the testimony of *Martín Fierro*, heroes such as San Martín or Artigas had integrated the libertarian and emancipatory values of the Enlightenment in their popular and democratic project. Later movements such as "Irigoyenism" or Peronism represent, respectively, the proper way of living the republican ideal and universal suffrage and the social concerns brought about by a later modernization and industrialization.

In this way, the "political values of democratic and participatory orientation... are finally incorporated into our national identity," and "social justice, taught by the popes, was gradually integrated into the social project of Argentinians" (ICN, 29), because in their origins these values had been, respectively, "political democracy, historically channeled by liberalism" and "the aspiration toward social democracy, marked by socialist trends" (ICN, 110).

This same capacity for "vital synthesis" was later noted by the workers in greater Buenos Aires, who frequently came to the city from the interior of the country and who, after an initial cultural clash and uprooting, assumed the urban and industrial way of life, as well as the problems of political and union participation. In other words, the traditional values (basically Christian) that they had brought with them were confronted by modernization.

Such assimilation of the new, even the antagonistic, has been and remains possible because our people have lived powerful and historical experiences, such as those previously mentioned of a foundational mestizaje, the struggles for emancipation, civil strife, "Irigoyenism," Peronism, the current return to democracy, and so on, which are political but also cultural phenomena. In these experiences, the "already" aspect of justice, unity, and liberation has been lived symbolically but efficaciously, albeit in partial and perhaps provisional realizations, which demand that it continue to accomplish the "not yet" of such aspirations more and more.[38] Such strong experiences form a line in a history that has made possible in our cultural ethos, despite so many oppressions, betrayals, and frustrations, the prevalence of: (a) the sense of *identity* above mere opposition, (b) the sense of *time* over impatient violence, and (c) *personal* mediations over the merely formal.

a) As stated above, the sense of our own *cultural identity* prevailed in our *ethos* over the mere dialectic opposition to its adversaries, even while acknowledging them. Hence, at important moments in our history, national *unity* was emphasized over internal antagonisms, as well as the priority of nationalism over regional or social factions if these tended to fracture. We were—and still are—facing a common external enemy: fracturing imperialism and its accomplices. Social injustice, because it *fractures fraternity*, is the first accomplice. This same idea is manifested in these well-known lines in *Martín Fierro*:

> Brothers should stand by each other because this is the first law.
> Keep a true bond between you always, at every time—
> because if you fight among yourselves you'll be devoured by those outside. (4691–96)

After the terrible clashes and ruptures endured by Argentinian society during the last military dictatorship (1976–83), in particular those originating in violent subversion and repression, the Falklands War (1982), and the constant increase of the "gap between rich and poor," the great consensus that reaffirmed democracy took place (1983), followed by the acceptance by referendum of the papal mediation in the border dispute with Chile: this gives us hope that the strength of our identity as a people-nation and the strength of the humanist sense of our *ethos* could help to overcome the profound crisis at all levels, whose roots are mainly ethical. The bishops have repeatedly pointed to the ethical roots of the crisis and the need for reconciliation, "which is built only on truth, justice and freedom, imbued by mercy and love" for adequate healing (see ICN, 34, and previous and later sections).[39] In another document, it affirms,

> The Falklands War has emphasized ... great values that seemed to be dormant and has shown at the

> same time, in all their harshness, the evils that have corroded the nation for many decades. The general consensus of all citizens around the cause of territorial integrity of the country, the yearning for participation in it with sacrifice of their own goods and even their own lives, the voluntary postponement of just social claims while the emergency lasted, the manifestations of Latin American solidarity, were all expressions of fundamental values that shape the national culture.

At the same time, however, it added, "The evil of discord, however, has gravely manifested itself at the moment in which unity was most urgent and was expected from the leadership" (see Permanent Commission of the Episcopal Conference of Argentina, *Camino de Reconciliación* [Buenos Aires, 1982], 4). Note the contrast between "general consensus" and the allusion to the "leadership."

b) I consider that, in spite of these violent antagonisms in the *ethos* of our people—the majority of whom rejected the terrorist methods of subversion and repression—there prevails the sense of time over violent imposition, in order to achieve the integration of spaces or parties in conflict. This had been the federal strategy. Artigas had already said it: first the peoples; then the provinces; and finally, the confederation of free peoples without prematurely imposing on them a constitution, copied from foreign constitutions. Something similar was affirmed by Juan Manuel de Rosas in his famous letter to Facundo Quiroga, written at the Figueroa hacienda, where he exposed his national political strategy.[40]

c) According to our cultural idiosyncrasy, we prefer *personal mediation* over the merely formal. This explains the federal *caudillo*, or leader, as a living channel, outstanding in our history over the written *constitution*, often fabricated from the outside, such as those of 1819 and 1826, both of which the people rejected. The living bonds of friendship, faithfulness, and loyalty are both indigenous and Spanish legacies; the latter is characterized by Visigothic jurisprudence, according to which a person—a judge—interpreted the written law in the here and now.

   Such a concept of law is opposed to a positivist and formal literalism, but it managed to integrate the values of the written law and the constitution, as the popular political movements of the twentieth century demonstrated new ways of institutional democracy and the rule of law. We have started a journey on this path by popular consensus; however, it does not exclude personal leadership but rather seeks to control and balance it.

In all these cultural characteristics, we see the influence of a human and Christian wisdom lived out in a way that is particular to us. It recognizes the drama of the struggle against evil and is not given to "tragedy." It affirms peace and hope; its relationship to time is patience, full of long-suffering, effort, and courage because it is hopeful; it prefers personal mediation, such as that of Christ, the Virgin Mary, and the saints (see EG 90), or those of a faithful and living interpretation of the tradition by the magisterium or of the law of a superior, living law, above merely formal and legalistic mediation. That is, it gives preference to the spirit above the letter, in order to vivify it by fulfilling it, not ignoring it.

A Humanism Open to Transcendence

Such cultural *ethos* is open to the true sense of God. However, this is not a relationship with him that one seeks, above all, beyond this world, as apparently occurs elsewhere—I am thinking of India—in one's relationship to the sacred. In the religiosity of our people, the sense of "incarnation" is primary (and through it, one attains true transcendence). It discovers God preferably as the one who grants ultimate transcendence and *final hope to human life and coexistence*, that is, as one who saves them in body and soul, without any dualism. He is a saving and provident God.

Our people, particularly the simple people, have the capacity to find God in joy, in pain, and in the limits of existence, such as the birth or death of a loved one. This is frequently lived with an attitude of trust in providence, as popular sayings put it: "God knows what he's doing," "God willing," and "God took him away." *Martín Fierro* is an example of this filial sense of providence, which does not remove but rather assumes freedom and effort.[41]

This "incarnate" understanding of God also appears in the popular songs of our different provinces, inherited from Baroque spirituality: the *glosas a lo divino*[42] are a typical case. These discover the divine in earthly—even erotic—realities, as well as their value as embodied and transcendent symbols, while they demonstrate the divine emphasis of the human in their earthly value. Popular religiosity, the heir of this same tradition, values human mediation (saints, rites) and prefers the more human mysteries of the life of the Lord: Christmas, the passion, the motherhood of Mary (cf. PD 454; EG).

This sense of transcendence accompanies not only personal life but political and social life as well. Both in *Martín Fierro* and popular sentiment, the church (chapel, shrine) is part of social life, symbolizing its transcendent value, as is obvious in schools and other public institutions, even if people do not attend church every Sunday.

A national symbol of the transcendent sense, even in the political realm is the Virgin Mary as patroness of liberating armies (Our Lady of Mercy, patroness of the Argentinian army with Belgrano; Our Lady of Mount Carmel, patroness of the Army of the Andes, along with St. Martin). According to Joaquín Alliende, this symbolized the paschal lordship of Christ over history, and through Our Lady the national identity was expressed in the struggles for the freedom of the homeland, for which these armies fought.[43] In a similar direction, this points out the religious reading of Artigas and his liberating and driving mission for the people. He interprets this in the light of biblical history, similar to the missions of Moses and Aaron in relation to the Israelites. Let us note that, in turn, such religious reading of the political reality implies a political rereading of Exodus without diminishing its religious meaning.[44]

Keeping all this in mind, it is not surprising that the people live common national events with a religious sense, such as the death of Perón, to give an example relatively close to all Argentinians, both Peronists and non-Peronists.[45] The pastoral interpretation of this moment was given by Archbishop Vicente Zaspe of Santa Fe when he said at the time that we touch "the Argentinian family, the deep Argentina, the one who prays."[46]

Something similar was experienced on May 25, 2010, on the occasion of the celebration of the bicentennial of the May Revolution, when a joy "was felt" beyond legitimate political divisions.[47] When the parade floats were going by, someone offered a partisan motto to President Cristina Fernández de Kirchner, who rejected it with a gesture that seemed to signify the recognition that unity—celebrated on this occasion—was beyond partisan ideologies.

Hope is born in these powerful moments (rooted in the faith of providence) for moments of disorientation and resurgence of unnecessary conflicts, such as the transfer of the presidential insignia on December 10, 2015.[48]

TOWARD A THEOLOGY CONSTRUCTED FROM OUR HISTORICAL-CULTURAL PERSPECTIVE

In the first part of this chapter, I attempted to show the power of Christian wisdom in the cultural *ethos* of our people. To that end, I stopped at different moments of history and various cultural phenomena, while trying to interpret them holistically. With different elements, which apparently are anecdotal (historical facts, political or literary texts, religious symbols, and so on), we have discovered *a trend of meaning* structuring them in a *space of cultural significance and values and in a historical tradition*. We must now demonstrate that through them a theological alternative emerges. I believe a similar method could be used by other people, their history, and culture.

First, I will list the theological assumptions on which this statement is based. Second, I will briefly state in which sense we can speak about an "alternative." Finally, I will demonstrate how this can be approached at the level of theological hermeneutics (corresponding to a fundamental theology). In this way, I will enrich what I stated in the last chapter about an inculturated and contextual theology.

Hermeneutical Assumptions

After presenting an understanding of our history and culture that underlies this approach, I will now indicate two pre-assumptions that are of a theological nature and refer to the relationship between faith, culture, and theology.

a) Christian wisdom, insofar as it is inculturated in the cultural *ethos* of a people, possesses—because it is wisdom—its own *rationale*, a historically determined theological *logos*. This determination is provided by the fact of its "incarnation" and inculturation, but it is an *open determination* because this *logos* transcends every historical and cultural situation, even if it is incarnated in it. It has a located universality.
b) This *logos*, or wisdom rationale, although historically inculturated, can be assumed in an articulated, reflective, and critical way by theology as a *science* (therefore, in concepts, judgments, and systematic lines with a *universal* value).

The same ideas can be affirmed in other words. In the two previous paragraphs, we focused on the issues beginning with Christian wisdom (or a global sense of life implied by Christian faith), insofar as this is historically inculturated. If the problem is approached from another angle, the cultural one, we can affirm the same thing in the following way: a sense of life is in force in the wisdom of life that forms the ethical and anthropological heart of a cultural *ethos*. If it refers to a people whose culture has been evangelized, this will be a Christianized sense, but always one of human wisdom. As such, it has a rationality or *logos* that can be philosophically conceptualized and taken up by theological reflection for an understanding of faith.

The possibility of making the same statements from both perspectives reflects the mutual interaction between faith and culture. This relationship can be approached both from a faith (and its theological rationality) and from a cultural perspective (and its implicitly philosophical sense of human existence).

Why Speak of an "Alternative"?

Elsewhere I have written about the qualitative steps taken by recent Latin American theology. Taking into account the current Latin American theological context, I will speak of a theological "alternative," in contrast with other approaches: (1) with those who tend to be *ahistorical* in their perspectives; (2) with those who have discovered their *historicity* (of the history of salvation and human reason) but who do not approach theologically the *inculturation* of faith and the understanding of faith in the *concrete history of the peoples*; and (3) with those who attempt to look at history, culture, and society through theological reflection but interpret them by using categories that are alien to the Christian understanding of humanity and society, such as *Marxist categories*, without subjecting them first to a deep critical rereading.

I am speaking of an alternative because I believe this is a possible and fruitful way, although not exclusive, to attain a reflective understanding of faith through historical experience and the cultural *ethos* of a people particularly, but not exclusively, when at its root there has been—and remains—the Christian meaning of life, as in the case of the peoples of Latin America.

A Theological Hermeneutic

This could become fruitful for theology at the following levels: (1) at the fundamental theology level of a *theological hermeneutic*; (2) at the *dogmatic theological* level of theological rereading of the principal mysteries of faith from a historical and cultural situation; and (3) at the level of a *theology of history or of historical action and passion* (specifically, those of a people or a set of peoples, e.g., at a continental level).[49]

The first basic level I will discuss is that found under the heading "Hermeneutical Assumptions" (see above). As was previously stated, the *popular wisdom* of every people whose culture has been evangelized, insofar as it has been, may be considered a *theological wisdom*. In the following section, I will try to briefly complete what was said in the last chapter, keeping in mind what was discussed above.

What the document on popular ministry of the Argentinian Bishops' Conference says may be applied to the different evangelized peoples, namely, that

> the Church is inserted and enfleshed in the national experience of the people... [and she] must discern about her liberating or salvific action from the perspective of the people and its interests, this being the subject and agent of human history "intimately linked to salvation history," the signs of the times become present and intelligible in the events proper of the people or affecting it....Therefore, the action of the Church must not only be directed toward the people but also, and mainly, from the people itself.[50]

So one of the moments of that salvific action of the Church is the theological and pastoral reflection, such as—in our case—the one posed by the Argentinian theology of the people.

This perspective assumes that the people of God, here and now, are the *subject of theological wisdom* and of a *sensus fidei,* which tends to inculturate, in communion with the universal people of God and the universal tradition of the Church. This theological wisdom can be articulated in a reflective, critical, and methodical way in theological *science.*

In this way, the *sensus fidei* of the faithful is revalued as a "theological locus" or *source* of theological knowledge, and it is interpreted contextually, at the level of the particular Church in communion with the *whole* Church.[51] The local cultural-historical perspective *does not* lead to expressions of different or new truths, but rather it influences the "style" or way of believing, with the *accent or the modality,* in the peculiar structuring of the experience, expression, and reflection of a *same* common faith. This is demonstrated not at the level of judgments of truth, but at the level of insight (understanding of meaning) and of hermeneutical options.[52]

The faithful people are not only the subject, however, but also the *recipient* of this theological task. Therefore, it is one of its *norms.* This allows for a reinterpretation of the *function of the theologian,* since it is part of his or her mission and charism, as a member of that inculturated faithful people, "to bring to concept,"[53] that is, to express reflectively, articulately, and systematically such theological wisdom as that people of God, "in each major socio-cultural area" (AG 22). In addition, because this has a hierarchical structure, our viewpoint serves to shed light on the function of discernment and control that is proper to the *local magisterium* within its insertion in the universal Church under the magisterium of St. Peter. The accent on the theological relevance of the faithful people, who are gifted with memory, likewise contributes to a better understanding of *living tradition* as a source of knowledge and faith, explaining how inculturation demands the unfolding, in *new* ways, of the inexhaustible richness of Christ's message.

The hermeneutical perspective that I present implies a theological *epistemology* that values practical and historical communitarian wisdom, without ignoring the role of the magisterium or that of the theology and its universal power. It is clear in this context, however, that the notion of *science* applied to theology must be rethought, not only to purify it from illuminist traces that it could have acquired in recent centuries, but also explaining that it is at the service of wisdom, and that this is communitarian and historical while at the same time spiritual and transcendent. In relation to this, the *analogical and symbolical* nature of the theological language is reaffirmed.

In this way, a *hermeneutical approach* is facilitated that allows, on the one hand, a rereading of divine revelation from the historical, practical, and cultural situation of a people—particularly if one is a believer—and, on the other hand, it makes possible a theological rereading of the history, praxis, and culture of that people and the cultural symbols in which they express themselves in the light of divine revelation. Theological discernment of God's action in the life of the people seen in that light contributes, in turn, to a deeper knowledge of the self-revelation of God.

Such a hermeneutical approach implies the contributions of the *scientific, political, and/or poetic interpretations* of history, culture, and society as mediation for theological knowledge.[54] Such mediation is possible thanks to the global human moment of meaning that such interpretations imply, that is, its implicit or explicit philosophical moment.[55] This global moment of meaning can be assumed by theology, but beforehand it must be critiqued in the light of faith, since this, as I mentioned previously, also implies a global human meaning.[56]

The indications that I have made in this chapter and the previous one about an inculturated theology may find a philosophical deepening according to the same trend of thought in my book *Nuevo punto de partida en la filosofía latinoamericana* ["The New Starting Point of Latin American Philosophy"].[57]

Chapter 6

POPULAR RELIGIOSITY, POPULAR WISDOM, AND POPULAR THEOLOGY

The revaluation of the "religion of the people, popular religiosity, or popular piety" (PD 444, quoting EN 48) is a sign of the times of the Church today (see EG 122–26). Not only is its pastoral reassessment taking place, which has enormous practical consequences, but also its theological reassessment, whose theoretical fruits have not yet been sufficiently explored. Pope Francis has recognized it as no less than a theological locus (EG 126).

This reevaluation is twofold. On the one hand, it is, in the words of Karl Rahner, the creative and normative significance of the religion of the people for theology[1] and, on the other hand, the question of so-called popular theology. The consideration of the people as the subject of religiosity, religion, and piety, as well as the subject of popular culture in which faith is incarnated, and of a popular spirituality and mysticism in which such faith incarnated in culture and expressed in piety flourishes, led to the question of the people as the *subject of the discourse* from and about faith, a faith thus situated in history, society, and culture, and, therefore, as the subject of theology.

I will take up the second question in this chapter: the relationship between popular piety and a popular theology whose subject is the people, proposing popular wisdom as an organic articulation between both. I have already suggested some of that in the previous chapter.

At the same time, I cannot help but allude once again to the first question indicated above: the relationship between the religion of the people and theology in general. This approach will have a universal nature, but as will become evident, I will do it by considering Latin American issues, understanding it as a universal whole situated in place.

First, I will briefly remember the meaning of two key words that shape the title of the chapter: *wisdom* and *theology*. Second, I will deal with the basic theological question that such a title suggests. Finally, in the third step, I will deal with the relationship between popular theology and scientific or academic theology.

TWO KEY CONCEPTS

Wisdom

When I speak of the wisdom of the people implied by popular piety, I refer to the contemplative or intuitive (*sapere*) knowledge of the ultimate meaning and first foundation of life and to everything else in light of it, which structures the human lifestyle of a people, their cultural *ethos*, and their unique way of relating to God, to other people, and to things. Theologically speaking, its character of authentic wisdom will be measured not only by anthropological-cultural or philosophical criteria, but above all by Christ, the Wisdom of God. He is the standard by which authentic Christian theological wisdom is measured, ultimately distinguishing it from ideology. In the case of Latin America, the Puebla Document affirms, as has been previously mentioned, "At its core, the religiosity of the people is a treasure trove of values that respond to the great questions of existence with Christian wisdom" (PD 448, cf. 413).

Theology

In what sense is this word used in the label "popular theology"? In the first place, it can be understood in a *broad* etymological sense as the word or speech (*logos*) of God, insofar as it speaks of him expressing his word (revelation) in human discourse. Also, if this term is used to name the *intellectus fidei* without further detail, it encompasses all intelligent discourse made from and about faith.

But in a more *restricted* sense—and according to current use—more ordinary and strict, when we speak of "theology" we generally think, above all (as *analogatum princeps* ["prime analogate"]), of theology as science, without denying its wisdom function. Recently, liberation theology has articulated a third function and task of theology as "critical reflection of the historical praxis in the light of the word" of God, a function that subsumes, preserves, and reinterprets its moments of wisdom and science.[2]

According to what has been said, the problem arises from a theology *of the people* (a subjective genitive!) in its relationship to the religion of the people insofar as it is an inculturated expression of Christian faith, particularly of a poor and believing people, as in Latin America.

Is this merely another name (whether improper or proper, derivative, and analogous) for religious discourse? What is its relationship to theology as a science? In what sense is the people a subject of theological reflection? Is this perhaps a displacing of the *analogatum princeps* in the use of the word *theology*? For now, suffice it to say that *at least* we are speaking of theology in the *broad* sense, considering it with its *own* meaning when we speak of "popular theology."[3]

THE RELATIONSHIP BETWEEN POPULAR PIETY AND POPULAR THEOLOGY

This relationship is mediated by popular wisdom, whether we consider it "from below" as the human wisdom that structures religiosity and popular culture, or "top down" as the *theological* wisdom implied by faith, as embodied and inculturated in this religiosity and culture, providing them with a new dimension of meaning. For an understanding of faith and, therefore, of theology (popular), such wisdom is first understood as the "seed of the Word" (PD 401, 451) and *manuductio,* or the instrument that faith illumines, purifies, and assumes in order to seek and find its inculturated understanding. In the second approach, however, it is considered as "fruit" of the word (PD 403), in a popular religiosity that, having been evangelized, "contains the word of God incarnate" (PD 450) and thus it is also "actively evangelizing" (PD 396).

To understand the first approach, we have suggested using a pair of concepts: *revelabile-manuductio,* which St. Thomas uses in the *Summa Theologica* to give reasons for the instrumental service that philosophy lends to theology as science, preserving the unity of its formal object (the light of revelation: *divinitus revelabilia,* "things that are divinely revealable," or *divino lumine cognoscibilia,* "understandable in the divine light").[4] The second approach also evokes the corresponding semantic "transignification" and "transvaluation," which, for Aquinas, are given when philosophy, enlightened by faith and assumed by and for the intelligence of the same is compared with the water transformed into wine, without losing its rational character.

The council guides us to that parallel between philosophical wisdom and popular wisdom when, proposing in *Ad Gentes* 22, a theological consideration proper to each great sociocultural region, it observes that in this way "it will be more clearly seen in what ways faith may seek for understanding, with due regard for the philosophy and wisdom of these peoples," as has been previously quoted. The present work deals precisely with of one of those last ways, which is undertaken from popular piety, through the wisdom of life that centers it.

We have been inspired by the Thomist conceptual pair *revelabile-manuductio* because it understands the "noetic unity" between faith and reason according to the Chalcedonian model (*inconfuse et indivise*), the incarnational and sacramental structure of the revelation of Christ and, hence, of its intellection by and in theology. In our case, however, we are concerned mainly with *wisdom* rationality.

This last statement can help us to take a new step, since in previous paragraphs we dealt with the relationship between popular religiosity and wisdom (human and/or Christian). Now we must deal with the problem of the relationship between this mediating wisdom and popular theology. First, I will indicate how the former implies *logos*. Then we take up the relationship of unity and rupture between the *logos* and of theology as *science*.

Without any doubt, popular wisdom, even if considered only as human, implies meaning, understanding, and consequently word and reason as well, since such meaning and understanding are expressed and articulated not only in significant symbols, practices, and rites but also in discourse (narrative, proverbial, poetic, examination of life, and so on), which has its own rules and its own logic.[5] Both a type of concrete and located *reflection* and a *critical judgment* rooted in common sense and wisdom discernment (connaturally) correspond to these. Therefore, we can properly qualify such language not only as meaningful but also as logical, rational, and capable of critique, since it not only moves in a world mediated by significance and value but is also capable of truth and of discernment of truth.

If we accept Bernard Lonergan's vision about the differentiations of human consciousness,[6] we could say that popular piety and wisdom, as well as popular theology, move in the realm of common sense and (given the conversion of faith) in the realm of "life in the Spirit," but in them there is also human rationality, even if it is not mediated by theory and science, or by an explicitly consciousness hermeneutic (as from the scholarly perspective).

Such characteristics gain prominence when we speak of a *Christian* popular wisdom. Because faith structurally seeks the *understanding* of itself and "to give reasons for hope," it leads to *joyous communication* and to missionary *witness*; it possesses a "feeling of faith" given by anointing of the Holy and an "evangelical instinct" to discern the *truth* of Christ; and it leads one not only to confess and announce it but also to articulate, teach, and defend it.

All that has been thus far said gains more strength if we remember that the poor—through the free will of the Lord—are not only the preferential recipients of the gospel message and of a privileged place to know the God of Jesus and his will, but they are also called to be active subjects in the Church, in the order of the intelligence of faith and its proclamation. Relative to the "evangelizing potential of the poor" (PD 1147), Jon Sobrino speaks of their "theologizing" potential.[7] Gutiérrez himself affirms also that the "small Christian communities themselves are the subject of theological reflection," as it is occurring in many places throughout Latin America: "It is not only a reflection done in common, 'in Church,' but also, and very particularly—of the subject of the theological reflection: communitarian, collective subject."[8]

This quote by Gutiérrez forces us to distinguish two levels in "popular theology": the more spontaneous, primary, and immediate one, rooted above all in the word of God incarnated in popular piety and spirituality, and the second, which, from that first "humus," is the fruit of a *new and renewed* contact of the poor and faithful people with the word of God, through popular organizations such as the Small Christian Communities or Biblical Circles, and so on. Both levels are closely related; thus, we cannot help but point out the *qualitative newness* of this last new encounter of the people with Scripture and its consequences for popular theology. We also must not forget that this new ecclesial experience—spiritual and theological—is rooted in the aforementioned incarnation of the gospel in popular religiosity and partly feeds on it. Even before this greater degree of organization, explicit reflection, and self-consciousness occurred, an evangelized popular piety was already evangelizing and also "theologizing" in its own way, although the awareness of this would not have been possible without the new step taken later. In this, there are two moments of great importance and consequence for popular theology, and even for theology in itself, which in the past had not been so relevant, namely, the *direct* contact of the poor and faithful people with the Bible and the enlightenment from its life and *historical* shared experience. Thus, there is a fruitful hermeneutical circle between Scripture and life (including popular pastoral and social praxis), whose fruit is a theological discourse of an articulation that is not scientific but sapiential.

However, in which sense is a popular theology thus understood? Is it, properly speaking, theology? Although this is in part a question of labeling, it is also a question of valuation. Therefore, some adopt the strict distinction that Clodovis Boff makes in his book, *Teologia e Pratica,* between religious discourse (prophetic, wisdom, revision of life, and so on) and the theological one, understood in the sense of theology as science. João Batista Libânio fears, however, that this distinction of terminology might hide a certain elitism and privilege exclusive to the latter; according to him, these are two different *theological* discourses, not only legitimate, but legitimizing.[9]

Gutiérrez states, "This reflection of evangelizing communities, that convoke in *ecclesia* (and therefore are precisely ecclesial) is doing theology, thinking the faith, the Christian condition. This is the exercise of the right of the poor to think." However, he also speaks of "those Christians whom we call more strictly theologian (qualified as 'professional theologians' in some environments)."[10] Well, the word *strictly* implies the acceptance of common terminology (as "analogous" of the term *theology*), but in no way does it mean a devaluation of popular theological discourse, but, on the contrary, the recognition of its *properly* theological nature.

For my part, I believe that with all propriety, but analogically, we can speak of such discourse as "popular *theology*," although—in current usage—it seems that, when we speak of theology alone, without any further clarification, he points to theology mainly as a science. But we do not affirm the nature of the *analogatum princeps* of this as something essential but as something *historical,* so that there could be a historical displacement of its use.

Nor is this a greater (or lesser) valuation, whether motivated by a certain scientific bent or rationality for which science is the only thing that guarantees *logos* and reason, whether it is out of Romantic or anti-

Enlightenment enthusiasm for the merely popular, the other side of the coin. We simply recognize the *specific* validity of both theologies, with each one having its own *logos* or rationality.

What is proper to theological discourse as a science is not that it has rules, logic, and critical capacity, since this is proper to any human discourse insofar as it is human and thus rational. As a science, it is characterized by a threefold note: First, it is a *theoretical* discourse, whose realm of meanings has been reflectively objectivized, analytically explicated, conceptually defined, and systematically interrelated. Second, not only does it have rules, but it is a reflexively and critically *methodical* discourse and is therefore *self-controlled*. Finally, its articulation is argumentative and *self-consciously* critical; it not only judges and rationally discerns but knows why it does so and can give reasons for it, in a methodical and systematic way. Evidently, such theological discourse does not correspond to popular consciousness as such, because this does not move in the realm of scientific theory or academic hermeneutics (*scholarship*, in Lonergan's terminology).

POPULAR THEOLOGY AND THEOLOGY AS A SCIENCE

From what has been said thus far, we can conclude that the model for thinking about the relationship between these two kinds of theological knowledge can in no way be the same as the relationships such as ignorance-knowledge, opinion-truth, *dóxa-epistēmē*, or ideology-science.

But neither is the paradigm (dialectical) "implicit knowledge–explicit knowledge" or that of "representation-concept" sufficient, since it is not a primitive, naive, inferior, and imperfect knowledge that becomes critical, superior, and perfect only in subsequent knowledge, explicated conceptually by science. Likewise, the *mere* relationship (of phenomenological inspiration) "realm of life–ideation," "what is experienced–what is reflected upon," or "factuality-*eîdos*" is inadequate, since in popular theology there is not only life and content but also form, idea, and reflection, which in their own way reach an essential meaning and truth. Although both dialectic exposition and phenomenological reduction value popular wisdom not only as *pre-* but also as *intra-*scientific (respectively, as a *moment* of science, insofar as immediate knowledge, or as its *horizon,* as the realm of life), they measure it both from and with the measure of science, as if this were the prototype (although not the only form) of rationality. Therefore, such models are inadequate for thinking about the relationship between popular and scientific theology.

Instead, I agree with Clodovis Boff in that the model for understanding the relationship between the knowledge of the people and of the intellectual[11] (which we are applying to this case) must not be unidirectional but the mutual exchange of specific, distinct, irreducible, and valid knowledge, each in its own kind. Thus, each one has an irreplaceable function in theology as the internal moment of the Church and as a task and charism given to her, so that, even if a specific contribution of theology is provided, there is also one proper to popular theology, both to theology and to the Church.

It is not exactly a bipolar or circular relationship, however, but a three-dimensional one since faith, which seeks knowledge, constitutes a kind of third priority and normative pole between the two extremes, orienting, guiding, and discerning the aforementioned exchange of knowledge as a *manuductive* instrument of its own intellection. Hence, the irreplaceable function of discernment of the magisterium of the Church is also derived, as the authentic interpreter of the faith, in this theological dialogue.

Although this exchange has deep roots in Sacred Scripture,[12] the history of the Church, and theology, there is a new form of awareness today, whose explication, accentuation, and deepening are due to a twofold event: the "irruption of the poor" into the consciousness of society, of the Church, and of theology, and the consequent reevaluation of religion and popular wisdom, an event that is a true sign of the times and to which Pope Francis is no stranger.

In this exchange, what is the contribution proper to popular theology? It is not that it is necessarily freer from deviations or ideological influences, but, above all, in the following:

1. First, it consists in what is proper to spiritual wisdom as a primary and original knowledge that is closer to the spiritual sources of religion and faith (both those flowing from the human thirst for God as well as those coming from the free gift of the Lord), without too many mediations or conceptual hindrances.[13] From there, it draws a more charismatic, prophetic, and eschatological nature.
2. Second, it contributes the wisdom of life: its closeness and intimate connection with daily human existence, its culture, praxis, and concrete historical reality.
3. Third, it is a constant critical reminder to academic theology of what is elemental and fundamentally Christian and human, thanks to a sense of reality, humanity, and faith that the poor faithful have.
4. Fourth, its constant witness to what in faith is not reducible to reason, both the transcendence and gratuitousness of the mystery of God and his saving plan as the essential role for all theology of what is contemplative and historic and, therefore, of the symbol and narration (particularly biblical narration),[14] at whose service theorization and systematization must place themselves.
5. Fifth, because it is the theology of the poor, it contributes to the professional theologian and to academic theology as a discipline and institution, a privileged hermeneutical locus in order to come to know the God of Jesus[15] through an evangelical, ethical, and historical conversion to the poor. Thus, respecting the autonomy of theology as science and hermeneutics, it gives them a new horizon and perspective that is more evangelical, more

human, and more historical. In relation to the change of the "from where" and the *horizon*, there is also the "how" (in an *inculturated* perspective) and "whereto," or the practical *relevance* (pastoral and historical). All this does not blur the "what" of faith but rather opens its most profound intellection, nor does it contaminate theoretical reason but liberates and places it in context.[16]

6. Sixth, popular theology could raise a "methodological suspicion"[17] in an academic theology too far removed from spiritual life, human life, or historical reality; it can also positively offer not only new questions, but also new patterns of response, certain expressions, and even categories and lines of articulation that scientific theology can assume and critically elaborate according to its own method, while contributing to popular theology its specific contributions (which I have already suggested when speaking about what is proper to theology as a science).
7. Finally, there is the contribution, when the faithful people *receive* the academic theology communicated to it, according to the mode of its own popular theology. This is primarily the "evangelical instinct" (PD 448) that helps it to accept or not, by connaturality, a certain theology as either congruent or discordant with faith and the teaching of the Church. However, it is also about the reception or rejection of contributions of scientific theology, where they help it to grow or not in its own spiritual, human, and historical life and in its piety.

There are theologies that are perfectly orthodox but irrelevant, perhaps due to lack of spirituality, inculturation, or historical impact. For the professional theologian, the guarantee lies in whether his or her theology, mediated by hermeneutics and theory, returns to the faithful—particularly to the poor faithful people—and is translated in its discourse, making it grow in faith, hope, and charity that are truly incarnated.

Note that this exchange occurs in the unity of knowledge, both because of the continuity of content and because of its formal object: the light of faith. Moreover, our approach leads us to raise the issue of the *unity of the subject* of popular theology and of theology as a science. In the first instance, we are talking about a communitarian, collective subject, although this does not deny but rather assumes the irreducible role of persons. What happens in theology as a science?

First, due to epistemological rupture—or better still, the methodological one—between both knowledges in interchange, the subject of this are professional theologians or the community of the same. However, we can also affirm that, due to the unity of the formal object (and perhaps even of the inculturated hermeneutical horizon), there is a true unity of subject (communitarian and organic) between both theologies.

Such unity is derived above all from the *ecclesiality,* both of faith and theology, since this is a charism and task given to the Church in which there is an organic diversity of charisms and functions. However, if the professional theologian as such has brought his conversion of faith to the preferential option for the poor and to the evangelical, ethical, and historical consequences of it, and even its cultural ones, that academic theology will share with popular theology the fact that he has made the same journey not only the light of faith and faithfulness to the doctrine of the Church (which are based in the *intrinsic* analogy between them as theologies), but also the hermeneutical horizon, the cultural consistency, and the pastoral and historical relevance. Thus, the organic and internally differentiated unity of the subject is demonstrated in and despite the epistemological or methodological rupture and the irreducible specificity of both theologies.

Just as the aforementioned exchange of theological knowledge is an intrinsic demand, a real possibility, a task, and a certain reality already, its full realization is eschatological (in the tension of the "already" but "not yet"), and something similar can be said of the full union and communion of the subject of both. This demands that we overcome any false division of labor based on more or less antagonistic oppositions of class and culture, in order to move toward a differentiation of charisms, functions, approaches, and theological tasks based on communion and integral participation, according to the Spirit of Christ.

Part III

THEOLOGICAL-PASTORAL APPROACHES OF POPE FRANCIS

The first and second parts of this book correspond to its title, namely, "the theology of the people," both in their historical emergence, with characteristics and authors, in the nature of inculturated theology. In contrast, the third part echoes the subtitle of the book, that is, "the pastoral and theological roots of Pope Francis." Without denying the intrinsic and universal value of that theology that originated in Argentina, interest in it, particularly outside of Latin America, arose—and continues to do so—because it constitutes one of the main theological roots of the content and form of the teaching, pastoral ministry, way of governing the Church, leadership (even the extra-ecclesial), and style of the Argentinian pope. It is one of his sources that he not only brings to a universal level but advances, both theoretically and practically.[1]

Thus, chapter 7 will deal with how Francis, adopting the paradigm shift of Vatican II and the method of the pastoral constitution *Gaudium et Spes*—in continuity with the Latin American social teaching from Medellín to Aparecida—complements the unfinished agenda of the council, especially in the evangelical approach of a "poor Church for the poor." Later, chapter 8 deals explicitly with the pope's roots in the Argentinian theology of the people and his going beyond in the same line. The last three chapters present three important themes of the apostolic exhortation *Evangelii Gaudium*, the roadmap of his pontificate (without forgetting the first encyclical that is entirely his, *Laudato Si'*), because they are devoted to inculturation, the communitarian subject of popular spirituality and mysticism, and the four principles for the formation of the peoples and especially of the people of God. Culture, inculturation, and popular piety are key to the theology of the people, which the pope both assumes and deepens. In contrast, the four principles are his own contribution, not only to popular ministry and the governance of the Church, but also to a national and international policy that seeks universal justice, peace, and the common good.

In this way, the third part complements and crowns the first two, closing the living and fruitful circle that interrelates the theology of the people, which gives this book its title, with the theology and pastoral ministry of Pope Francis, as the subtitle indicates.

Chapter 7

THE UNFINISHED AGENDA OF VATICAN II

Gaudium et Spes *and Pope Francis*

For St. John XXIII, Vatican II was a new Pentecost, a salvation event that inexhaustibly "gives food for thought" for celebration and action in the Church. Its agenda remains open, and its texts are a permanent source of renewal. In my opinion, we are still living in a post–Vatican II period because we still have not done enough theological reflection, nor has it been fully brought to practical ministry, much less expressed in adequate canonical forms.

Because it is impossible in a brief text to deal with, even summarily, the entire unfinished agenda of the council, I will limit myself here to one of its main documents, *Gaudium et Spes,* without trying to encompass the broad wealth of its contents. This is precisely the one conciliar document that has had the most influence both on the theology of the people and on Pope Francis.

I will touch on three key points: (1) the general theological *paradigm shift* of the council, particularly the one given in this pastoral constitution; (2) the change of *methodology* in it and the relevance it continues to have in order to complete the unfinished agenda of the council; and (3) one of the fundamental *contents,* in accordance with the gospel, that emerged from the said changes in paradigm and method, namely, the *option for the poor,* which the council was unable to make explicit or deepen. In our current era of "globalization and exclusion,"[1] Pope Francis emphasizes this principle by saying, "I want a Church which is poor and for the poor" (EG 198).[2]

PARADIGM SHIFT

The new Pentecost and the *aggiornamento* of the Church desired by St. John XXIII was already felt at the first session of Vatican II, when a large majority of the council fathers objected to the documents prepared under the direction of Cardinal Alfredo Ottaviani, then prefect of what today is the Congregation for the Doctrine of Faith, and Pope John decided to have them rewritten. This was more than just mere criticism of each isolated document; it was also, implicitly, a radical rejection of a theological *paradigm* and the search for another, analogous to the "paradigm shifts" proposed by Thomas S. Kuhn in the hard sciences. As the Brazilian Dominican theologian and former professor of the University of Freiburg (Switzerland), Carlos Josafat Pinto de Oliveira, says, the emergence of a new paradigm—in our case theological—manifests its primary intentions and the foundational options above all through what it *rejects,* because in moments of transition we know well what we don't want, even if we still don't know what we *do* want.[3] According to Oliveira, the interventions of cardinals, patriarchs, and bishops during the first session of the council coincided with the criticism of the *ahistorical* and unmistakable atemporality of the previous documents, which failed to take into account the new historical consciousness of Western culture and philosophy, nor the advances in this field already made by biblical, patristic, liturgical, and systematic studies, nor the proposals of Pope John about a faith-filled reading of the signs of the times and the corresponding theological and pastoral actualization of the Church in a new and rapidly changing world. All these characteristics imply a *historical* vision of reality.

For my part, I add to Oliveira's considerations that philosophy, with Heidegger, even in conspicuous representatives of Catholicism and Thomism (e.g., Etienne Gilson of the school of Louvain or theologians like de Lubac, Congar, Rahner, or von Balthasar), had already overcome the mere classic paradigm of substance and was overcoming the modern one of subject, moving toward a new paradigm that was not only theological but also historical-cultural. While the first two paradigms privileged identity, need, intelligibility, and eternity as characteristic traits of the first principle and therefore of the understanding of God, the emerging paradigm, which implies a reassessment of the category of relationship over that of substance, without denying those characteristics, rethinks them from the basis of difference of alterity (the relationship), the mystery revealed *as* mystery, the gratuitousness of the gift, and therefore the unpredictable historical novelty.[4]

The shift of the ethical-social paradigm, a consequence of the theological one, is evident if GS is compared to the previous document, which was rejected by the council fathers, titled *De Ordine Morali Christiano*. According to Oliveira, it defends a static "objective and absolute order," one that does not sufficiently consider the reality and objectivity of *subjective and historical* human factors. It conceives of God as "avenger of the moral order" and takes a condemnatory, negative, and authoritarian attitude;[5] in my opinion, this would be an "ethicism without kindness" such as the one Pope Francis criticizes in the exhortation *Evangelii Gaudium* (EG 231). Kindness knows how to keep in mind the *uniqueness* of each person and situation, and *ethicism* is nothing but a caricature of ethics.

In contrast, the fundamental ethical paradigm of GS is not negative but positive because it is guided by the principles of human dignity and responsibility. It is not a merely "natural" ethical-social paradigm, but also a historical one that recognizes the historical realities of the *plurality* of peoples and cultures as well as of social, political, and economic structures.

CHANGE OF METHOD

The turn from an ahistorical paradigm to a historical one implied a change of method, which is not deductive but takes as its starting point and hermeneutical locus the historical, social, and cultural situation.[6] The new method thus became a precious instrument to bring out, in accordance with temporal and cultural circumstances, the riches still unexplored in the open agenda of Vatican II.

Thus, GS adopted the method that John XXIII attributes in *Mater et Magistra* 236 to the social teachings of the Church, formulated by the *Juventud Obrera Católica* as "see, judge, act" and later taken up by the general conferences of the Latin American episcopate in Medellín, Puebla, and Aparecida. Such a method helps the pastoral constitution to "scrutinize" and "interpret in the light of the Gospel" (therefore, theologically) the signs of the times, understanding them not only as characteristic of the times (GS 4) but also as signs "of God's presence and purpose" (GS 11) in it. This vision is not only sociological but one of faith, because it is exercised "in the light of the Gospel" and discovers signs of the will of God in history. Later, the Puebla Document would speak of a "pastoral vision of reality" (PD, title of the first part), and Aparecida would recognize a trinitarian framework in it (AD 19).

Even if seeking the truth within a specific area, a method maintains a close relationship with the *sense,* that is, with the way of *understanding* that truth and with its horizon of comprehension, so new methods often imply a change of paradigm and vice versa. This respect for the truths—and therefore the adaptation of judgment to corresponding realities—nonetheless interprets them in a new and renewed form in accordance with another perspective and with new eyes, so that it becomes possible to discover or explain new truths or change the hierarchical ranking and systematization of the known ones, shifting the emphasis in their interconnection and exposition. It was in this way that what was true in the modern science of Galileo and Newton continued to be true, but the global *paradigm* of physics was transformed after Max Planck, Einstein, and Heisenberg.

Bernard Lonergan, with his theory of method—based on four intentional operations: experience, insight, judgment, and decision—helps us to understand the distinction between meaning and truth, between paradigm (confrontation of the meaning) and doctrine (teaching the truth), both in theology and in the various sciences, at least those that deal with the "world mediated by meaning and motivated by value."[7] Hence, it is possible, without altering the truth of doctrines, to reinterpret them in faithfulness and creativity, finding in them undiscovered nuances and explanations until a particular historical and cultural moment.

In both binomials (sense and truth, paradigm and doctrine), the first term refers to *insight* (understanding) and the second to the *judgment* of reality. The Canadian theologian distinguishes among them in order to unite them and interrelate them according to the order of the four intentional operations, or in the inverse order, depending on whether it is the first or second phase of the hermeneutical circle and its method. The eight functional specializations of theology correspond to the four mentioned operations, with four in each phase, as successive steps of its method.

The first phase of the theological method, according to Lonergan, starts with a functional specialization, "research," which in my opinion must refer not only to Scripture, patristic scholarship, or the history of the Church, but also to the current situation when it deals with, as in GS, theologically reading the signs of the times. This corresponds to the level of the first intentional operation (experience); in the case of the signs of the times, it must be helped by the mediation of the sciences of humanity and society.[8] The second specialization is the "hermeneutical," which corresponds to insight (understanding of the experience). The third specialization ("history") corresponds to the judgment that affirms or denies the truth of such interpretation (insight) of experienced reality. In turn, the dialectic—the fourth and final specialization of the first part of the method—accompanies, conditions, and complements the affirmation of truth through the reasonable option of a particular interpretation as being true in the face of its contrapositions. It moves at the level of value (i.e., of the fourth intentional operation) through a critique of possible affective disorders that ideologically blur the understanding of a pure and integral perception of truth and its correct assessment. Therefore, Lonergan says that, after the "masters of suspicion" (Marx, Freud, and Nietzsche), an affective conversion is necessary in every science that has a hermeneutical moment.[9] Aristotle (in the *Nicomachean Ethics* 6.2) affirmed that, in issues of ethics and politics, a right passion is a sine qua non condition of an unbiased knowledge of practical truth, and Ignatius of Loyola advocated, to gain a better understanding, the liberation of disordered passions. In the case of reading of the signs of the times in circumstances of injustice and violence, as in Latin America, such a conversion is made concrete in a historical conversion toward the poor who endure these sufferings.

I consider this fourth functional specialization extremely important because, although it does not provide arguments for the respective science, it *conditions* the three previous specializations and those that follow, since it frees them from biases or ideological limitations and (pseudo-)rationalizations, by releasing the unlimited desire for truth and goodness that lies in the heart and mind of every man and woman.

In the second phase of the theological method, the fifth specialization ("foundations") also moves at the level of option, because it expresses in foundational categories a new horizon of understanding open by conversion (in theology, religious conversion includes ethical and affective conversion) insofar as it is possible to thematize it. As you can see, in this specialization the foundational lines of a new paradigm have already been drafted (whether because the historical experience is new or because its interpretation has been liberated from prior ideological biases), which, as I will soon explain, will be made explicit in the seventh specialization, the "systematic" one that corresponds to insight, which will then be put into practice in the eighth and final step—practical "communications"—thus returning to experience, in order to transform it through *action,* in which the intellectual and evaluative judgment *see* and culminate.

Between the "foundations" and the seventh and eighth steps, however, there is another: "doctrines." This corresponds to judgment because both are true doctrines that are eventually reinterpreted according to the historical context ("epochal" and cultural) without changing their truth. These are the same, although not always equally formulated, except for what is denied in them (e.g., by anathema). On the positive side, in order to formulate them, *analogical* language is used, which is proper to the theological expression of the mystery and its gradual inculturation in history. These doctrines are then ordered and ranked among themselves in the following seventh specialization, the "systematic," which corresponds to insight or intelligibility of meaning. There is a global and systematic understanding that remains open; that is, it does not close itself off from the system, because it deals with mystery.

In fact, this paradigm shift does not imply a shift in doctrine, because there is a distinction between the realm of meaning and that of truth, although many times—due to the interrelation between both—the paradigm shift involves both an enriching reinterpretation of known truths as well as the historical unfolding of new truths, that is, a homogeneous evolution of dogma and doctrine. Pope Francis alludes to this when he quotes—quite frequently—St. Vincent of Lérins and his teachings on the evolution of doctrine.[10]

Many of the "novelties" of Vatican II that are still being discovered, for example, in the teachings of Pope Francis about the poor or marriage, are due to this paradigm shift and, therefore, to the method facilitated by the council. Without changing them, doctrines are reinterpreted in creative faithfulness, in accordance with an analogical hermeneutic[11] that responds to a reading of the signs of the times in the light of the word of God that is found and lived in the tradition of the Church. All this is part of the unfinished agenda of Vatican II, which continues to unfold in accordance with the cultural and individual time and place, thanks to the new method.

OLD AND YET "NEW" CONTENT: THE OPTION FOR THE POOR

From John XXIII to *Evangelii Gaudium*

According to the instruction *Libertatis Conscientia* of the Congregation for the Doctrine of Faith (1986), the preferential option for the poor, announced messianically by the prophets, manifested itself not only in Jesus, his person, life, and teachings, but also in the entire history of the Church. However, theological reflection based on new historical experiences, for example, the "irruption of the poor" in Latin America, "makes possible a highlighting of aspects of the Word of God, the richness of which had not yet been fully grasped" (*Libertatis Conscientia* 70). In this sense, this is something *new,* but faithfulness to its evangelical meaning will always depend on the theologian's interpretation of "the experience from which he or she begins in the light of the experience of the Church herself," who "shines with a singular brightness and in all its purity in the lives of the saints" (no. 70). Therefore, semantic fidelity (in meaning) will depend on pragmatic correspondence—that is, in attitudes and feelings—between the new experience, on the one hand, and the experience narrated by the biblical text, on the other, as well as that of the Church in its history, especially that of the saints. This correspondence is given at the fourth intentional level of Lonergan, that is, the one of value and decision.

Thus, when the Church in Latin America and the Caribbean attempted to apply the method of GS to its historical circumstances, reading the signs of the times in those regions, it intuited in Medellín (1968) and explicitly formulated in Puebla (1979) the preferential option for the poor, given the new experience of the "irruption of the poor" in Latin American history, that is, in the social and the historical consciousness of the subcontinent and its Church. The poor had always been with us, and there was always the evangelical option for the poor in the Christian community, but the novelty, comparable to an "irruption," consists in the *acute awareness of the structural injustice* that causes poverty and in the "major fact" of the corresponding *central role* of the poor in society and in the Church, as it appears in Pope Francis's speeches during his encounters with popular movements in Rome and Santa Cruz de la Sierra, Bolivia.

So, an element of fundamental evangelical relevance belonging to the unfinished business of Vatican II started making itself more and more present. Without a doubt, this new experience, lived out by a whole episcopacy and even more by many of its local churches and confirmed by popes, is in creative continuity with the biblical experience and the experience of the Church and the saints throughout history.

In the above paragraph, I connected this ecclesial novelty to the unfinished agenda of Vatican II. St. John XXIII had already affirmed in his radio message of September 11, 1962, "Before the poor countries, the Church presents itself as what it is and wants to be: The Church of all, but especially, the Church of the poor." Consequently, during the first session of the council, Cardinal Giacomo Lercaro proposed that this be *the* "great theme of the council."[12] Despite all this, even though the issue was present, for example, in GS, it did not attain due relevance in accordance with the gospel. For this reason, the historian Giuseppe Alberigo even said that the "main omission of the Council was the commitment to poor peoples as John XXIII had requested, and the poverty of the Church."[13]

The remedy for this omission led to the method of GS being applied in Latin America and the Caribbean, regions that are simultaneously Christian and poor, in its reading of the signs of the times. Now, a pope "from the ends of the earth" is applying it to this globalized world and proclaims it for the universal Church, making explicit and radicalizing even more what his two predecessors had already taught. He recognizes that "for the Church, the option for the poor is primarily a theological category rather than a cultural, sociological, political or philosophical one" (EG 198) and that the "expressions of popular piety of the poor and simple," according to the words of Paul VI (EN 48), are a *theological locus* that "demands our attention, especially at a time when we are looking to the new evangelization" (EG 126), both of the poor and of the not so poor, in our "common home," the earth.

It was in this way that the biblical and *Levinasian* topic of the "face of the poor" was first taken up in Puebla (1979) by the Latin American bishops, beginning with their use of the theology and philosophy of liberation. It was then gradually renewed and historically enriched with new faces of poverty in the conferences of Santo Domingo (1992) and Aparecida (2007), where there was a discussion about the excluded, the "rejected," and the "remnants." Today, among the vulnerable whom we must take care of (EG 209–16) is our "sister earth." This was addressed in EG, but particularly in LS. This is a new reading of another sign of the times, taking another step toward the completion of the unfinished agenda of the council, in accordance with the method of GS and within the new conciliar paradigm.

Vatican II was the first council that dealt not only with directly religious topics but also, in its pastoral constitution, those of society, culture, politics, economics, and international relations in the light of the gospel. Later, the Synod of 1971, which focused on justice in the world, affirmed that this struggle—intertwined with the option for the poor—is a *constitutive* dimension of evangelization. Following the Synod of 1974, EN (1975), though it recognized the close bonds between it and human promotion, development, and liberation (and therefore with the preferential option), that is, anthropological, theological, and strictly evangelical bonds, did not discern the question of whether it is an *essential* component—without which there would be no evangelization—or only an *integrating* one, however important that may be. Thus, both the Synod of 1974 and Puebla (January 1979) interpreted this component as *integral* to the preaching of the gospel.

My arms, my legs, and my eyes are important components of my person, but, if they are removed, I continue to exist and be myself, which does not take place with my essential components: soul and body. Therefore, if social promotion is an essential element of evangelization, there is no evangelization if this is limited only to its specifically religious and cultural aspects. Hence, the importance of this question.

Shortly after Puebla (March 1979), St. John Paul II, in his first encyclical, *Redemptor Hominis,* declares,

> Inspired by eschatological faith, the Church considers an *essential,* unbreakably united element of her mission this solicitude for man, for his humanity, for the future of men on earth and therefore also for the course set for the whole of development and progress. (*Redemptor Hominis* 15; italics mine)

He immediately adds its christological foundation: "She finds the principle of this solicitude in Jesus Christ himself, as the Gospels witness" (no. 15). This essential character was later reiterated by the pontiff himself, referring to the social teaching of the Church as "an essential part of the Christian message" and providing the following reason for it: "Since this doctrine points out the direct consequences of that message in the life of society and situates daily work and struggles for justice in the context of bearing witness to Christ the Savior" (*Centessimus Annus* 5). In the following paragraph, he adds, "The 'new evangelization'... must include among its essential elements a proclamation of the Church's social doctrine" (no. 5). Later, in the inaugural discourse of Aparecida (2007), Benedict XVI reaffirmed such christological foundation, saying, "The preferential option for the poor is implicit in the Christological faith in the God who became poor for us, so as to enrich us with his poverty (cf. 2 Cor 8:9)."[14]

In my opinion, Pope Francis's teachings not only advance the same line of creative fidelity with respect to the council, prolonging the paradigm shift of GS and the use of its method, along with the Latin American teaching on the option for the poor, which was assumed at the universal level by his predecessors; he also manifests it very concretely with gestures and words and in a language that, like that of the gospel, is pastoral, simple, and accessible to all, even though it is theologically profound. Hence its profound impact, which corresponds to the new signs of the times in this epoch of "globalization and exclusion."

Pope Francis, the Option for the Poor, and the Unfinished Agenda of Vatican II

In what remains of my exposition, I will not attempt to make a synthesis of the teachings of Pope Francis about a "Church which is poor and for the poor"; rather, I will suggest two converging lines of work, using especially EG and LS. These are the two faces, the negative and the positive, of the same evangelical option for the poor that is proclaimed not only for the universal Church but also in and for a global society, along the lines of the unfinished agenda of Vatican II.

The "No!" of Pope Francis and the New Sociocultural Paradigm

In EG, Francis rejects "an economy of exclusion and inequity," because "such an economy kills," creating the rejected, dregs of society, and "remnants" (EG 53), since "inequality is the root of social ills" (EG 202). He says *no* to "the idolatry of money and the dictatorship of an impersonal economy lacking a truly human purpose" (EG 55), *no* to a "socioeconomic system that is unjust at its root" (EG 59), *no* to "ideologies which defend the absolute autonomy of the marketplace and financial speculation" (EG 56), *no* to the "globalization of indifference" (EG 54), and so forth and so on.[15] In no way, however, does he reject a market economy or free enterprise,[16] but rather the *neoliberal ideology* that proposes absolutization and self-regulation of the market, turns it into an end and not the means, and accepts the hegemony of finances over productive capital and work.

In LS, Pope Francis delves into the common denominator of everything that he rejects, indicating what lies beneath so much inequity and injustice, and its personal and structural causes, namely, the current sociocultural paradigm and the logic derived from it at all levels: individual, social, cultural, political, economic, international, and even religious; in this case, for example, when in EG he criticizes "spiritual worldliness" (EG 93–97, 207) and other pastoral temptations (EG 76–109).

According to Francis, although a radical change of structures is necessary, it is not enough, since "changing structures without generating new convictions and attitudes will only ensure that those same structures will become, sooner or later, corrupt, oppressive and ineffectual" (EG 189). Therefore, the idea is to transform the present sociocultural paradigm, which dominates many institutions, as well as minds and hearts; sometimes he calls it *technocratic* (LS 106ff.) and at other times *technoeconomic,* because its virulence shows particularly in this latter realm. Note that it is not technology or technoscience but rather technocracy. This vision seems very abstract, but it is not, as it serves to unify all the concrete "no's!" that affect all of us, especially the poor and the excluded, as well as the earth, to penetrate them to their very foundations. This is not economic infrastructure (Marx), despite its importance, but rather the *cultural-ethical core* (Ricœur speaks of the "mythical-ethical core")[17] that is at stake because of our freedom and the "interrelation" of our freedoms incarnated in culture and society, even in the markets.

Therefore, in the face of the gravest ecological problems—and, we might add, the social problems of human ecology—Francis urges us to "move forward in a bold cultural revolution" (LS 114), that is, with a "distinctive way of looking at things, a way of thinking, policies, an educational program, a lifestyle and a spirituality which together generate resistance to the assault of the technocratic paradigm" (LS 111). Purely technical remedies are insufficient, although they must be used; rather, we need a new integral paradigm, without forgetting the human heart, with a new spirituality.

The pope agrees, at least in part, with the philosophical diagnosis of our contemporaneous historical situation, both by Heidegger and his successors in the Frankfurt School. Heidegger's critique of the *Gestell* (the "position" of being the modern subject, thus reducing it to a mere object) and, on the other hand, the rejection of the same school of the absolutization of *instrumental reason* (Adorno, Horkheimer, Habermas, and others) seem to converge with Francis's interpretation of the present negative challenges. In this context, he quotes Romano Guardini, who was announcing the "end of modern times."[18]

In turn, the inflection (*Kehre*) of this and of *post-Heideggerian* phenomenology and hermeneutics, toward the reception of the *gift and donation* (e.g., in Marion)—as opposed to the position of everything by the transcendental subject—as well as of the second generation of the Frankfurt School (Habermas, Apel) toward *a communicative rationality and ethics* (as well as in economy[19]) and even the pragmatic-linguistic turn of analytic philosophy (the second Wittgenstein, Austin, Searle), which rediscovers the cognitive importance of the active and affective, seem to point to a direction convergent to that of Francis, with his criticism of the self-reference of the Church and societies, his openness to the free gift as well as others, his "culture of encounter," his communication and dialogue, and his "revolution of tenderness" and mercy. That is, they seem to point to the real possibility of a new integral *sociocultural* paradigm.

The New Sociocultural Paradigm and the New Signs of the Times

Although during the emergence of a new paradigm it is easier to know what to reject than what to keep, it is possible to discover in the present experiences, in the light of the gospel, the possible "seeds of the future," which challenge us to allow and foster their growth. For the believer, these are both signs and fruits of the action of the Holy Spirit of the risen Lord throughout history.

I think that the pope indicates at least two clues that lead us in this direction, which intersect and mutually enrich each other. The first one takes place in the life of the poor; the second, in popular movements.

a) "Experiences of Community Salvation" in the Daily Life of the Poor

The first clue is given, among other places, in the section "Ecology of Daily Life" in LS. There, Francis praises the "admirable creativity and generosity...shown by persons and groups who respond to environmental limitations by alleviating the adverse effects of their surroundings" (LS 148). Thus, he alludes to family homes with their well-kept interiors, in spite of their shabby facades; to the "commendable human ecology...practiced by the poor despite numerous hardships"; to the "network of solidarity and belonging," thanks to which "any place can turn from being a hell on earth into the setting for a dignified life" (no. 148); and so on. All this was often experienced by Bergoglio in the *villas miseria* of his Archdiocese of Buenos Aires.

Moreover, in the following paragraph he refers to something, even in environments of extreme scarcity, in which "daily experience of overcrowding and social anonymity can create a sense of uprootedness which spawns antisocial behavior and violence" (LS 149); however, "love always proves more powerful." "Many people in these conditions are able to weave bonds of belonging and togetherness which convert overcrowding into an experience of community in which the walls of the ego are torn down and the barriers of selfishness overcome." Francis calls these "experiences of communitarian salvation" (LS 149) and recognizes them, for example, in "creative ideas for the improvement of a building or a neighborhood." Let us observe that these are experiences and not merely theories, and that they are not only individual but also communitarian. Moreover, he interprets them theologically as experiences of salvation in this world, though not yet full and final.

In a footnote, the pope quotes one of my works.[20] Later, I will, in a similar context, discuss what the Venezuelan theologian Pedro Trigo observed in the slums of Greater Caracas. It is something we have also experienced

> in Greater Buenos Aires, namely, that even in the midst of circumstances of death, there is an overabundance of life, solidarity, and freedom, which—with the pope—we can call "experiences of community salvation." These are signs of the times, seeds of the emergence of something new, and the active presence of the Lord throughout history.[21] The title of the book quoted by the Holy Father in this note alludes to the "irruption of the poor" in Latin American consciousness and society—an expression that I borrowed from Gutiérrez. I characterize this as "an event of life and freedom" because where death would be expected, there is strength and overabundance of life, and in the midst of oppression and exclusion, there is the experience of personal dignity and freedom for oneself and for others, which is transformed into human liberation for everyone.

In this article quoted by the pope and other later ones, I relate these phenomena of life and coexistence among the poor with wider processes such as the one that the Brazilian economist Euclides André Mance denominates "the revolution of the networks" of popular economy in solidarity. The Argentinian political scientist Daniel García Delgado calls it "basic neo-communitarianism,"[22] which is taking place in different parts of the world, at all levels of common life: economic, political, social, cultural, and religious. Both phenomena introduce us to the second type of the positive signs, which, in my opinion, the Holy Father discovers among the poor of the world: the popular movements.

b) Popular Movements

> The pope not only emphasizes the dignity of the poor but also knows how to read the sign of the times represented by these movements, and he fosters and supports them as a way of implementing the option for and with the poor, insofar as they are the active *collective subjects*

(see EG 122). When he received the representatives of these movements on October 28, 2014, he affirmed and encouraged them, saying,

> You feel that the poor want to be protagonists: they organize, study, work, demand, and above all, they practice that special solidarity that exists among those who suffer....Solidarity...means to fight against the structural causes of poverty, inequality, lack of work, land and housing, the denial of social and labor rights. It means to confront the destructive effects of the empire of money: forced displacements, painful migrations, human traffic, drugs, war, violence.[23]

We are not dealing only with the suffering of the poor—the crucified of history—but we see glimpses of Easter already manifested in their central role, their creativity, their active struggle for justice—without violence—and against the idolatry of money and, above all, in their solidarity, because this, as Francis states, "is...to think and act in terms of community, of the priority of the life of all above the appropriation of goods by the few....Solidarity, understood in its deepest sense, is a way of making history, which is what popular movements do."[24]

Trigo had already spoken of the culture of the barrios, in which unexpected human and Christian values shine in circumstances that would make one expect only selfishness and violence. For the Holy Father, "it is precisely in the barrio where that great family of humanity is built from the concrete, from life shared with neighbors."[25] Likewise, he mentions that "settlements are blessed by a rich popular culture: there the public space is not a mere place of transit but an extension of the home itself, a place where bonds can be generated." Thus, he emphasizes their creativity, affirming,

> You, the excluded workers, remnants of this system, gradually invented your own work with what already seemed exhausted; but you, with your God-given craftsmanship, with your search, your solidarity, your community work, your popular economy, have achieved it and continue to achieve it....Let me say this to you: besides work, this is poetry.[26]

In this way, the act of "making history" poetically, which the Holy Father attributes to them in this same text, is demonstrated. And my assertion is affirmed that this is both a fact of life and of freedom.

Moreover, the encounters of such movements, at a global level, fostered and accompanied by the pope and the Church, are in themselves signs of the times, indicators of newness, even that of an alternative globalization, whose model is the polyhedron (EG 236). Therefore, Francis states,

> I know that among you there are people of different religions, professions, ideas, cultures, countries, and continents. Today you are practicing here the culture of encounter, so different from the xenophobia, discrimination, and intolerance that we so often see. Among the excluded there is this an encounter of cultures where the whole does not eliminate the particularity. That's why I like the image of the polyhedron, a geometrical figure with many different faces. It reflects the confluence of all the parts that in it maintain their originality. Nothing is dissolved or destroyed, nothing is dominated, but everything is integrated. Today you are also looking for that synthesis between the local and the global.[27]

In summary, Francis's recognition and support of the organizations, the struggles, and solidarity with the poor is all part of his desire for a poor Church for the poor. Just as he predicts—at a specifically Christian level—a relevant role in the new evangelization for the poor, he also foresees for them a historical and central role in the project of a new humanity: a more just, more fraternal, and more humane one, within an alternative globalization that is not a hegemony but a polyhedron.

In Santa Cruz de la Sierra, the pope answered the question that the small and vulnerable ask themselves—"What can I do?"—by telling them,

> They can do a lot.... You, the lowly, the exploited, the poor and underprivileged, can do, and are doing, a lot. I would even say that the future of humanity is in great measure in your own hands, through your ability to organize and carry out creative alternatives, through your daily efforts to ensure the three "L's"... (labor, lodging, land) and through your proactive participation in the great processes of change on the national, regional and global levels. Don't lose heart![28]

CONCLUSION

The council's theological paradigm shift and method in GS continues to unfold the richness of the unfinished agenda of Vatican II. Among so many possible subjects, I have paid special attention to one privileged by Christ himself, the Church, the recent popes, and particularly the current pope, namely, the preferential option for the poor as an Evangelical and theological category. I believe this is not only *essential* for the new evangelization of the Church and the world but also necessary to effectively impact the emergence of a new sociocultural paradigm that is more humane, just, and democratic, in accordance with a globalization that serves as an alternative to the one in use today.

Chapter 8

EVANGELII GAUDIUM AND THE THEOLOGY OF THE PEOPLE[1]

Ever since he walked out on the balcony of St. Peter's after his election, Pope Francis has made symbolic gestures, given interviews, spoken as head of the Church, and published a kind of "roadmap" of his pontificate in the post-synodal exhortation *Evangelii Gaudium* (EG), which, in many ways, echoes the Argentinian theology of the people.[2] Hence the question about the likely convergences of his pastoral perspective with this theology.

In this chapter, I will consider (1) his understanding of the faithful people of God; (2) his understanding of the *peoples* of the earth, their relationship with it, and their own historical/cultural development as peoples; (3) a pastoral and theological assessment of *popular piety*; and (4) the relationship of this to the *poor*.

THE FAITHFUL PEOPLE

The pope's gesture of asking the people for a blessing almost immediately after presenting himself in public attracted immediate attention. Those of us who knew his theological appreciation of the "faithful people of God," which implies a specific way of thinking of the Church, a recognition of the *sensum fidei,* and the role of the laity in it, were not surprised. Hence, his predilection for the expression "faithful people" repeated in EG (e.g., nos. 95, 96) that explicitly recognizes it as "a mystery rooted in the Trinity, yet she exists concretely in history as a people of pilgrims and evangelizers, transcending any institutional expression" (EG 111; cf. no. 95).[3] The people as a whole announce the gospel. God "has chosen to call them together as a people and not as isolated individuals....God attracts us by taking into account the complex interweaving of personal relationships entailed in the life of a human community" (EG 113).

Both the Scriptures and Vatican II echo in these texts, as well as the theology of the people, especially regarding the peoples, their cultures, and their history: "The People of God is incarnate in the peoples of the earth,[4] each of which has its own culture....It has to do with the lifestyle of a given society, the specific way in which its members relate to one another, to other creatures and to God....Grace supposes culture, and God's gift becomes flesh in the culture of those who receive it" (EG 115). I emphasize that Francis adopts the rereading of the Puebla Document, following the theology of the people, of the first paragraphs of GS 53, beginning with the third one. Likewise, I remember that when Fr. Bergoglio was rector of the Philosophical and Theological Faculty of San Miguel, he organized the first congress on the evangelization of culture and inculturation of the gospel ever held in Latin America (1985); he scheduled it with theologians from North and South America, Europe, Asia, and Africa, and in his keynote address, he spoke of inculturation, citing Pedro Arrupe, a pioneer in the use of this new word.[5]

Therefore, Pope Francis, when speaking of the people of God, refers to its "varied face" (EG 116) and its "multifaceted harmony" (EG 117), thanks to the diversity of the cultures that enrich it, as when he speaks about the peoples, using the image of the polyhedron, in order to point to the plural unity of the irreducible differences within it.

Along the lines of the theology of the people, he *emphasizes* traditional doctrine when he recognizes that "God furnishes the totality of the faithful with an *instinct of faith—sensus fidei*—which helps them to discern what is truly of God. The presence of the Spirit gives Christians a certain connaturality with divine realities, and a wisdom which enables them to grasp those realities intuitively, even when they lack the wherewithal to give them precise expression" (EG 119). Moreover, at times, the bishop must allow "the flock to strike out on new paths" (EG 31) of evangelization.

THE FOUR "BERGOGLIAN" PRIORITIES IN BUILDING AND LEADING THE PEOPLE

The Argentinian bishops, including Cardinal Bergoglio, following and enriching the approaches of the theology of the people, adopted the proposal of the Argentinian Commission of Peace and Justice on the subject of transitioning "from inhabitants to citizens." This illuminates what Pope Francis, with still greater depth, writes in EG 220 about the people-nation: "People in every nation enhance the social dimension of their lives by acting as committed and responsible citizens, not as a mob swayed by the powers that be.... Yet becoming a people demands something more. It is an ongoing process in which every new generation must take part: a slow and arduous effort calling for a desire for integration and a willingness to achieve this through the growth of a peaceful and multifaceted culture of encounter." Notice the characteristic expression: "multifaceted culture of encounter."

First as a provincial of the Jesuit order and later as archbishop of Buenos Aires, Bergoglio explained in greater detail the governing priorities that lead to the common good,[6] namely, (1) the superiority of the *whole over the parts* (while being *more* than the *mere* sum of the parts, (2) that of the *reality over the idea,* (3) that of *the unity over conflict,* and (4) that of *time over space.* It is said that these are taken from a letter of Juan Manuel de Rosas, the governor of Buenos Aires Province, to

Facundo Quiroga, the governor of La Rioja Province, about the Argentinian national organization, written from the hacienda de Figueroa in San Antonio de Areco (December 20, 1834);[7] Rosas does not make them explicit, although he keeps them in mind. Later, Pope Francis introduced the last two priorities in his encyclical *Lumen Fidei* (nos. 55 and 57). Finally, he develops and articulates them in EG 217–37, presenting them as a contribution based on Christian social thought "for the building of a people" (first of all, the peoples of the world, but also the people of God).

Theological-Pastoral Sense of Time

The exhortation begins with the priority of time over space. This means initiating processes that build a people (EG 223, 224) in history, rather than occupying spaces of power and or possession (land or wealth).

In my opinion, the spiritual feeling of the right time for the right *decision*, be it existential, interpersonal, pastoral, social, or political, is part of the Ignatian charism, which is intimately connected to the discernment of spirits. In his theology, Gera recognizes its importance for prophets, pastors, and politicians, and Methol Ferré is known for his geopolitical analyses and his Christian interpretation of the signs of the times and of the Latin American Church as a font of salvation. For his part, Bergoglio, as a Jesuit, participates in this charism of discernment, and he understands the theoretical contributions of these thinkers. Despite all this, he does not ignore space but considers it as starting with time. He crowns his considerations by saying, "Time governs spaces, illumines them and makes them links in a constantly expanding chain, with no possibility of return" (EG 223).

Plural Unity and Conflict

The theology of the people thought of the people from a starting point of unity, but it also recognized the reality of the "antipeople," of conflict and of the struggle for justice. In the pope's thinking, there is not only an intelligently received influence but also an Evangelical and theological deepening. He affirms that conflicts cannot be ignored, but neither can we remain trapped in them or make them the key to progress. On the contrary, the idea is "the willingness to face conflict head on, to resolve it and to make it a link in the chain of a new process. 'Blessed are the peacemakers!' (Matt 5:9)" (EG 227). This is not the peace of the grave but that of the "communion amid disagreement," "a life setting where conflicts, tensions and oppositions can achieve a diversified and life-giving unity" (EG 228), a "cultural covenant," "a reconciled diversity" (EG 230). I remember that Bergoglio wanted to do his doctoral thesis on Romano Guardini, consulted his archives, and then devoted himself to the understanding of the dialectic dynamism (but not in the Hegelian or Marxist sense) of the contraries[8] in order to apply it to praxis and to history since its union is perfectly achieved in Christ (EG 229). This is the ultimate foundation of his favored "culture of encounter" in the absence of ignorance of the reality of conflict.

Reality Superior to the Idea

There also exists a bipolar tension (see EG 231), because the second is dependent on the first, without separating itself from it; otherwise, there is the danger of manipulating it. "Formal nominalism has to give way to harmonious objectivity" (EG 232), the pope tells us. According to him, "principle has to do with incarnation of the word and its being put into practice," because, he adds, "not to put the word into practice, not to make it reality, is to build on sand, to remain in the realm of pure ideas and to end up in a lifeless and unfruitful self-centeredness and gnosticism" (EG 233).

I do not see an immediate connection between this priority and theology of the people—as in the previous cases—unless it is the critique of both liberal and Marxist ideologies, and in the search for hermeneutical categories from the Latin American historical reality, particularly of the poor.

The Whole Is Greater than the Sum of Its Parts

The pope connects this principle with the tension between globalization and localization (see EG 234). Regarding the latter, it converges with the cultural-historical *rootedness* of the theology of the people, located socially and hermeneutically in Latin America and Argentina and with its emphasis on the *incarnation* of the gospel, which is in itself transcultural, *inculturating* it in popular Catholicism.

Regarding globalization, COEPAL did not keep it explicitly in mind when it was still just emerging. Later, those who continued its work did, however, such as Methol Ferré, Gerardo Farrell, and the interdisciplinary works of the Group of Social Thought of the Church, who took its name from Farrell after his death.[9] Farrell had belonged to and was secretary of COEPAL, although because of his age he is thought of as part of the second generation of the theology of the people, and he was a founding member of the group that bears his name today.

At this point, Bergoglio advanced toward a higher synthesis, which did not erase tensions but understood them, enlivened them, made them fruitful, and opened them to the future. As I said, however, for him, "the model is not a sphere, which is not superior to the parts, where each point is equidistant from the center, and there are no differences among points. The model is the polyhedron, which reflects the confluences of all sides and retains their originality." Almost immediately, Bergoglio added, "It is the convergence of peoples who, within the universal order, maintain their own individuality; it is the sum total of persons within a society which pursues the common good, which truly has a place for everyone" (EG 236). Without using the word, the pope is hinting at *interculturality*.

Previously, Pope Francis had offered a trinitarian foundation for this: "The same Spirit is that harmony, just as he is the bond of love between the Father and the Son. It is he who brings forth a rich variety of gifts, while at the same time creating a unity which is never uniformity but a multifaceted and inviting harmony" (EG 117). This attraction to beauty characterizes many of Francis's expressions, which brings him closer in many ways to Benedict XVI.

POPULAR PIETY

A distinctive characteristic of the theology of the people is its theological and pastoral reassessment of the religion of the people, so that it recognized a "popular mysticism [*mística*]" as found in AD 262. On two occasions, EG refers to this, for example, when it exemplifies the superiority of the whole over the parts, stating, "The genius of each people receives in its own way the entire Gospel and embodies it in expressions of prayer, fraternity, justice, struggle and celebration" (EG 237; cf. no. 124).

EG also converges with the theology of the people when it relates popular piety to other topics that are key to both, such as the inculturation of the gospel (EG 68–70) and that of the "most in need" and their "social promotion" (EG 70). Both distinguish this clearly from a "Christianity made up of devotions reflecting an individual and sentimental faith life" (no. 70), without denying, however, the need for a further "purification and maturity" of this religiosity, for which "popular piety itself can be the starting point" (EG 69), as stated in the same exhortation.

In referring to "new relationships generated by Jesus Christ," it spontaneously connects them to popular religiosity, recognizing that its "genuine forms of popular religiosity are incarnate, since they are born of the incarnation of Christian faith in popular culture. For this reason, they entail a personal relationship, not with vague spiritual energies or powers, but with God, with Christ, with Mary, with the saints. These devotions are fleshy, they have a face. They are capable of fostering relationships and not just enabling escapism" (EG 90).

One of the richer and more profound insights of Pope Francis about popular religion was the one he shared in Rio de Janeiro with the CELAM, when he presented it as an expression of *the creativity, healthy autonomy, and freedom of the laity,* in the context of the conference's critique of the temptation of clericalism in the Church. He recognized it as a manifestation of "the Catholic Church as a people" in its communitarian and adult character in faith, while recommending the organizations characteristic of Latin America, such as Bible study groups and small faith communities.[10]

A tangible example of convergence with the theology of the people is presented in EG when, quoting PD 450 (as well as AD 264), it concludes that, through its popular piety, "a people continuously evangelizes itself" if they are a people in which the gospel has been inculturated (EG 122; cf. no. 68). Each one of them is "the creator of their own culture and the protagonist of their own history. Culture is a dynamic reality which a people constantly recreates; each generation passes on a whole series of ways of approaching different existential situations to the next generation, which must in turn reformulate it as it confronts its own challenges" (no. 122). Then, "in their process of transmitting their culture they also transmit the faith in ever new forms; hence the importance of understanding evangelization as inculturation. Each portion of the people of God, by translating the gift of God into its own life and in accordance with its own genius, bears witness to the faith it has received and enriches it with new and eloquent expressions" (no. 122). Note that he does not speak of a merely cultural external transmission but of a living collective testimony. Thus, he adds, "This is an ongoing and developing process, of which the Holy Spirit is the principal agent" (no. 122).

I will not quote extensively from these important paragraphs of EG but only observe that they mention "the people's mysticism" a second time as "a spirituality incarnated in the culture of the lowly," and that even in "the act of faith greater accent is placed on *credere in Deum* than on *credere Deum*." This reminds me of Tello's expressions, but it is not "devoid of content; rather it discovers and expresses that content more by way of symbols than by discursive reasoning." Moreover, "it brings with itself the grace of being a missionary, of coming out of oneself and setting out on pilgrimage" (EG 124).

A little later, almost duplicating Lucio Gera and the PD, he teaches that "only from the affective connaturality born of love can we appreciate the theological life present in the piety of Christian peoples, especially among their poor" (EG 125).

Moreover, the exhortation concludes its treatment of popular religiosity, accepting, with the theology of the people, its relevance, not only pastoral, but strictly theological, as it ends by saying, "Expressions of popular piety have much to teach us; for those who are capable of reading them, they are a *locus theologicus* which demands our attention, especially at a time when we are looking to the new evangelization" (EG 126).

The Holy Spirit breathes whenever and wherever it wills. It seems to me that today, in the secularized areas of the north, "where God shines because of his absence,"[11] and from the south, the lived sense of piety of the "poor and simple" and their "popular mysticism" is humbly offered as a contribution to the new evangelization (see EG 126).

The pope is not naive and does not ignore that "in the last decades there has been a breaking in the generational transmission of Christian faith in the Catholic people," to which he had referred in EG 122. He had already warned of this as archbishop of Buenos Aires. Now, he is not only exploring its causes (EG 70) but is committing to urban pastoral ministry (EG 71–75), since "God lives in the city" (AD 514), though his presence must be "found, uncovered" (EG 71), no less in the "non-citizens," the "half citizens," or the "urban remnants" (EG 74), that is, the poor and excluded in their "struggle for survival," which "contains within it a profound understanding of life which often includes a deep religious sense" (EG 72).

THE PREFERENTIAL OPTION FOR THE POOR

I have emphasized the close connection between this and popular piety as experienced in Latin America, above all, in impoverished areas. Although the whole Church, including the popes, have taken this option, without a doubt, liberation theology in all its trends, including the Argentinian, is characterized by making this the starting point and hermeneutical locus.

Beginning with his choice of name, the pope revealed his emphasis on the preferential love for the poor, the marginalized, the excluded, the unemployed, the sick, the handicapped, the "rejected," and the "remnants," so much so that many have said that his first visits outside of Rome, to Lampedusa and Sardinia, and his encounter there with migrants, refugees, and the unemployed worked symbolically as true encyclicals.

Not only does he declare that "solidarity is a spontaneous reaction by those who recognize that the social function of property and the universal destination of goods are realities which come before private property" (EG 189), according to Catholic teaching, but he then affirms, "For the Church, the option for the poor is primarily a theological category rather than a cultural, sociological, political or philosophical one" (EG 198). Hence, he repeats what he said on other occasions: "This is why I want a Church which is poor and for the poor. They have much to teach us. Not only do they share in the *sensus fidei,* but in their difficulties they know the suffering Christ. We need to let ourselves be evangelized by them" (no. 198).

However, Francis also sees the other side of the coin. Hence, he criticizes an economy that kills (EG 53) and the "idolatry of money" (EG 55), and he notes that a "socioeconomic system is unjust at its root" (EG 59) due to ideologies that defend the absolute dominion of the markets and financial speculation (EG 56, 202). He affirms that "God, in Christ, redeems not only the individual person, but also the social relations existing between men [and women]" (EG 178), so that Christians must fight, without violence but with historical efficacy, for "the inclusion of the poor in society" (EG 185) and against "the economy of exclusion and inequity" (EG 53) and the "evil crystallized in unjust social structures" (EG 59).

I will not attempt to develop here the topic of the poor according to Pope Francis, because it is too obvious and well known. However, in the present context, I cannot help but mention it as an essential point of convergence between his teaching, the social teaching of the Church, and the theology of the people. In these three cases, we are not dealing with mere theory but with its incarnation in existential and social (including structural) practices that make the "incarnation of the gospel" and the "revolution of tenderness" a reality (EG 88).

CONCLUSION

Because reality is superior to the idea, I believe that in addition to the new ideas that Francis brought to his papacy—about which I have spoken in this chapter—there is something still more important that is contributed by the *reality* of his person and his charism, namely, a radical transformation of *morale* in the Church, as well as outside of it.

Along with Ricœur, I accept that history, including that of the Church and its relationship with the world during Francis's papacy, can be interpreted as a text.[12] According to the same philosopher, part of the meaning of a text is not only *what* is said in it but also the pragmatic moment of *how* it is said, what existential *attitude* it conveys, what spiritual *meaning* it reflects, and what affective *tone* and what lived *experience* accompany it. Hence, there are objective indicators in the style of the text, the repetition of words, and so on.

So, the time of the present pontificate, seen as a text, and the text of EG seem to me to reflect a new mood in the Church, both in the pope's interventions and in the creative response of the faithful. Such a mood is transparent in the repetition of texts and gestures and experienced in certain *leitmotivs,* such as the "joy of the gospel," "the revolution of tenderness," "the culture of encounter," and so on. These are opposed to attitudes of *discouragement, disillusionment,* and *individualistic isolation*. Above all, they testify to the transparent *joy* of evangelizing and being missionary disciples, joyful *detachment,* the *preferential option for the poor,* the *mercy* of Jesus, the *hope* of the kingdom, and the "possibility of another world." However, these are not separate tonalities; rather, they configure a harmonic "system of attitudes" (EG 122) in accordance with those of Jesus and his gospel.

Chapter 9

INCULTURATION IN *EVANGELII GAUDIUM*

The importance that Pope Francis gives to inculturation in his apostolic exhortation *Evangelii Gaudium* is not surprising, since it had been a pastoral concern of his for several years. I noted earlier that, when Bergoglio was the rector of the Philosophical and Theological Faculty of San Miguel in Argentina, he organized the first congress on the topic in Latin America (1985), bringing together Cardinal Paul Poupard, the recently appointed president of the Pontifical Council for Culture, numerous Latin American bishops, theologians from every continent, and a large interested audience. Then, as rector, he gave an inaugural address,[1] alluding to the Jesuit tradition of inculturation with figures such as Frs. Matteo Ricci, Roberto de Nobili, José de Acosta, and the important intervention of Fr. Pedro Arrupe at the Synod of 1974 on evangelization, who had already used the neologism *inculturation*, later adopted by John Paul II. The latter, for his part, emphasized the analogical parallelism of inculturation with the incarnation.

Hence, the *incarnation* becomes the most important *key for reading*, and I propose to study this issue in EG. The second is the other side of the first, namely, the *pneumatological*, which continues the trinitarian analogy with the inculturation of the word. The third is one of its extensions, namely, *popular piety*, since this, thanks to the Holy Spirit, has become intimately linked to the ecclesiology of the faithful people and their evangelizing mission. Thus, we are dealing with three interconnected moments of a single event: the *incarnation* in culture by the work of the Spirit.

Inculturation is one of the guiding concepts, not only of EG, but also of the pastoral-theological thinking of the pope, who conceives "evangelization as inculturation" (see EG 122), even if that does not exhaust it. The Spirit moves the faithful people, incarnated in those who are the protagonists of their history and their culture, especially the poor and simple, both to live and to share their popular piety and mysticism according to their cultural idiosyncrasy, to constantly evangelize themselves, and to be missionary disciples in the face of the present challenge of a new evangelization.

THE ANALOGY OF THE INCARNATION AND ITS PNEUMATOLOGICAL COUNTERPART

The analogy of incarnation was used even before the term *inculturation*, since, for example, the Puebla Document—the third general conference of the Latin American bishops (1979)—referred to the "incarnation of faith in culture." As stated, the neologism *inculturation* had been used by Arrupe at the Synod of 1974. It was later used by John Paul II in his meeting with the Pontifical Biblical Commission, where he referred to the inculturation of the word of God in biblical cultures as incarnation. Later, he took up the term again in *Catechesi Tradendae* 53 and developed his christological analogy, expanding it to Easter—death and resurrection—in *Redemptoris Missio* 52ff.

Challenges of the Inculturation of Faith

As it is an important power idea (*idea-fuerza*) of Pope Francis, the key of *incarnation* appears several times in EG, even in the face of the current ambiguity of a return to the sacred.

Sometimes people seek to quench their thirst for God in "alienating proposals or in a Jesus Christ without flesh and without commitment to the other" (EG 89). Note that these are two basic criteria for discernment:

> Genuine forms of popular religiosity are incarnate, since they are born of the incarnation of Christian faith in popular culture. For this reason they entail a personal relationship, not with vague spiritual energies or powers, but with God, with Christ, with Mary, with the saints. These devotions are fleshy, they have a face. They are capable of fostering relationships and not just enabling escapism. (EG 90)

As we see, the pope connects the three moments indicated above. He does not always use the word *incarnation* of faith in culture, but he does assume it. Thus, he speaks of the "living reality" of the "Christian substratum of certain peoples—most of all in the West" (EG 68), an expression that reminds us of the PD referring to Latin America. It is demonstrated, according to the text, in a "moral resource which preserves the values of an authentic Christian humanism" (no. 68). Bergoglio does not only give sociological reasons, but some that are strictly theological and pneumatological, and also of experience illumined by faith, when he argues:

> Seeing reality with the eyes of faith, we cannot fail to acknowledge what the Holy Spirit is sowing. It would show a lack of trust in his free and unstinting activity to think that authentic Christian values are absent where great numbers of people have received baptism and express their faith and solidarity with others in a variety of ways. (EG 68)

Note, on the one hand, the allusion to the Spirit, to a "look of faith," and to baptism; on the other hand, there is empirically proven data, read with the eyes of faith. Christian humanism and solidarity appear as other discernment criteria.

The pope then takes up the Argentinian theology of the people, already present in the PD: "There we must recognize much more than a 'few seeds of the Word,'" since these are *fruits* of the same that have been inculturated. Thus, following its principle that "the whole is superior to the sum of the parts," that is, a people is greater than the sum of its individual components, he affirms,

> The immense importance of a culture marked by faith cannot be overlooked; before the onslaught of contemporary secularism an evangelized culture, for all its limits, has many more resources than the mere sum total of believers. (EG 68)

Such capacity to resist and overcome, which is typical of an "evangelized popular culture," originates, he goes on to say, in "values of faith and solidarity" that are "capable of encouraging the development of a more just and believing society," because it "possesses a particular wisdom." This is, undoubtedly and without division, a theological and human wisdom.

People often speak of the evangelization of culture and of the inculturation of the gospel as a kind of systole-diastole movement, as two symmetrical faces of the same coin. In the next section, the pope introduces a "what for" that gives *definitive primacy* to the second, giving more meaning to the mentioned "evangelization as inculturation." He proposes that "it is imperative to evangelize cultures *in order to* inculturate the gospel" (EG 69; italics mine), and then he distinguishes the cases of countries of Catholic tradition from those of other religious traditions and from those that are deeply secularized. In the latter two cases, "it will mean sparking new processes for evangelizing culture, even though these will demand long-term purification and growth" (EG 69).

Despite inculturation, Francis acknowledges failings and weaknesses in "popular cultures of Catholic peoples" (EG 69). And he adds that "popular piety itself can be the starting point for healing and liberation from these deficiencies" (EG 69), insofar as it is in them that the gospel is incarnated.

Another challenge, to which he already referred in Buenos Aires before the fifth conference of the Latin American bishops in Aparecida (2007), consists in that "we cannot overlook the fact that in recent decades there has been a breakdown in the way Catholics pass down the Christian faith to the young" (EG 70). Suffice it to say here that, given the sequence of the paragraphs, he seems to respond to this new challenge with his exposition about urban ministry because "God dwells in the city" (see EG 71–75), inculturating in new forms the gospel in the multiculturalism of its citizens. I mentioned this in the last chapter.

He recognizes, therefore, the present cultural pluralism, especially in the cities, but he knows how to find there, if not the fruit, then at least the seeds of the Word. Thus, the "struggle for survival" of the citizens in their daily life "contains within it a profound understanding of life which often includes a deep religious sense" (EG 72) and is thus open to a new evangelization.

THE MANY FACES OF THE PEOPLE OF GOD ON EARTH

After speaking of the Church as God's people (EG 114), the pope uses the analogy of the incarnation, saying, "The People of God is incarnate in the peoples of the earth, each of which has its own culture" (EG 115). Let us observe that, in this context, speaking in the plural, he is referring to the *peoples-nation,* considering them as protagonists of their respective history and culture. However, he does not value this one primarily in relationship to its respective people but in its ecclesiological function, thinking of it as a valuable "concept for understanding the various expressions of Christian life present in God's people" (EG 115), namely, to understand inculturation.

He then rereads the conciliar constitution *Gaudium et Spes* 53 from a Latin American perspective, as DP, 386–87 (which he quotes) had already done, and in which the humanistic concept of culture of the first two paragraphs is reread in the more ethnologic and sociological third paragraph. The pope defines culture thus:

> It has to do with the lifestyle of a given society, the specific way in which its members relate to one another, to other creatures and to God. Understood in this way, culture embraces the totality of a people's life. (EG 115)

He immediately underscores, with the council, the autonomy of the temporal, affirming that "each people in the course of its history develops its culture with legitimate autonomy." And, because "nature and culture are intimately linked," he applies to the latter what is usually said about the former, turning for help to the analogy of the incarnation: "Grace supposes culture, and God's gift becomes flesh in the culture of those who receive it" (EG 115). The words "those who" refer to each person, but also the peoples in themselves. So, despite the ultimate internal multiculturalism of a people-nation, a common "lifestyle" is recognizable, uniting it in a plural unity, distinct from that of other peoples.

In the next paragraph, he refers to the gift of God, affirming that "whenever a community receives the message of salvation, the Holy Spirit enriches its culture with the transforming power of the Gospel" (EG 116). Thus, in its twenty centuries of history, having been evangelized by "countless peoples... in the language of their own culture," "the Church expresses her genuine catholicity and shows forth the 'beauty of her varied face'" (EG 116). In this admirable exchange, each people and culture becomes more itself, according to the analogy of the incarnation, and, in a parallel fashion, by the grace and work of the Holy Spirit, the Church becomes more attractive and, in fact, more Catholic. Even revelation itself is better demonstrated to the Church and the world, as it is made flesh of culture, since "in the Christian customs of an evangelized people, the Holy Spirit adorns the Church, showing her new aspects of revelation and giving her a new face... for 'every culture offers positive values and forms which can enrich the way the Gospel is preached, understood and lived'" (EG 116).

Carlos Galli, in his unpublished doctoral dissertation, "The People of God and the Peoples of Earth," wondered about the intrinsically ecclesiological value of cultures that Hans Urs von Balthasar denies and that he, on the contrary, affirms. Both John Paul II's quote, taken from *Ecclesia in Oceania* 16 (2001), and the affirmations of Pope Francis leave no doubt. These "ways" are not extrinsic, in a kind of ecclesiological Nestorianism, but rather intrinsic, as the flesh of inculturation. Moreover, their value is not just ecclesiological but at least also theological-fundamental and theological-epistemological, since they manifest for the Church new "aspects of the revelation."

The pope's profound trinitarian theology helps us better understand the incarnational and pneumatological value, not merely pastoral, but also theological, of inculturation. In the following section, from the perspective of the trinitarian mystery, he explains in a new way the plural and multiform unity of the Church:

> The Holy Spirit, sent by the Father and the Son, transforms our hearts and enables us to enter into the perfect communion of the blessed Trinity, where all things find their unity. He builds up the communion and harmony of the people of God. The same Spirit is that harmony, just as he is the bond of love between the Father and the Son. It is he who brings forth a rich variety of gifts, while at the same time creating a unity which is never uniformity but a multifaceted and inviting harmony. (EG 117)

Next, the pope alludes to the "logic of the incarnation," which is the key we are dealing with and whose other side is pneumatological, just as Word and Spirit are the "two hands of the Father" (St. Irenaeus). Thus, it excludes thinking of Christianity as "monocultural and monotonous" (EG 117).

Here, Francis takes a theological and pastoral position in favor of the inculturation of the gospel in all cultures, although recognizing, on the one hand, "that some cultures have been closely associated with the preaching of the Gospel and the development of Christian thought," since, if he had not recognized this, he would be opposed to the "logic of incarnation" and its sense of history, which is contingent but real. On the other hand, he affirms once again that the "revealed message is not identified with any of them [i.e., with cultures such as the Greek, Latin, German, etc.]; its content is transcultural" (EG 117). Hence, in terms of mission, "it is not essential to impose a specific cultural form, no matter how beautiful or ancient it may be, together with the Gospel."

Such affirmations recall the discussions about the inculturation of the liturgy in Africa that took place at the Congress of San Miguel in 1985, as well as later ecclesial theological debates in India and the indigenous theology in Latin America. In EG, when Francis speaks about the "varied face of the Church," the "multiform harmony" in the communion of differences, the image of the polyhedron instead of the sphere, and decentralization, I consider that, without naming it, he is alluding to the interculturality of the Church as another face of inculturation. Although he primarily deals with the plurality of the peoples, I deem that the image of the polyhedron is also applied to the previously mentioned multiculturality within a people in its plural unity.

He is then inspired by the highest mysteries of the faith, namely, the Trinity and the incarnation, as models to live by and to understand the Church and its evangelizing mission, following the trinitarian line of thought of the first paragraphs of LG and AG, according to an ecclesiology of communion (unity in differences). Here, both pastoral and theological guidelines and criteria for discernment of genuine inculturation are born.

POPULAR PIETY AS INCARNATION OF THE GOSPEL

The Second Vatican Council did not take popular religion into account. Its reassessment—not only pastoral, but also theological—began, in my opinion, with the Argentinian theology of the people, led by Lucio Gera and his colleagues of the COEPAL, and was taken up again by at least three successive generations,[2] as I explained in the first chapter of this book.

Latin American bishops brought the topic to the 1974 Synod on Evangelization and, through the intervention of the Argentinian bishop, later cardinal, Eduardo Pironio, it was taken up by Paul VI in *Evangelii Nuntiandi*. Later, it was explicitly applied to Latin America by Puebla (1979). In this conference, the topic was further enriched, above all, in the parts of the PD devoted to the evangelization of popular culture and piety, whose main redactors were, respectively, the aforementioned Gera and the Chilean pastoralist Joaquín Alliende, the promoter of what he would call the "Argentinian school of popular ministry," referring to the "theology of the people." Thus, the issue went from Latin America to Rome and returned to Latin America, spiraling the process ever deeper. The Aparecida Document (2007) seemed to take it to its highest point in its explicit assessment of popular spirituality and mysticism (AD 258–65), but now the universal teaching of Francis has once again deepened it and made it more fruitful.

Inculturated Self-Evangelization of the People and Popular Piety

The pope deals with this in the context of the whole people of God as evangelists and missionary disciples. Puebla had already acknowledged that Latin American popular Catholicism, in which the gospel was incarnated in the piety of the poor and simple, is the way that our people have been historically self-evangelized (PD 450;

AD 264). Francis extends this affirmation to all the "different peoples among whom the gospel has been inculturated" (EG 122) and explains this return to the historical concept of "culture," respecting its secular autonomy, saying,

> This is because each people is the creator of their own culture and the protagonist of their own history. Culture is a dynamic reality which a people constantly recreates; each generation passes on a whole series of ways of approaching different existential situations to the next generation, which must in turn reformulate it as it confronts its own challenges....Once the Gospel has been inculturated in a people, in their process of transmitting their culture they also transmit the faith in ever new forms. (EG 122)

Here he adds the important phrase that I previously alluded to: "Hence the importance of understanding evangelization as inculturation" (EG 122). This is not merely an external transmission but a creative, dynamic, and testimonial transmission, alive to each new generation as a "system of attitudes" and values, in the face of new historical challenges that also involve faith. This is evident in that "by translating the gift of God into its own life and in accordance with its own genius, [it] bears witness to the faith it has received and enriches it with new and eloquent expressions" (EG 122).

In this context, Francis alludes to the "importance of popular piety, a true expression of the spontaneous missionary activity of the people of God" (EG 122; AD 263), which is in no way static or dead since it is "an ongoing and developing process, of which the Holy Spirit is the principal agent" (EG 122). Here again, note the constant remembrance of the *pneumatological* nature of inculturation, according to the analogy of the incarnation.

In the next paragraphs, he focuses on this incarnation of faith in culture through such piety, in its reassessment by previous popes, and once again he connects the people and its culture with the "poor and simple" (EG 123; EN 48). Later, without ceasing to affirm the central role and free initiative of the Spirit, he returns to the affirmations of Aparecida (AD 262) on popular piety, recognizing it as "a spirituality incarnated in the culture of the lowly" (EG 124; AD 263) and even as "popular mysticism" according to the expression coined by Jorge Seibold.[3] And he warns against misunderstandings by "scholars," asserting, "Nor is it devoid of content; rather it discovers and expresses that content more by way of symbols than by discursive reasoning, and in the act of faith greater accent is placed on *credere in Deum* than on *credere Deum*" (EG 124).

To appreciate this, however, we need an adequate theological epistemology, proper to the "gaze of the Good Shepherd," who lives out theological virtues in the form of pastoral charity. "Only from the affective connaturality born of love can we appreciate the theological life present in the piety of Christian peoples, especially among their poor": "No one who loves God's holy people will view these actions as the expression of a purely human search for the divine. They are the manifestation of a theological life nourished by the working of the Holy Spirit who has been poured into our hearts (cf. Rom 5:5)" (EG 125).

It is precisely the wisdom *per connaturalitatem*—masterfully explained by St. Thomas, whom the pope quotes—that is the appropriate epistemological and methodological tool in these cases, which is not a substitute for science but rather root it and accompany its analysis and arguments with a state of mind (*Stimmung*) that is adequate to its hermeneutic as it pragmatically complements and confirms it.

Finally, Pope Francis demonstrates the depth of his consideration of popular piety by pointing to it as the source of his theological reflection, saying, "Expressions of popular piety have much to teach us; for those who are capable of reading them, they are a *locus theologicus* which demands our attention, especially at a time when we are looking to the new evangelization" (EG 126).

This was not the proper place for the pope to explain why this is the case. I will continue along this line of reflection, venturing out at my own risk, in this chapter's conclusion.

Personal Reflection on Popular Piety as *Locus Theologicus* for the New Evangelization

The life of the Church is a source of theology and a lived and experienced *locus theologicus* (Congar). So, in the piety of an evangelized people we find "the two hands of the Father," that is, both the word of God historically and ethnologically incarnated in culture and religiosity and the guiding, purifying, and transformative action of the Spirit that inspires, guides, and moves the process of inculturation, providing

> an instinct of faith—*sensus fidei*—which helps them to discern what is truly of God. The presence of the Spirit gives Christians a certain connaturality with divine realities, and a wisdom which enables them to grasp those realities intuitively, even when they lack the wherewithal to give them precise expression. (EG 119)

Note the allusion to *per connaturalitatem* knowledge and to wisdom whose (symbolic) expressions lack the precision of science. Thus, the first criterion for discernment has an affective though no less objective nature, that is, "the affective connaturality born of love" (EG 125).

Thus, theological reflection, at the service of the theological wisdom of the inculturated faithful, can, in the light of the same word, provide the living criteria and critically distinguish a "kind of Christianity made up of devotions reflecting an individual and sentimental faith life" (EG 70) from authentic theological piety. Because this always opens itself up to the other, and particularly to those who suffer, it is communitarian, socially committed, and fully humanizing.

In addition, as previously mentioned, theology can, following an adequate method, categorize and "conceptualize" with greater precision the human and evangelical riches lived out with wisdom in theological piety, particularly that of the poor, the favored ones of God.

On the other hand, what about the allusion, in EG 126, to the "new evangelization"? Above all, we have said repeatedly that "the option for the poor is primarily a theological category rather than a cultural, sociological, political or philosophical one" (EG 198), arising from the very life of Jesus and of the early Christian community, as well as over twenty centuries of the life of the Church. Therefore, because it is essential to evangelization (*Redemptor Hominis* 15; *Centessimus Annus* 5), it is also essential to the new evangelization in every region and circumstance. The option for the poor implies a theological assessment of its popular piety in its Christian totality, since "the genius of each people receives in its own way the entire Gospel and embodies it in expressions of prayer, fraternity, justice, struggle and celebration" (EG 237). That is why it has much to teach every one of us, including academic theologians (EG 126). From the south, it represents an answer to the secularized north's search for meaning, where "God shines by his absence" (Bernhard Welte), but the postcritical naiveté, at least in philosophy, is beginning to be experienced, as is the second naiveté (Paul Ricœur) of "remaining adults but becoming like children."

Chapter 10

THE COMMUNITARIAN SUBJECT OF POPULAR SPIRITUALITY AND MYSTICISM[1]

As I said earlier, Karl Rahner, though he was not personally familiar with Latin America, had a fine sense for the new theological contributions and therefore edited two books about what was coming from the continent: *Teología liberadora* and *Religión popular-religión del pueblo.*[2] The first dealt with liberation theology. Regarding the second subject (popular religion), Vatican II had not addressed it, but it emerged from Latin American reality and from postconciliar ministry and reflection, particularly in Argentina. Today, Pope Francis, who knows it firsthand, has given special relevance to it in the exhortation *Evangelii Gaudium,* resuming the approach of the Aparecida Document (Brazil, 2006)—the fifth general conference of the Latin American and Caribbean bishops—since this exhortation deals with, but now at the universal level, popular spirituality and mysticism.

In this chapter, I will strive to answer questions about this issue, following the approach of both documents. In addition to the obvious personal subject of spirituality and mysticism, I will also address the collective subject and how it must be understood.

First, I will explain how the question was raised. I will then shed light on this from a theological perspective, turning for the most part to what has been explained or assumed by EG. Finally, to deepen our understanding, I will explain elements of a philosophy that will somewhat explain the mystery, once again along the lines proposed by the papal exhortation.

FROM POPULAR RELIGIOSITY TO POPULAR MYSTICISM

Although popular religiosity has been present in Latin America since the first evangelization and the foundational cultural mixing, there was no theological reflection on it until after Vatican II. A key role in this shift was played by the pastoral, theological, and interdisciplinary reflections of the Pastoral Episcopal Commission, which was created by the Argentinian bishops after the council and lead by two professors of the Faculty of Theology of Buenos Aires: Lucio Gera and Rafael Tello.[3]

Later, it was the Latin American bishops, inspired by this incipient "theology of the people," who brought the topic to the Synod on Evangelization (1974). It was then taken up by Paul VI in his post-synodal exhortation *Evangelii Nuntiandi* (48). This marked a major step forward in its pastoral description, no longer calling it "popular religiosity" or "religion of the people," but "popular piety."

Puebla, the third general conference of the Latin American bishops (1979), applied the papal exhortation to Latin America and recognized popular Latin American Catholicism as "the incarnation of the gospel" in culture. One of the main redactors of the section "Evangelization of Culture" was the aforementioned Gera. The one dedicated to "Popular Religiosity" was done by Joaquín Alliende, a Chilean priest of the Schönstatt Apostolic Movement who adhered, at this point, to what he called the "Argentinian school of popular ministry."[4]

The fourth conference (Santo Domingo, 1992) already spoke expressly of "inculturation" and continued the previous steps. However, it was Aparecida (2006) that explained a new character of the popular piety by speaking several times of "popular spirituality" and once of "popular mysticism" (AD 262–63). In the meantime, the reputed "father" of liberation theology, the Peruvian theologian Gustavo Gutiérrez, a Dominican friar, had written—among other things—valuable pages on popular spirituality, and the Argentinian Jesuit Jorge Seibold, a philosopher, pastor, and pastoralist, had forged the concept of "popular mysticism."[5] This was used by the Argentinian bishops at Aparecida and was incorporated into the document, whose editorial committee was chaired by then-Cardinal Bergoglio. Thus, a way was paved for a pastoral and theological reassessment of popular religiosity, until it reached the point at which the universal magisterium considered it a "theological locus" and gave it a key role in the new evangelization (EG 126).

THE SUBJECT: PERSONAL AND COMMUNITARIAN

In the aforementioned work, Gutiérrez emphasizes that this spirituality corresponds to the "journey of an entire people"—not only individuals—as in the case of Israel in the desert and of the early Church, according to Acts.[6] In this case, it applies to what was affirmed by John Paul II in *Dives in Misericordia* (no. 4) regarding the experience of the Jewish people, both "communal and personal." Likewise, the unpublished writings of the aforementioned Rafael Tello, some of which have recently been published, deal with the actions and habit of theological virtues, particularly of faith, lived out not only personally but also communally when speaking, for example, about "popular Christianity according to the theological virtues" (1996).[7] Then the question arises about how to understand this theological experience, as a collective, both theologically and philosophically.

Seibold has expanded on "popular mysticism," pointing to phenomena and events common in Latin American popular piety. However, as he begins to explain the mystical moment, he correctly turns to the experiences of St. Teresa of Avila or St. John of the Cross, but consequently without considering the communal factor. Piero Coda, in expositions unrelated to popular piety, compares and contrasts the mysticism of the Carmelite saint with Chiara Lubich, opening up new ways of reflection.[8] For Lubich, there is a fourth dark night, the cultural one—therefore, experienced socially; in St. John the cell is the other one—but not one in a monastery or friary. The figure of "Jesus in the midst" helps us to understand the ecclesial community and that of the *focolares* as communities in themselves. All these elements can help us to illuminate Pope Francis's approach when he speaks of popular mysticism, not as something individual but communal, while at the same time remaining very personal.

POPULAR SPIRITUALITY AND MYSTICISM IN EG

For Pope Francis, the Church is a mystery rooted in the Trinity, as was already stated by Vatican II in the opening paragraphs of *Lumen Gentium,* the dogmatic constitution on the Church, and in *Ad Gentes,* on the Church's mission, but this mystery is made concrete "in history as a people of pilgrims and evangelizers, transcending any institutional expression" (EG 111).

To this end, the pope frequently links trinitarian pneumatology and ecclesiology, that is, the divine initiative led by the action of the Holy Spirit, on the one hand, and, on the other, the Spirit's action in the people of God as a collective subject, for example, when he asks us to remain "attentive to the promptings of the Holy Spirit who helps us together to read the *signs of the times*" as a community (EG 14; author's italics).

Likewise, both aspects appear to prioritize the pneumatological, when the pope deals with the evangelization of cultures and its expression in popular piety, above all, that of the poor. Thus, when he says, "The Christian substratum of certain peoples—most of all in the West. Here we find, especially among the most needy, a moral resource which preserves the values of an authentic Christian humanism," he attributes this to "what the Holy Spirit is sowing" and to the baptism received by most of the population. Therefore, "This means more than acknowledging occasional 'seeds of the word'" (EG 68), that is, its fruits can also be contemplated (EG 126).

However, this is not about each individual taken in isolation and added to others but about the people as a whole, considered communally as a collective subject of culture. Because, as the pope notes, an evangelized culture has many more resources than a mere sum of believers in the face of the attacks of present secularism, and it "possesses a particular wisdom" (EG 68).

This popular wisdom may be interpreted as undoubtedly and decisively theological and human. At the same time, it is acted upon as a community by the Spirit as a fruit of the inculturation of the gospel in a people, and it naturally arises from them, in whose human wisdom theological wisdom is incarnated. This is because grace assumes not only nature but also culture and becomes flesh in it (EG 115). Note that the subject of a culture is not only each individual separately; it is, above all, the lifestyle of a people (see GS 53c).

As something obviously connected to wisdom and to popular culture, explicit reference is made by the pope to this subject, acknowledging that it can suffer from deficiencies: "Popular piety itself can be the starting point for healing and liberation from these deficiencies" (EG 69). It assumes that the subject of such piety is collective, namely, the inculturated "People of God ... incarnate in the peoples of the earth, each of which has its own culture" (EG 115). It is incarnated thanks to the free action of the Spirit in each and every one, according to the analogy of the incarnation of the Word, as I explained in the previous chapter.

Nevertheless, Francis clearly distinguishes this piety from a devotional Christianity that is individualistic and sentimental. The criteria to distinguish them are related to the community; they are concerned with the "advancement of society or the formation of the laity" (EG 70). Because God "has chosen to call them together as a people and not as isolated individuals. No one is saved by himself or herself, individually, or by his or her own efforts. God attracts us by taking into account the complex interweaving of personal relationships entailed in the life of a human community" (EG 113).

Humanity is not the sum of individuals, with each one on his or her own; rather, it is historically shaped by various peoples,[9] in reciprocal interrelation, with each subject to his or her culture. God summons all who belong to those peoples in order to form his faithful people, the Church. Thus, the "concept of culture is valuable for grasping the various expressions of the Christian life present in God's people" (EG 115). This concept has an ecclesiological and pastoral function, therefore, in addition to a sociological or ethnological one. It helps to reflect on and to bring to fruition the "varied face" of the Church, which is the work of the unique Spirit of the Father and of the incarnate Son.

> Whenever a community receives the message of salvation, the Holy Spirit enriches its culture with the transforming power of the Gospel. The history of the Church shows that Christianity does not have simply one cultural expression, but rather, "remaining completely true to itself...it will also reflect the different faces of the cultures and peoples in which it is received and takes root" [*Novo Millennio Ineunte* 40]. In the diversity of peoples who experience the gift of God, each in accordance with its own culture, the Church expresses her genuine catholicity and shows forth the "beauty of her varied face." (EG 116)

In the manifestations of an evangelized people, the Holy Spirit beautifies the Church, "showing her new aspects of revelation and giving her a new face" (EG 116).

Note that it is beauty that attracts, because in this way elements that are unarticulated in revelation unfold, which is, another facet of the face of Christ in the light of his Spirit that continues to be "incarnated" in humanity.

As was previously mentioned, the ultimate root of this plurality in unity (of communion) of the same communal subject—of "we, the people of God"—is in the Trinity. Pope Francis adds,

> When properly understood, cultural diversity is not a threat to Church unity. The Holy Spirit, sent by the Father and the Son, transforms our hearts and enables us to enter into the perfect communion of the blessed Trinity, where all things find their unity. He builds up the communion and harmony of the people of God. The same Spirit is that harmony, just as he is the bond of love between the Father and the Son. It is he who brings forth a rich variety of gifts, while at the same time creating a unity which is never uniformity but a multifaceted and inviting harmony. Evangelization joyfully acknowledges these varied treasures which the Holy Spirit pours out upon the Church. (EG 117)

It is not only pneumatology and trinitarian theology, however, that illumine this ecclesiology of the people of God—the communitarian subject of divine convocation and of evangelization—in and from the peoples of the earth (the communal subjects of culture), but it also receives the light of Christology, as was have seen in the analogy of inculturation and the seeds and fruits of the Word. Following this same train of thought, Pope Francis adds, "We would not do justice to the logic of the incarnation if we thought of Christianity as monocultural and monotonous" (EG 117).

A few paragraphs later, Francis explicitly mentions the "active collective subjects" (EG 122),[10] referring to the peoples of the world and implicitly to the faithful people—insofar as all of them announce the gospel communal—and to popular piety, since

> we can see that the different peoples among whom the Gospel has been inculturated are active collective subjects or agents of evangelization. This is because each people is the creator of their own culture and the protagonist of their own history....Once the Gospel has been inculturated in a people, in their process of transmitting their culture they also transmit the faith in ever new forms; hence the importance of understanding evangelization as inculturation.... One can say that "a people continuously evangelizes itself." (EG 122)

The reflection on the evangelization of a people's culture and the inculturation of the gospel in it[11] naturally ends in the mention of its evangelized and evangelizing religiosity, proper to the Lord's people, understood both as subject and communitarian agent, under the guidance of the Spirit. Therefore, he continues,

> Herein lies the importance of popular piety, a true expression of the spontaneous missionary activity of the people of God. This is an ongoing and developing process, of which the Holy Spirit is the principal agent. (EG 122)

Under the central role of the work of the third person of the Trinity, the pope interweaves the action of the evangelized peoples of the world, on the one hand, and, on the other, that of the people of God embodied by them, because he recognizes that the latter is *laós ex ethnôn,*[12] that is, "a people formed from peoples," without mistaking one for the other but also without separating them, if the latter are evangelized in their respective cultures. Thus, he immediately adds, "Popular piety [of the people of God in community] enables us to see how the faith, once received, becomes embodied in a culture [of a concrete people as a collective subject] and is constantly passed on" (EG 123). Later, I will address how the pope proposes the current problem of multicultural societies as he approaches the issue of the multicultural community.

The following paragraphs are dedicated to popular piety and allude to its reassessment by Paul VI and Benedict XVI. Quoting the last conference of the Latin American bishops, he uses the expressions that give this chapter its title:

> The Aparecida Document describes the riches which the Holy Spirit pours forth in popular piety by his gratuitous initiative....The bishops also refer to it as "popular spirituality" or "the people's mysticism" [AD 262]. It is truly "a spirituality incarnated in the culture of the lowly" [AD 263]. (EG 124)

Without quoting it directly, he reflects the thinking of Enrique Ciro Bianchi, commenting on the theology of Rafael Tello in which he uses Thomistic categories to discuss faith.[13]

In addition, the pope refers to symbolic mediation and to pilgrimages, both phenomena of popular culture, as typical of the subject. On the one hand, he affirms that such spirituality discovers and expresses content via symbols, not using theoretical reason, and that in the act of faith it places greater emphasis on the *credere in Deum* (believing in, trusting, and loving God) than the *credere Deum* (believing what God has revealed about himself). On the other hand, it values the "journeying together to shrines" as a believing and evangelizing action (EG 124).

As he has previously done, he turns once again to inborn knowledge (as theorized by St. Thomas) to explain his thinking. This is an important key to understanding it. Of course, here we are not dealing with, as before, the popular communitarian subject (EG 119) but rather the other side of the coin, that is, that of a pastor in reference to the people, whom he knows "from the affective connaturality born of love," and that this piety, especially in the poorest, is the manifestation of theological life and therefore, a gift of the Holy Spirit (EG 125). Therefore, "expressions of popular piety have much to teach us; for those who are capable of reading them, they are a *locus theologicus* which demands our attention, especially at a time when we are looking to the new evangelization" (EG 126).

This affirmation crowns and, for now, brings full circle what was said earlier about the teaching of the last popes and the Latin American bishops about this topic.

Moreover, it seems that "popular mysticism" is dear to the heart of Pope Francis, because later he unexpectedly alludes to it once again when he applies the principle of "the whole is greater than the sum of its parts" to the "totality and integrity of the gospel" (see, respectively, nos. 237 and 235) in previously quoted texts about an evangelized culture being greater than—and has more resistance than—the mere number of the believers (EG 68). He completes these affirmations by saying,

> The genius of each people receives in its own way the entire Gospel and embodies it in expressions of prayer, fraternity, justice, struggle and celebration. . . . The Gospel has an intrinsic principle of totality: it will always remain good news until it has been proclaimed to all people, until it has healed and strengthened every aspect of humanity, until it has brought all men and women together at table in God's kingdom. The whole is greater than the part. (EG 237)

From the perspective of this rich text, we will now consider only what refers to this mysticism, because it encompasses not only moments of communal prayer and celebration but also the whole of Christian life, which is totally transfigured by the Spirit, who operates both individually and collectively in every human dimension. He operates collectively through his action, which is at once personal and interpersonal in and through Christ, the Head. Hence, the five words chosen by the pope for this are *prayer*, *fraternity*, *justice*, *struggle*, and *celebration*. Every one of them must be interpreted in both modes, that of community and of each individual in their mutual interaction and reception, all of whom actively welcome the initiative of the Spirit, the main actor of evangelization. Once again, the image is not that of a sphere but of a polyhedron (EG 236).

UNDERSTANDING POPULAR SPIRITUALITY

When Paul VI spoke of the evangelization of cultures, he was also referring to "collective consciences" (EN 18). Along these same lines, Pope Francis approaches both the faithful people of God and the peoples of the world as "active collective subjects" (EG 122), unquestionable in the light of theology. However, when we speak in that context of "conscience," "subject," "agent," "evangelizer," and so on, what does philosophical reflection tell us? Are these words perhaps *mere* metaphors? Is there in the individual and collective use of these words a true intrinsic analogy, or are we falling into error?

To discern this, I will first refer to Gerard Whelan's interpretation of how Bernard Lonergan thought of the plural subject of a common culture, applying it to our topic. I will then comment on Paul Ricœur's rejection of the Hegelian spirit in order to think about "we" as a communitarian subject, accepting his critique of Hegel. This will give us an opportunity not only to delve into the aforementioned analogy of the polyhedron—opposed to the Hegelian circular model—but also to respond to the question about multicultural societies and to see whether the image applies to them or not.

The Communitarian and Historical Subject of Culture according to Lonergan

In an unpublished study, "Pope Francis, Bernard Lonergan and Contextual Theology," Gerard Whelan explains the communitarian nature of the subject of culture according to Lonergan, based on the four transcendental operations, namely, experience, insight, judgment, and decision. A common experience leads to common insights; these to shared judgments of reality and values; and finally to common options, so that a "common sense" is achieved, proper to any given society.[14] I think this is a good basis on which to propose our question, although we might need another step to take us from the common to the communitarian.

The pope explains that popular spirituality is expressed, above all, through symbols (EG 124). So, if we apply what has been said to shared symbols, particularly religious ones, but also national, political, athletic, and the like, and to the affective spirits provoked by them, for example, the veneration of an image of Christ or of Mary, participation in a pilgrimage or procession, or the celebration of a popular feast, it seems that it not only is a common phenomenon, but also a communitarian one, insofar as the people share in it as individuals and also as an interpersonal community, according to a common culture, that is, the same "world of meaning and value" (Lonergan).

The following section, based on what has been said so far, will attempt to take a further step, that is, to understand the communitarian "we" as such, avoiding two pitfalls: individualism, which rests on a mere sum of particular characteristics, and collectivism, which dilutes them into a collective uniform subject.

Ricœur's Rejection of the Hegelian *Plus* of the Spirit and Francis's Pluriform Communion in the Spirit

To respond to the philosophical issue of the other and of the "we," Paul Ricœur prefers Husserl and his analogy of the alter ego (the other I), from the I itself, rather than Hegelian mutual recognition.[15] He fears an authoritarian, often totalitarian use of that *plus* when Hegel refers, for example, to the "spirit of the people" or resolves it in a dialectic totalization of the relationship of the I, the other, and we. Ricœur is correct in rejecting both the functionalization of the I and the other to mere moments in the totality of the we, and the "spirit" dialectically understood in Hegelian fashion, since Hegel thinks of this as the Greek *noûs,*[16] interpreted as the cognitive and dialectic subject-object relationship.

For Pope Francis, the issue does not concern these categories but rather the interrelation of love and the Christian *pneûma*. This, as the bond of love between the Father and the Son (EG 117), respects and guarantees, in the identity of the one God, the interpersonal distinctions between both, and of both of them with the Spirit. This, in communion with the people of God, reinforces the personality of each of its members in their mutual interrelation but irreducible to each other and to a "we" conceived as a dialectic totality. When the exhortation speaks of popular piety, therefore, it emphasizes that "they entail a personal relationship, not with vague spiritual energies or powers, but with God, with Christ, with Mary, with the saints. These devotions are fleshy, they have a face" (EG 90). The analogy is understood not with either the cognitive and dialectic subject-object relationship but with the ethical (and even super-ethical) interrelation of communion in the distinction that is proper to God, who is Love, and to persons as relationships. Thus, its reality is not represented in the Hegelian figures of the circle or the spiral:

> Our model is not the sphere, which is no greater than its parts, where every point is equidistant from the center, and there are no differences between them. Instead, it is the polyhedron, which reflects the convergence of all its parts, each of which preserves its distinctiveness. (EG 236)

In this text, it is evident that Francis is thinking both of the people of God and of the peoples-nations, in which the poor occupy a special place and in whom the original contribution of each individual must not be ignored. He goes on to say, "Pastoral and political activity alike seek to gather in this polyhedron the best of each. There is a place for the poor and their culture, their aspirations and their potential. Even people who can be considered dubious on account of their errors have something to offer which must not be overlooked" (EG 236).

In contrast to both Hegel and Husserl, our understanding of the pope could be helped by turning to what Jean-Luc Marion says about mutual recognition (of love) and the third party, referring to the trinitarian doctrine of Richard of St. Victor, in which the third is the Spirit as *condilectus* (co-loved).[17] Thus, the "we" is understood not as a compact or dialectical whole, but thanks to the ethical interrelation (already given in the language) between the "I," the "you," and the "he/she" in that they are distinct and irreducible among themselves, conceived in plural unity and in communion, which does not reduce them to mere moments of a totality, but also does not include them as a mere addition of unrelated individuals. Furthermore, let us keep in mind that for Marion the third is, in the male-female couple, the son (or at least the possibility)[18] and that Gaston Fessard bases his concept of "people" on the fraternity of sons and daughters, considered as third parties.[19] Once again, the *avant la lettre* phenomenology of Richard of St. Victor illuminates what was stated previously in this chapter about the peoples of the world (and the people of God), just as, on the other hand, the experience of the fraternal "we," of a mystical, contemplative fraternity (EG 92), and of "being a people" and "belonging to a people" (EG 270) can help us to better understand the trinitarian mysteries and the role played by the Spirit.

In a meeting that took place in Paris in 1982,[20] Lévinas rejected the we-people concept because he considered it as "walking together with each other," according to a consideration of Heidegger's "being-with" (*Mitsein*), to which he counterposed the "face-to-face" or "in front of" (*coram*) of the ethical alterity of the other, as he conceived it. Both Carlos Cullen and I responded that the "we" is not a collective I or a sum of individual "I's," but rather that it is the configuration as "I, you, he/she" in their ethical interrelations that makes them form a community, in which the persons constituting it are irreducible. In order to understand the "we," therefore, it is necessary to think of interpersonal relationships, not only according to the preposition *with*—one with another—but also according to *coram* (facing each other) and even in the "between" of the interpersonal and, in the case of the Church, of "Jesus in the midst." Marion's recourse to the trinitarian theology of Richard of St. Victor came sometime later to confirm his intuitions, and it now helps us to better understand Francis's thinking about the people of God and the peoples of the world, the "active collective subject" (EG 122) of popular spirituality and mysticism, and the original use that he makes of the polyhedron.

Multicultural Society and the Figure of the Polyhedron

From his own pastoral experience, the pope has firsthand knowledge of multicultural societies like that of Buenos Aires. Thus, he recognizes that we must remember that "cities are multicultural" (EG 74). What he says about this can also be applied to any society with cultural plurality, be it urban or otherwise, namely, "in the larger cities a connective network is found in which groups of people share a common imagination and dreams about life, and new human interactions arise, new cultures, invisible cities. Various subcultures subsist side by side and often practice segregation and violence. The Church is called to be at the service of a difficult dialogue" (EG 74).

In the same way that in each great city various "invisible cities" cross over one another, each with their respective cultural visions, today's globalized society has both the "culture of encounter," which must be fostered by the Church, and even the cultural mixing of visions with a true interculturality,[21] as well as cultural discrimination.

The faithful people of God can thus perfect its "multifaceted face," not only with the riches of the nations or at various historical times, but also with those of distinct "invisible cities" in one single sociocultural space as a city. The fruitful encounter among them and their respective visions can be illustrated with the image of the polyhedron.

This geometric figure and the assessment of the best of each individual within it apply, then, both to the multicultural people of God and to the peoples of the world where the intersection of cultures and their relationships takes place, since it is always possible to seek a genuine, just, symmetrical, and supportive interculturality. When the pope rejects the model of the sphere and chooses that of the polyhedron instead, he concludes by affirming, "It is the convergence of peoples who, within the universal order, maintain their own individuality; it is the sum total of persons within a society which pursues the common good, which truly has a place for everyone" (EG 236).

Adding to this thought, we could also say that it is the faithful people whose cultural face is multifaceted in the communion of differences, because it is guided by the Spirit, the bond of love in the irreducible distinction between the Father and the Son.

Chapter 11

POPE FRANCIS'S FOUR PRINCIPLES FOR BUILDING A PEOPLE[1]

The exhortation *Evangelii Gaudium* develops four principles when it speaks about social peace, both within a people and among the peoples, without forgetting the faithful people of God. Therefore, its objective is a peace that implies "a more perfect justice among men" and arises as a fruit of the integral development of all (EG 219).

For the pope, who is an assiduous student of Romano Guardini,[2] these principles are related to the "constant tensions present in every social reality" (EG 221) that could threaten the peace but that, on the contrary, can and ought to help to reaffirm it.

Not just any human group dwelling in the same territory can be called a "people" in the strictest sense. That is why Francis, beginning with the concept of nation (rather than class),[3] will counterpose it to a "mob swayed by the power that be" (EG 220). To be a people, living together and sharing life is not enough; rather, "People in every nation enhance the social dimension of their lives by acting as committed and responsible citizens" (EG 220). Such free assumption of responsibility is insufficient, however, without the historical dimension, which needs time because "becoming a people demands something more. It is an ongoing process in which every new generation must take part." It also demands, on the one hand, "a desire for integration"—let us recall that for Hannah Arendt political power is generated in the common action and will[4]—and, on the other hand, "a willingness to achieve this through the growth of a peaceful and multifaceted culture of encounter" (EG 220). A people is always in the process of building—for which it will help to keep the four principles in mind—and to understand this, the static category of substance does not help us, but rather those of relation and process. In addition, in the just quoted text, there appear two key ideas for Francis's understanding: the culture of encounter, to which corresponds a method of dialogue but which also assumes conflict, and the model of the polyhedron as a figure of consonance ("harmony") in the respect and assumption of the irreducible differences ("multifaceted").

This emphasis on the dynamic, process-oriented, and historical dimension reminds us of the concept of "people" of the Argentinian theology designated with this name, since it underscores in a people—following the three moments of time—its common history, a common lifestyle (culture), and a project for the common good ("common action and will"). This does not exclude that there might be different interpretations of that history, various subcultures in plural unity, and different proposals for the common good. What prevails, however, is the will to live together and to act consequently, to seek that good together. On the other hand, it remains clear that the people is thought of as a subject and communitarian agent of a common history and culture, of historical action and passion, and—when dealing with the faithful people of God—even of evangelization (EG 111–34).

With Mario Toso, we need also to reflect on what he calls a "precondition"—I would say *affective and experiential*—to experience peace, justice, respect for human dignity, and social inclusion of the poor in a high-intensity democracy, namely, *essere, sentirsi e farsi incessantemente popolo* ("to be, to feel, and to incessantly become a people"), thanks to the daily experience of such culture of encounter in "a peaceful and multifaceted culture of encounter" (EG 220).[5] Although, as we will see, this experience implies a constant elaboration of conflicts from the previous feeling of belonging. According to my interpretation, this affective moment—not meaning irrational, but rather imbued by correct "reasons of the heart"—is related to Bergoglio's affirmations when he was archbishop of Buenos Aires about the "people" as a category, not a logical one, but rather a "historical and mythical" one that, therefore, "enjoys an increase of sense that would escape us if we did not turn to other ways of understanding, to other logics and hermeneutics."[6] This historical novelty is not logically deduced but rather experimented and discerned, and the symbolical-mythical meaning is grasped not with rational reason but rather with the *feeling* intelligence.[7]

In EG 221, the pope affirms that the four principles, related to the constant tensions proper to any society, "derive from the pillars of the Church's social doctrine," but without explaining how. Certainly, all of them are oriented to the common good, both of each people-nation and internationally. They assume as their foundation the unconditional dignity of the person and of the human community, and they likewise move within another bipolar opposition, namely, between solidarity and subsidiarity. Therefore, they are closely connected to the principles of that doctrine.

In this chapter, I will begin by briefly explaining how this reflection on the four principles originated in Francis's thinking, as far as I know. Then I will comment on them one by one. Finally, I will present a sort of conclusion, relating the principles to another of Bergoglio's key ideas: that of *discernment*, not only personal, but communitarian, pastoral, and historical.

THE ORIGIN OF THE STATEMENT OF PRINCIPLES

Behind these four principles, there is apparently the explanation by the Argentinian Jesuit Ernesto López Rosas, from his implicit implementation of the advice given by Juan Manuel de Rosas, the governor of Buenos Aires, to Facundo Quiroga, the governor of La Rioja, regarding the Argentinian national organization in a letter dated December 20, 1834, and sent from the Figueroa hacienda.[8] Bergoglio first applied it in his address of February 18, 1974, to the Fourteenth Provincial Congregation Jesuit province of Argentina when he was a provincial.[9] He took up some of those principles at a later occasion in 1990 when he referred to the "union of spirits" in the Jesuit communities and the contraposition of "unity-diversity" harmonized by hope and love.[10] Later, in 2010, as archbishop of Buenos Aires, he further elaborated this in "Hacia un bicentenario en la justicia y la solidaridad 2010–2016. Nosotros como ciudadanos. Nosotros como pueblo."[11] As a pope, he introduced two of these principles in the encyclical *Lumen Fidei*, nos. 55 ("unity is superior to conflict") and 57 ("time is always superior to space"). Finally, he presented them to the universal Church as part of his roadmap for his pontificate in EG 217–37, and he has taken them up on many occasions, for example, in his encyclical *Laudato Si'* (nos. 110, 141, 178, 198, 201). In my commentary, I will mainly refer to the exhortation EG, illumining it with the earlier texts, particularly that of 2010, although I will also devote a section to LS.

TIME IS SUPERIOR TO SPACE

In EG 222, Francis, in beginning to deal with these principles, refers to the "constant tension between fullness and limitation," in which the priority of time over space arises. In contrast, the document of 2010 framed the four in three bipolar oppositions, mentioning from the beginning—in addition to the previously mentioned tension—those that take place between idea and reality as well, and between the global and the local (NCNP, 59). According to this same text, by reason of the polarity of fullness-limitation, the first two principles are generated: time over space and unity over conflict.

In addition to the fullness sought out by every person because of his or her thirst for transcendence, there are the following corresponding expressions: "time," "the horizon which constantly opens before us," "brighter horizon of the utopian future as the final cause which draws us to itself" (EG 222). Moreover, according to *Lumen Fidei* 57, "time propels towards the future and encourages us to go forward in hope," so that utopia, goal, and hope are linked together. In all of these formulations, the word "time" is equivalent to the always open horizon toward a positive and full future, without conditions, and calls us, both theologically and as our ultimate goal, to live in hope.

Against the fullness, the "limitation [of] ... the wall set before us," "each individual moment has to do with limitation as an expression of enclosure" (EG 222), and "the conjunction of the moment" is set in contrast, that is, the present conditions that are also loaded with those derived from the past. Bergoglio then concluded, "Here we see a first principle for progress in building a people: time is greater than space" (EG 222), although one cannot occur without the other.

In contrast to the other three principles, this formulation is not as easily understandable at first glance. It is more clearly understood, however, when the pope, referring to the sociopolitical activity, criticizes "privileging the spaces of power instead of the times of the processes" (EG 223). Those who attempt to "have everything solved in the present ... attempt to own all the spaces of power and self-affirmation." In contrast, "giving priority to time is to be concerned with initiating processes rather than owning spaces." Thus, "what is at stake is to privilege actions that generate new dynamics in society and that involve other persons and groups who will develop them until they fructify in important historical events" (EG 223). In summary, occupying spaces in order to possess and control is opposed by putting into motion historical dynamics in which others intervene and which, therefore, will require some time.

For Franz Rosenzweig, the new thinking, which, in my opinion, the pope shares as a man aware of his era, "takes the other and time seriously."[12] Taking others into account demands time, and it also demands that I, in their favor, lose control of the spaces. Spaces are still valued, but without being concretized and fixed, because they must be ruled by time, which "transforms them into links of a chain in constant growth, without turning back" (EG 223).

The practice of this principle demands a change of attitude, from vicious to virtuous. On the one hand, it prevents the danger of "being obsessed with immediate results." On the other, "it allows us to work at long-term range" and "to patiently endure difficult or adverse situations, or the changes of plans that the dynamism of reality imposes." Let us remember that reality is superior to idea. Hence, Francis summarizes this point by affirming, "Without anxiety, but with clear convictions and tenacity" (EG 223).

He then returns to Guardini by providing us with the criteria to judge an era—our own, for example—by asking us "to what extent the fullness of human existence is developed and reaches its true meaning in it, according to the peculiar nature and the possibilities of such epoch" (EG 224).[13] Once again, let us note that this is a polar opposition between fullness and limitation. This now appears to have a double face: as a singular "character"[14] of the epoch insofar as there is a real "possibility" and "impossibility."

Although in his first approach Francis is referring to peoples-nations, his gaze immediately moves from them to the faithful people of God, because he applies the aforementioned criteria of Guardini (and therefore, the polarity and the principle). He adds, "This criterion is also very proper of evangelization, which requires to have the horizon very present, to assume possible processes and a long journey" (EG 225). Now he himself is doing it with his desired missionary and "pastoral conversion" and with the corresponding reform of "obsolete structures" of the Church.[15]

Finally, to illustrate this priority of time over space, he turns first to the Lord's affirmation to "his disciples: that there were things they still could not understand and it was necessary to wait for the Holy Spirit." Then he turns to the parable of the wheat that matures with time and the parable of the weeds sown by the enemy in the kingdom of God (EG 225). In the 2010 conference in Buenos Aires, the pope contrasted the mother of the sons of Zebedee begging Jesus to give them places of power with Jesus's proposal to follow him in his redeeming process in time (NCNP, 62).

UNITY PREVAILS OVER CONFLICT

In EG, Francis does not explicitly relate this principle to the polarity of fullness-limitation, but he did so in 2010, linking time to conjunction (NCNP, 61). There are echoes of this connection both in the previously quoted text of EG 222, about the "conjuncture of the moment" insofar as limitation, as in no. 226, where he applies what he said to the "conflictive conjuncture."

Social and political life is never free of conflict. According to EG, there are three possible attitudes in the face of conflict. The first one is ignoring or masking it (EG 226), since "some simply look on and go on as if nothing happened; they wash their hands in order to be able to go on with their lives" (EG 227), as the Levite and the priest in the parable of the Good Samaritan selfishly did, to which Bergoglio alludes in the 2010 document (NCNP, 63). The second attitude concerns those who "get so involved in the conflict that they are trapped in it" (EG 227), so that we "lose perspective, the horizons are limited and reality itself is fragmented," because then we "lose the sense of the deep unity of reality" (EG 226), which prevails over the concepts we create about it, causing our perspective to be biased from the beginning of the conflict.

Thus, the interrelation of the principle that "unity is superior to conflict" (EG 228) becomes clear. The pope uses this to prioritize reality over the idea, but also its arising from the tension of fullness-limitation, since in these texts he criticizes the limitation of horizons and perspectives as well as "stopping at the conflictive conjuncture" (EG 226). This, as I said, functions as limitation—in this case, stopping progress toward a shared common good.

The third (and adequate) way of facing the conflict is to *assume* it (EG 226): "It means accepting to suffer conflict, resolve it and change it into the link for a new process" (EG 227), as Francis said earlier about the spaces that are ruled by time (EG 223). Notice the three verbs that he uses in EG 227 to signify the "long journey" (EG 225) toward human fullness, without getting ourselves trapped in conflictive conjunctures that stop the advance. They are *suffering, resolving,* and *transforming* the conflicts.

To *suffer* the conflict reminds us that Bergoglio also affirms that Christ "'makes peace through the blood of the cross' (Col 1:20)" (EG 229), as well as the theory of René Girard, according to which the Lord overcame violence by suffering it himself.[16] Hence, the pope indicates that the profound meaning of biblical texts leads us to "discover that the first environment where we are called to that peacemaking of differences is our own interiority" (EG 229). This is the social or pastoral agent, the politician, the citizen, and so on. Christians contribute to peace by first pacifying their own hearts, but this is not enough for social peace, though, on the other hand, "with hearts broken into a thousand fragments, it would be difficult to build it" (EG 229).

How, then, to *resolve* the conflict by assuming it, without ignoring it or letting ourselves be trapped in it? In my opinion, the pope's proposal joins three key elements, which correspond to his anthropological vision. The first element provides him with the *premise* and *basis* for it, the second indicates the *way* toward the resolution of conflict, and the third is the goal that one aspires to achieve, even in a precarious and partial way.

The *premise* is the human dignity of each and every one, whether it is an adversary or an enemy, encouraging us to "go beyond the conflictive surface" (EG 228) and to accept such dignity. The *objective* is not a type of "syncretism or the absorption of one into the other," nor is it a "negotiated peace" (EG 230), but rather the "communion of differences," the "social friendship" that assumes irreducible otherness, a "pluriform unity" (EG 230). Later, the pope will say, as I have repeatedly explained, that the corresponding geometrical model is the polyhedron, since this configures diversities into a unity that does not reduce them or make them uniform, but rather respects them (EG 236).

The *mediating way* between such foundations and objective consists in "setting the stakes ... for the resolution at a superior level that conserves in itself the valuable virtualities of the opposing polarities" (EG 228). The condition is to not *make an absolute* of one's own position, as if this exhausted the truth of reality, or to demonize the opposite position, as if it had nothing to contribute. Thus, this points to gradually approaching the previously mentioned "multiform harmony" (EG 220) and "communion of differences" (EG 228). This is achieved, however, by rising up to a *superior level,* from which it is possible to understand and assume as such the bipolar oppositions in their life-giving tension.

In the context of a religious community, Bergoglio connects the union of spirits with hope and love, affirming that "unity also goes through overcoming... the conflict: this overcoming which can be accomplished at a superior level, conformed by a loving hope. The only way in which unity is superior to conflict."[17] If we applied this text to the social peace of a people, it seems to me that we should talk about the utopia of a shared quest for the common good, in the line of hope and the experience of social friendship, based on the mutual recognition of the dignity of all, as it corresponds to love, that is, "the loving hope."

Hence, this concerns not only *suffering and resolving* the conflict, but "*transforming* it into the link of a *new* process" (EG 227)[18] for the good of all—even adversaries—and at the same time prioritizing time over space.[19] The method is dialogical, even if it is painful (suffering conflict), since adversaries must give up their own absolutization—ideologically *making a fetish* of their own position—so as to recognize the partial truth of the other because "even the persons who can be questioned because of their error have something to contribute that must not be lost" (EG 236). That is why Francis gives so much importance to the "culture of encounter."[20] By practicing it, an ever-fuller mutual civil recognition will gradually be achieved, without giving up the acceptance of the limitations proper to the human condition. Within the tension of fullness-limitation, pacification will gradually be discerned historically, which, in each case, would be politically possible and ethically established and therefore more just.

For the pope, as a believer, social peace is based on "the conviction that the unity of Spirit harmonizes all diversities" (EG 230), not only within the people of God, but also within and among the peoples of the earth. Therefore, "the unity of Spirit... overcomes any conflict in a new and promising synthesis," which is not the product of the necessary logic of thesis and antithesis, but rather a free fruit of civil liberty as a response to this first action (which is often anonymous) of the Spirit. "Diversity is beautiful"—we are talking about harmony—"when it accepts to constantly enter a process of reconciliation leading to seal a kind of cultural pact from which emerges a 'reconciled diversity'" (EG 230). Thus, beauty attracts as a final cause and a shared common good.

REALITY IS MORE IMPORTANT THAN THE IDEA

In this case, the formulation of the bipolar tension coincides with the principle, which fosters the implementation of a "constant dialogue, preventing the idea from being separated from reality" (EG 231); otherwise, this would be hidden or deformed by the mere idea, which would become *ideological.* The pope then lists various forms of that separation between both, namely, "angelical purisms, totalitarianisms of the relativism, nominalist declarations, projects that are formal rather than real, ahistorical fundamentalisms, ethics without goodness, intellectualisms without wisdom" (EG 231). Notice that all of these are expressed by substantives ending in "-isms," which frequently indicates a reduction to a single aspect of reality or making an absolute out of it. It is thus that the idea is made "exclusive," deforming the perception of the real.

What do these "-isms" have in common, and what are they opposed to? Outside of the "nominalist declarationism," which remains in the exterior of a mere sophistic rhetoric, the others are linked to each other because they remain in what is abstract, ahistorical, formal, and "pure," both at the theoretical and practical levels (ethicism); they are opposed to historical concreteness, to what is relative and contingent on historical reality, to the "impure." This last one, because it is ambiguous, is limited to contents that are irreducible to a total formalization. I am particularly struck by the opposition of ethicism—which is formalistic, casuistic, and rigorous—to *goodness,* without which there are no true ethics, and even less a Christian ethic, and, on the other hand, that of intellectualism (not true intelligence!), which is rationalistic and calculating, to *wisdom,* since this is at the same time intellective and affective, with right affections. According to St. Thomas, wisdom knows affectively by *connaturality,* or "feeling and tasting internally" according to the Ignatian expression, which is reminiscent of the *sapere* (taste, wisdom) of St. Bernard. In both cases, ethics without kindness and "intellectualism without wisdom," only *what* and not *how* it is known is considered, namely, *with* or *without* kindness or, respectively, wisdom. As the philosophy of language claims, however, the pragmatic moment of the *how* is part of the significance, that is, of the *what.*[21] If this is neglected with an inadequate existential or pragmatical attitude, there are aspects—perhaps very relevant ones—that are not fully perceived, biasing, then, the integral knowledge of the same.[22]

This need for kindness and wisdom for a right knowledge is, in my opinion, a deep conviction of Pope Francis, which can be linked to other affirmations of EG, for example, to the critique to the second form of "spiritual worldliness." Those who "feel superior to others because they fulfill certain norms or because they are unflinchingly faithful to a certain Catholic style that belongs to the past," with a "supposed doctrinal or disciplinarian security that gives rise to a narcissistic and authoritarian elitism," which "spends energies in controlling" (EG 94), are lacking precisely in the goodness and wisdom flowing from it. On the contrary, "the look of the Good Shepherd ... does not seek to judge but to love" (EG 125) and thus knows well the reality of his sheep.[23] The "revolution of tenderness" to which the pope constantly calls us and to which the "Son of God, in his incarnation, invited us" (EG 88) helps us to "overcome suspicion, permanent mistrust, the fear to be invaded, and defensive attitudes" (EG 88), because it implies a good and wise heart, with the wisdom given by a discreet love.

For this same reason, the mere idea, in its abstraction and disconnect from reality, is not efficacious, does not convoke, does not touch a profound affectivity, and thus is not faithful to its function of "grasping, comprehending and leading." "What convokes is reality illumined by reasoning," so that, in order to be efficient, we must "go from a formal nominalism to harmonious objectivity" (EG 232). Truth, goodness, and beauty must go together: they attract, call, and *con*-voke.

Finally, the Holy Father, as in the previous cases, also connects this principle and criterion of an anthropological character—"reality is superior to the idea"—to the faith and pastoral ministry of the Church, particularly with the flesh of Christ, to which the exhortation frequently turns (see, e.g., EG 24, 198). He affirms that "this criterion makes the incarnation of the Word and its placing into practice" (EG 233), since the "criterion of reality, of an already incarnated Word and seeking to be incarnated, is essential to evangelization" (no. 233).

THE WHOLE IS GREATER THAN THE PART (AND THE MERE SUM OF ITS PARTS)

The fourth principle is framed in the bipolar opposition between globalization and localization. When the life-giving tension between both is not maintained, or on the side of the latter, one falls into "daily pettiness" in which one becomes "a folkloric museum of local hermits, condemned to repeat the same over and over, incapable to allow themselves to be challenged by the different and to value the beauty that God pours out outside their limits" (EG 234). Or, on the other extreme, one ceases to "walk with their feet on the ground," moving in "an abstract universalism" as "mimetic passengers in the last car of the train, admiring the fireworks of the world which belongs to others, gaping and with programmed applause" (no. 234). In the latter case, therefore, without tension, one's own creativity, the solid rootedness, the concrete reality, and the living identity are lost, thus falling in a "mimetic" alienation, a "world ... of others," with "gaping and programmed applause." On the opposite side, one can close up in what has already happened (as in a "museum"), with a static and dead identity ("always repeating the same" without "allowing oneself to be challenged by the different"), in isolation ("local hermits"), and without renewal beyond its narrow confines.

Therefore, "the whole is superior to the part and also more than the mere sum of parts" (EG 235). As a Jesuit, Bergoglio is used to seeking the greater glory of God; therefore, he advises us to "always widen the look in order to recognize a greater good that will benefit us all," while, of course, remaining in the dynamic tension that makes us fruitful, without remaining exclusively in the "global sphere that annuls us" or in the "isolated partiality that makes us barren" (EG 235). Such a vision, for it to be more encompassing and global, must be "without evasions, without uprootedness," because it is necessary to plant roots into a "fertile ground and in the history of one's own place, which is a gift from God" (no. 235).

Likewise, in his writings, Francis was likely reminded of the sixteenth-century epitaph of St. Ignatius: "Not to be daunted by the greatest enterprise, yet to invest oneself in the smallest one, this is divine."[24] We "work in the small, in the familiar, but with a wider perspective" (EG 235), namely, a universal one.

I mentioned earlier that, for Francis, the model is the polyhedron, "which reflects the convergence of all its parts, each of which preserves its distinctiveness" (EG 236). Each one has something particular to contribute to the common good, which only it can provide to the others and to the whole, since it does not make uniform or homogenize, but rather makes the differences come together in consonance and harmony, as in an orchestra. Thus, the figure is not "the sphere, which is no greater than its parts, where every point is equidistant from the center, and there are no differences between them" (EG 236). Once again, we see how Guardini's dialectic of polar contraposition (*Gegensätze*) has a very different result from that of Hegelian contradiction (*Widerspruch*)—whose figures are the sphere or the spiral—or the Marxist class struggle, as I previously noted on the topic of conflict and superior unity that respects the original diversity of each part, without being reduced to a mere sum, as in liberal individualism.

Francis immediately applies what has been said to the Church and civil society, as he adds, "Pastoral and political activity alike seek to gather in this polyhedron the best of each" (EG 236). For him, however, both in one and in the other, the contribution of the poor is essential because, as in an *ex abrupto,* he interposes an important allusion to them. "There is a place for the poor and their culture, their aspirations and their potential" (no. 236), which are essential for the wholeness of the faithful people of God and of the peoples of the earth.

In regard to them, the pope is thinking both of the international sphere and the national realm, favoring peace and justice in both cases, because he summarizes all of the above by affirming, "It is the convergence of peoples who, within the universal order, maintain their own individuality; it is the sum total of persons within a society which pursues the common good, which truly has a place for everyone" (EG 236). The image of the polyhedron and its contrast with the sphere help us to better comprehend how he understands the criterion of the whole as superior to the part.

Just as he did in his treatment of the previous principles, he applies faith to the fourth, since he says that, for Christians, this "evokes the totality or integrity of the Gospel" (EG 237). He then lists various categories of Christians, with the intention of encompassing all: entrepreneurs, workers, academics, artists, and so on. Once again, he remembers the poor and their spirituality in a kind of new *ex abrupto,* which for me speaks of the fullness of his heart, adding, "The genius of each people receives in its own way the entire Gospel and embodies it in expressions of prayer, fraternity, justice, struggle and celebration" (EG 237). This criterion of totality is intrinsic to the gospel, "which is not totally good news until it is announced to all, until it makes fruitful and heals all dimensions of man" (no. 237), that is, until it embraces and redeems every man and woman, all humanity.

THE FOUR PRINCIPLES IN *LAUDATO SI'*

The pope frequently refers to one or several of these principles in his allocutions and writings. Thus, it is not surprising that he used them in his first encyclical, although he does not do it systematically, as in EG, but in different contexts.

Thus, Francis touches on the specialization and fragmentation of knowledge and partial perspectives on different sciences, which make it difficult to solve the "more complex problems of today's world, particularly those regarding the environment and the poor." Therefore, he concludes by saying, "Once more we see that 'realities are more important than ideas'" (LS 110). Later, after having alluded yet again to the dialogue among different religions and the sciences—to prevent them from isolation and making an absolute out of their own knowledge, as well as among the ideologies that separate the ecological movements—he repeats the same principle (LS 201). Thus, the dialogue among different ideas approaches the possibility of grasping the ever-complex reality.

Likewise, when Francis notes that the analysis of environmental problems is inseparable from their distinct human contexts and that "there is an interaction among ecosystems and among the different worlds of social reference," he reminds us once again that "the whole is greater than the part" (LS 141).

Later, criticizing political expediency and the "myopia of power politics" that removes the environmental issue from the public agenda because of electoral reasons, he observes, "Thus we forget that 'time is greater than space,' that we are always more effective when we generate processes rather than holding on to positions of power" (LS 178), so as to project the common good in the long term.

Finally, seeing that "politics and economics tend to blame each other when it comes to poverty and environmental degradation," the Holy Father advises them to recognize their own error and to work together for the common good. On this occasion, he reiterates, "Here too, we see how true it is that 'unity is greater than conflict'" (LS 198).

These principles thus conform in an important way to Bergoglio's ideology and way of proceeding that they can easily be resourced in the various circumstances of his political counsel and pastoral action. LS is yet another example of this.

CONCLUSION: THE FOUR PRINCIPLES AS CRITERIA FOR DISCERNMENT

As I have pointed out, Francis sometimes refers to these four ideas as "principles." At other times, they are called "criteria," and even "polarities" or "tensions," and he contemplates the four of them in their mutual interrelation and with the three bipolar oppositions. They are *criteria* because they serve to judge and discern the situation of a people (or the people of God) by their function of their building and leading in peace, justice, and, fraternity (EG 221).

One way—but not the only one—to organize such an interrelation of the four is made possible by the concept, which is key for Bergoglio, of the whole as a polyhedron. This gathers in itself the unity of the diversities, assuming and overcoming conflicts in the harmony of the differences of the parts, each one with a specific contribution. The transversal priority of time demonstrates, then, that it is not only hope and utopia that act as a goal, but also a dynamic process—unpredictable and historical—that can contribute directly toward the goal. This cannot be controlled, however, because it involves many people. Consequently, the profound unity of reality appears superior to any idea that interprets it. Thus, making an absolute out of the part, of conflict, of space, and of the idea, is renounced, conceiving them in polar tension with their opposites, oriented and ordered by hope. Hence, there is a need to discern—politically, pastorally, and prophetically—the historical situation and to transform it gradually into the greatest possible human fulfillment.

I mentioned that in EG 229 the pope gives the example of inner pacification in order to better understand social peace. Thus, in the

1990 writing quoted earlier,[25] he developed the parallelism between the resolution, at a superior level, of inner conflicts through spiritual discernment and that of conflicts that affect the social union of spirits, specifying that, in both cases, these are not contradictions but rather polar contrapositions whose temporal discernment process moves from unity in diversity, previously reached at a certain level—whose sign is peace—toward a greater one, at a superior level, as links in an ascending process.[26]

For Diego Fares, Bergoglio coincides with Guardini in the quality that he attributes to von Balthasar, namely, "having eyes that listen,"[27] giving space—through the renunciation of the contemplating subject—so that what is looked at (the particular living being) may gain space so that his or her history is manifested to him. Guardini's method of polar oppositions, which, in my opinion, Bergoglio applies through the four criteria, is therefore a method that contributes to historical discernment. For Guardini, "the particular living being" par excellence is Christ, but also people, the peoples of the earth, and the faithful people of God in the process of their history, which, respectively, the director of spiritual exercises, the politician, and the pastor must help to discern in order to seek and find the new steps that need to be taken in order to achieve an ever-greater peace and justice of a higher quality.

Fares himself illustrates this by turning to Bergoglio's personal notes about a dream narrated by Guardini. According to Guardini, the dream told him that everyone, at birth, receives a word—a call, I would say—that serves as a password for everything that happens to them. It is something that must be translated during their lifetime and achieved through action, and by which they will be judged. In his notes from that time, the pope interpreted these words as an "existential *kerygma*," which comes even before the *kerygma* of the gospel. The consonance with this "word," in consolation and peace, is oriented to the straight path, while the dissonance (desolation) indicates either that the person is still searching or that there has been some sort of disagreement (with oneself, with others, with reality, or with God).

My hypothesis is that Francis uses Guardini's method and the Ignatian practice of discernment through consolations and desolations (consonances and dissonances) for the life not only of people but also of the peoples of the earth and even of the people of God, in order to "seek and find—for them—the will of God." The four criteria studied in this book serve him on that path of pastoral discernment.

For Bergoglio is not only the "pope of the people" (of the faithful people of God and of the peoples of the earth) but also the "pope of discernment" of the signs of our times.[28]

NOTES

FOREWORD

1. Pope Francis, "Welcoming Ceremony," South Lawn of the White House, Washington, DC, Wednesday, September 23, 2015, http://www.vatican.va/content/francesco/en/speeches/2015/september/documents/papa-francesco_20150923_usa-benvenuto.html.

2. Austen Ivereigh, *The Great Reformer: Francis and the Making of a Radical Pope* (New York: Henry Holt, 2014).

3. Massimo Borghesi, *The Mind of Pope Francis: Jorge Mario Bergoglio's Intellectual Journey* (Collegeville, MN: Liturgical Press, 2018).

4. Thomas Rourke, *The Roots of Pope Francis's Social and Political Thought: From Argentina to the Vatican* (Lanham, MD: Rowman & Littlefield, 2016).

5. *Porteño* refers to a resident of Buenos Aires since the port of that city was critical in the development of the city and the nation.

6. *Laudato Si'* note 117, citing Juan Carlos Scannone, "La irrupción del pobre y la lógica de la gratuidad," in *Irrupción del pobre y quehacer filosófico. Hacia una nueva racionalidad*, ed. Juan Carlos Scannone and Marcelo Perine (Buenos Aires: Bonum, 1993), 225–30.

7. Juan Carlos Scannone, *La teología del pueblo. Raíces teológicas del papa Francisco* (Maliaño, Spain: Sal Terrae, 2017), 245–46. [This is found in chap. 10 of the present volume.] Whelan is an Irish-born Jesuit who taught for many years at Hekima College in Nairobi and since 2007 has been a professor at the Pontifical Gregorian University in Rome.

8. This teaching of Pope Francis is explicitly stated in the Spanish version of *Evangelii Gaudium* and is for that reason underscored by Scannone (*La*

teología del pueblo, 237). The English translation, however, simply speaks about listening to the promptings of the Spirit "together."

9. *Evangelii Gaudium* 32, 106, 145, 166, 175, 177, 201, 254, 261, and 270.

10. *Evangelii Gaudium* 254.

11. See Peter Casarella, "Pope Francis, Theology of the People, and the Church in the United States," in *Discovering Pope Francis: The Roots of Jorge Mario Bergoglio's Thinking*, ed. Brian Y. Lee and Rev. Thomas L. Knoebel (Collegeville, MN: Liturgical Press, 2019), 177–208.

12. For a deeper appreciation of the pivotal role of Lonergan's multiple conversions to the philosophical method of Scannone, see Lorenz Bruno Puntel, "Consideraciones acerca de la concepción y el manejo del metódo filosófico en J. C. Scannone," in *Filosofía y teología en diálogo desde América Latina. Homenaje a Juan Carlos Scannone, sj en su 80 cumpleaños*, ed. José María Cantó, SJ, and Pablo Figueroa, SJ (Córdoba: Editorial de la Universidad Católica de Córdoba, 2013), 296–306.

13. Pope Francis, "Welcoming Ceremony."

14. See Stuart Squires, *The Pelagian Controversy* (Eugene, OR: Wipf & Stock, 2019), 278–94.

15. From the Preamble of the U.S. Constitution.

PREFACE

1. I am referring to my *Evangelización, cultura y teología* (Buenos Aires: Guadalupe, 1990; 2nd ed., Buenos Aires: Docencia, 2011, with a foreword by Guillermo Rosolino) and *Weisheit und Befreiung. Volstheology in Latinamerika* ("Sabiduría y liberación. Teología popular en América Latina") (Dusseldorf: Patmos, 1992).

PART I

Chapter 1

1. The first part of this article corresponds to the first part of the article "Papa Francesco e la teologia del popolo," *La Civiltà Cattolica* 3930 (March 15, 2014): 571–79.

2. Cf. E. C. Bianchi, *Pobres en este mundo, ricos en la fe: la fe de los pobres en América Latina, según Rafael Tello* (Buenos Aires: Ágape, 2012); F. Forcat, "En las nacientes de la Pastoral Popular. Rafael Tello entre los peritos de la COEPAL," *Stromata* 71 (2015): 145–49.

3. See my *Le pape du people. Bergoglio raconté par son confrère théologien, jésuite et argentin. Entretiens avec Berndadette Sauvaget* (Paris: Cerf, 2015).

4. See J. C. Maccarone, "La teología en la Argentina. Segunda mitad del siglo XX. ¿Tradición o ruptura?" *Teología* 60 (1992): 155–68; the author studies it from the 1930s.

5. See R. Oliveros, *Liberación y teología. Génesis y crecimiento de una reflexión. 1960–1977* (Lima: CEP, 1977), 52ff.

6. It was later published in Montevideo, see MIEC-JECI 1969.

7. About COEPAL, see S. Politi, *Teología del pueblo. Una propuesta argentina a la teología latinoamericana 1967–1975* (Buenos Aires: Guadalupe, 1992), chap. 4; M. Gonzalez, *Reflexión teológica en Argentina (1962–2010). Aportes para un mapa de sus relaciones y desafíos hacia el futuro* (Buenos Aires: Docencia, 2010), chap. 2 (henceforth, RTA). Regarding Priests for the Third World, see J. P. Martin, *El Movimiento de Sacerdotes para el Tercer Mundo* (Buenos Aires: Guadalupe, 1991).

8. For a selection of his works, see V. R. Azcuy, C. M. Galli, M. Gonzalez (Editorial Theological Committee) *Escritos Teológico-Pastorales of Lucio Gera, I: Del preconcilio a la Conferencia de Puebla (1956–1981)* (Buenos Aires: Ágape, 2006); *II: De la Conferencia de Puebla a nuestros días* (Buenos Aires: Ágape, 2007). See also my "Los aportes de Lucio Gera a la teología en perspectiva latinoamericana," in *Presente y futuro de la teología en Argentina. Homenaje a Lucio Gera*, ed. R. Ferrara and C. Galli (Buenos Aires: Paulinas, 1997), 121–41; and "Lucio Gera: un teologo 'dal' Popolo," *La Civiltà Cattolica* 3954 (March 21, 2015): 539–50.

9. About the "polo" in Justino O'Farrell, see M. Gonzalez, RTA, 75–83 (with bibliography); about the "polo" in Rafael Tello, see M. Gonzalez, RTA, 83–84. Unpublished manuscripts by Tello are now being published, among others: *La Nueva Evangelización. Escritos teológico-pastorales I* (Buenos Aires: Ágape, 2008); *Pueblo y Cultura* (Buenos Aires: Patria Grande, 2011).

10. See C. M. Galli, epilogue of the book cited in n. 8, vol. 1, 879.

11. See Third General Conference of the Latin American Bishops, *Documento de Puebla* (Buenos Aires: Episcopal Conference of Argentina, 1979), n414 (henceforth, PD).

12. About the problems of the last paragraph, see F. Boasso, *¿Qué es la Pastoral Popular?* (Buenos Aires: Patria Grande, 1974); the author affirms that he is expressing not just his own thought but that of COEPAL.

13. This expression means *anyone* from among the people, similar to "John Doe" in English.

14. "Religiosidad popular," in C. Floristán and J. J. Tamayo, *Conceptos fundamentales de pastoral* (Madrid: Cristiandad, 1983), 879.

15. Alliende refers positively to what he calls the "Argentine school of popular ministry" in "Diez tesis sobre pastoral popular," in Equipo SELADOC, *Religiosidad popular* (Salamanca: Sígueme, 1976), 119.

16. See my book *Evangelización, cultura y teología* (Buenos Aires: Guadalupe, 1990; 2nd ed., Buenos Aires: Docencia, 2011).

17. My article mentioned in the text is "La teología de la liberación. Caracterización, corrientes, etapas," *Stromata* 48 (1982): 3–40; see also K. Neufeld, ed., *Problemi e prospettive di teología dogmatica* (Brescia: Queriniana, 1983). Above I mention J. L. Segundo, *Liberación de la teología* (Buenos Aires: Lohlé, 1974), 264; S. Politi, op. cit. in n. 7 of this chapter; G. Gutiérrez, *La fuerza histórica de los pobres*, 2nd ed. (Lima: CEP, 1988), 372; and R. Oliveros, op. cit. in n. 5 of this chapter.

18. Cf. A. Quarracino, "Algunos aspectos de la 'teología de la liberación.' Líneas doctrinales y pastorales del documento," *L'Osservatore Romano* (Spanish ed.) 819 (September 9, 1984): 567; J. B. Libânio, *Teologia da libartação. Roteiro didáctico para um estudo* (São Paulo: Loyola, 1987), 258ff.; A. Methol Ferré, "Da Rio de Janeiro a Puebla; 25 anni di storia," *Incontri* 4 (1982): 4; and the oral exposition of Cardinal Moreira Neves at the CELAM talk on "El método teológico de América Latina," Bogotá, October 28 to November 1, 1993.

19. See his message to the Brazilian bishops. *L'Osservatore Romano* (weekly Spanish edition) 904 (1986): para. 5.

20. There I had already made my presentation from the perspective of the theology of the people. See "Teología y política. El actual desafío planteado al lenguaje teológico latinoamericano de liberación," in *Fe cristiana y cambio social en América Latina. Encuentro de El Escorial, 1972*, ed. Instituto Fe y Secularidad (Salamanca: Sígueme, 1973), 247–81. There you can also see the abstract of my talk "Necesidad y posibilidades de una teología socioculturalmente latinoamericana," 353–75.

21. Cf. J. Comblin, J. I. González-Faus, and J. Sobrino, eds., *Cambio social y pensamiento cristiano en América Latina* (Madrid: Trotta, 1993).

22. Cf. Monsignor L. Mendes de Almeida, et al., *El futuro de la reflexión teológica en América Latina* (Bogotá: CELAM, 1996). My presentation's title was "El comunitarianismo como alternativa viable," 195–241.

23. See G. De Shreijver, ed., *Liberation Theologies on Shifting Grounds: A Clash of Socio-economic and Cultural Paradigms* (Leuven: Leuven University Press/Peeters, 1998).

24. See C. M. Galli, "Evangelización, cultura y teología. El aporte de Juan Carlos Scannone a una teología inculturada," *Stromata* 47 (1991): 205–16; M. González, RTA, 124–44.

25. See, among other writings, O. Yorio, "El acontecimiento argentino como lugar teológico," *Revista Bíblica* 37 (1975): 61–92; Id., *Tanteando pactos de amor. Reflexiones en los Seminarios de Formación Teológica,1989–1997* (Buenos Aires: Nueva Tierra, 1999).

26. It was published by the press of the Catholic University of Córdoba (Argentina) in 2006. In it, twenty-two women and men theologians, both Catholic and non-Catholic, contributed to it; it was edited by Marcelo González and Carlos Schickendantz.

27. Among other works, see A. M. Grande, *Aportes argentinos a la teología pastoral y a la nueva evangelización* (Buenos Aires: Ágape, 2011). This is a doctoral dissertation (by a fourth-generation theologian) directed by Carlos Galli (third) about Gera, Farrell, and Scannone (first and second generations).

28. The complete title is *El Pueblo de Dios en los pueblos del mundo. Catolicidad, encarnación e intercambio en la eclesiología actual.* It was defended at the School of Theology of UCA in 1993. One of the chapters was published as "La encarnación del Pueblo de Dios en la Iglesia y en la eclesiología lationamericanas," *Sedoi* 125 (1994).

29. In the text I resume what I said in my article "Perspectivas eclesiológicas de la 'teología del pueblo' en la Argentina," in *Ecclesia Tertii Millennii Advenientis. Omaggio al P. Ángel Antón*, ed. F. Chica, S. Panizzolo, and H. Wagner (Casale Monferrato: Pienme, 1997), 686–704, particularly 701ff.

30. A classic on this subject is J. L. Cohen and A. Arato, *Civil Society and Political Theory* (Cambridge, MA: MIT Press, 1992). Regarding Latin America, see my article referred to in n. 22 (with bibliography) of this chapter.

31. See P. Trigo, "Imaginario alternativo al imaginario vigente y al revolucionario," *Iter. Revista de Teología* 3 (1992): 61–99; Id., *La cultura del barrio* (Caracas: Centro Gumilla, 2004); Id., *Relaciones humanizadoras. Un imaginario alternativo* (Santiago [Chile]: Universidad Alberto Hurtado, 2013);

J. R. Seibold, "Imaginario social, trabajo y educación. Su problemática actual en medios populares del Gran Buenos Aires," in *Ética y economía. Economía de mercado, neoliberalismo y ética de la gratuidad*, ed. J. C. Scannone and G. Remolina (Buenos Aires: Bonum, 1998), 369–408; Id., "Ciudadanía, transformación educativa e imaginario social urbano," in *Lo político en América Latina. Contribución filosófica a otro modo de hacer política*, ed. J. C. Scannone and V. Santuc (Buenos Aires: Bonum, 1999), 463–511.

32. Regarding Brazil, see P. Rubens, *Discerner la foi dans des contexts religieux ambigus. Enjeux d'une théologie du croire* (Paris: Cerf, 2004), 24. I believe something similar could be said of the non-Catholic popular religiosity of greater Buenos Aires.

33. See J. R. Seibold, "Imaginario social, religiosidad popular y transformación educativa. Su problemática en medios populares del Gran Buenos Aires," in G. Farrell, et al., *Argentina, tiempo de cambios* (Buenos Aires: San Pablo, 1996), 323–88. What the author says about Greater Buenos Aires—still current—is analogically applied to the great suburbs of the large Latin American cities.

34. Regarding the *vital synthesis* of visions, see my article "La religión en la América Latina del tercer milenio. Hacia una utopía realizable," *Stromata* 51 (1995): 75–88. Today, however, there are still ambiguous elements: see my "Situación religiosa actual en América Latina," *CIAS. Centro de Investigación y Acción Social* 55 (2006): 157–72.

35. See the Fifth General Conference of Latin American and Caribbean Bishops, *Aparecida. Documento conclusivo* (Buenos Aires: Conferencia Episcopal Argentina, 2006), nn258–65, particularly 262.

36. See G. Gutiérrez, *Beber en su propio pozo. En el itinerario espiritual de un pueblo* (Lima: CEP, 1983); J. R. Seibold, *La mística popular* (Mexico City: Buena Prensa, 2006).

37. See my "La transcendencia como intrínsecamente constitutiva de ética y política," *Budhi: A Journal of Ideas and Culture* 13 (2009): 325–34; about *saturated phenomena*, see J. L. Marion, *Étant donné. Essai d'une phénoménologies de la donation* (Paris: PUF, 1997); Id., *De surcroît. Etudes sur les phénomènes saturés* (Paris: PUF, 2001). See also J. C. Scannone, R. Walton, and J. P. Esperón, eds., *Transcendencia y sobreabundancia. Fenomenología de la religión y filosofía primera* (Buenos Aires: Biblos, 2015).

38. Congregation for the Doctrine of Faith, Instruction *Libertatis Conscientia* (1986), no. 70.

39. Cf. H. Simián Yofre, "Epistemología y hermenéutica de liberación," in *Actas del IV Simposio Español and I Simposio Bíblico Hispanoamericano* (Granada: Fundación Bíblica Española, 1992).

Chapter 2

1. This chapter was published as an article under the title "Lucio Gera: un teólogo dal popolo," *La Civiltà Cattolica* 3954 (March 21, 2015): 539–50.

2. See Lucio Gera, *Religiosità popolare, dipendenza, liberazione* (Bologna: Dehoniane, 1978), 5.

3. Some people prefer to call it "theology of culture," as it conceives the people as creative subjects of culture.

4. Both texts are: "Pueblo, religión del pueblo e Iglesia" (henceforth, PRP) in CELAM, *Iglesia y religiosidad popular en América Latina. Ponencias y documento final* (Bogotá: Secretaria General del CELAM, 1977), 258–83; and "La Iglesia frente a la situación de dependencia" (henceforth, ISD), in Lucio Gera, Aldo J Büntig, and Osvaldo Catena, *Teología pastoral y dependencia* (Buenos Aires: Guadalupe, 1974), 9–64. In part 2, I particularly take into account "Evangelización y promoción humana," *America Latina y la doctrina social de la Iglesia. II. Identidad cultural y modernización en América Latina,* comp. Carlos María Galli and Peter Hünermann (Buenos Aires: Paulinas, 1992), 23–90. These three works have been republished in *Escritos Teológicos Pastorales de Lucio Gera. I: Del Preconcilio a la Conferencia de Puebla (1956–1981),* ed. Virginia R. Azcuy, Carlos María Galli, and Marcelo Gonzalez (Buenos Aires: Ágape, 2006), 717–45 and 661–717, respectively; and *Escritos teológico-pastorales de Lucio Gera 2: De Puebla a nuestros días (1982–2007),* ed. Virginia R Azcuy, José Carlos Caamaño, and Carlos M Galli (Buenos Aires: Ágape, 2007), 297–364.

5. See Pope Francis, apostolic exhortation *Evangelii Gaudium* 125 and 119. The relationship is obvious, on the parts of both Gera and the pope, with the "knowledge by connaturality" of Thomas Aquinas, which he develops by speaking about the gift of wisdom. I relate it not only with the theology of *spiritual senses* (Origen, Bernard de Clairvaux, Bonaventure, Ignatius of Loyola, Karl Rahner, Hans Urs von Balthasar) but also with the "*sentient intelligence*" of the Spanish philosopher Xavier Zubiri: see his *Inteligencia sentiente I: Inteligencia y realidad* (Madrid: Alianza Editorial, 1980).

6. I believe that behind Gera's concept is that of Suárez, reinterpreted by giving relevance to culture. See my "Lo social y lo político según Francisco Suárez. Hacia una relectura latinoamericana actual de la filosofía política de Suárez," *Stromata* 54 (1998): 85–118.

7. See Paul Ricœur, "Civilisation universelle et cultures nationales," in *Histoire et Verité* (Paris: Seuil, 1955), 286–300.

8. See Carlos M. Galli, "Introducción al tomo Segundo," in Carlos María Galli and Peter Hünermann, *America Latina y la doctrina social de la Iglesia. II. Identidad cultural y modernización en América Latina.*

9. Gera himself complements ISD in his nearly contemporary "Cultura y dependencia a la luz de la reflexión teológica," *Stromata* 30 (1974): 169–224. It consists of the exposition of the previous year during the Jornadas Académicas de las Facultades de Filosofía y Teología de San Miguel on "Dependencia cultural y creación de cultura en América Latina."

10. Recall that Gera's role was relevant in the preparation of Puebla and, during the conference, in the redaction of its texts about the evangelization of culture.

11. The references are the following: (1) AAS 77, no. 1 (1985): 354–61, cf. *L'Osservatore Romano* 825 (1984): 668ff.; (2) *L'Osservatore Romano* 825 (1984): 671–74; (3) AAS 75 (1983): 771, cf. *L'Osservatore Romano* (1983): 179ff.

12. My italics. Later, John Paul II in *Centesimus Annus* 5 will say, "In effect, to teach and to spread her social doctrine pertains to the Church's evangelizing mission and is an essential part of the Christian message, since this doctrine points out the direct consequences of that message in the life of society and situates daily work and struggles for justice in the context of bearing witness to Christ the Savior."

PART II

1. About inculturation, see International Theological Commission, *Faith and Inculturation* (1987), accessed October 23, 2020, http://www.vatican.va/roman_curia/congregations/cfaith/cti_documents/rc_cti_1988_fede-inculturazione_en.html; Andrés Tornos, *Inculturación Teología y método* (Madrid: Universidad Pontificia de Comillas; Bilbao: Desclée, 2001).

2. Cf. Karl Rahner et al., eds., *Befreiende Theologie. Der Beitrag Lateinamerikas zur Theology der Gegenward* (Stuttgart: Kohlhammer, 1977); *Volksreligion-Religion des Volkes* (Stuttgart: Kohlhammer, 1979). Rahner himself wrote the prologue to the first work as well as the text, "Einleitende Überlegungen zum Verhältnis von Theologie und Volksreligion" (9–16) for the second. I had the honor to participate in both.

3. See "Documento final" of the Encuentro Interdepartamental of CELAM on popular religiosity in *Iglesia y religiosidad popular en América Latina. Ponencias y documento final* (Bogotá: Secretaría General del CELAM, 1977), 385.

4. I explain the distinction and interaction between "theological locus" in a strict sense, hermeneutical locus, and the matrix of a concrete theology in my "Los ejercicios espirituales: lugar teológico," *Stromata* 47 (1991): 231–47.

5. See Melchor Cano, *Opera I* (Madrid, 1779; the first edition is from 1563). See also Albert Lang, "Loci theologici," in *Lexikon für Theologie und Kirche 6* (Freiburg: Herder, 1961), col. 1110–14, and *Die loci theologici des Melchior Cano und die Methode des dogmatischen Beweises* (Munich: Kösel and Pustet, 1925).

6. See G. Gutiérrez, *Teología de la Liberación. Perspectivas,* 2nd ed. (Salamanca: Sígueme, 1972), 35; on page 29 he quotes Chenu and Laurentin.

7. See H. J. Pottmeyer, "Normen, Kriterien und Strukturen der Überlieferung," in *Handbuch der Fundametaltheologie 4: Theologische Erkenntnislehre* (Freiburg: Herder, 1988), 139 and 144.

8. See Hans Urs von Balthasar, "Theologie und Heiligkeit," in *Verbum Caro. Skizzen zur Theologie,* vol. 1 (Einsiedeln: Johannes, 1960), 220.

9. See Peter Hünermann, "Konkretion und Geist. Der qualitative Sprung im Verständis von Weltkirche," *Theologische Quartalschrift* 165 (1985): 224–25.

10. Cf. M. Seckler, "Die ekklesiologische Bedeutung des Systems der loci theologici. Erkenntnistheoretische Katholizität und strukturale Weisheit," in *Weisheit Gottes, Weisheit der Welt: Festschrift für Joseph Kardinal Ratzinger zum 60. Geburtstag,* ed. W. Baier et al. (St. Ottilien: EOS, 1987), 37–65.

11. See Giuseppe Maria Zanghì, *Leggendo un Carisma. Chiara Lubich e la Cultura* (Rome: Città Nuova, 2013). Bernhard Welte speaks of a new religious experience in the light of nothingness (dark night); see his *Das Licht*

des Nichts. Von der Möglichkeit neuer religiöser Erfahrung (Düsseldorf: Patmos, 1980).

12. This distinction is made by K. Lehmann, "Methodisch-hermeneutische. Probleme der Theologies der Befreiung," in Internationale Theologenkomission, *Theologie der Befreiung* (Einsiedeln: Johannes, 1977), 18–21.

13. Jon Sobrino quotes Ellacuría in "Hacer teología en América Latina," *Theologica Xaveriana* 34 (1989): 155n13.

14. The decree *Ad Gentes* (henceforth, AG) of Vatican II states in no. 22, "It is necessary that in each major socio-cultural area, such theological speculation should be encouraged, in the light of the universal Church's tradition, as may submit to a new scrutiny the words and deeds which God has revealed, and which have been set down in Sacred Scripture and explained by the Fathers and by the magisterium. Thus it will be more clearly seen in what ways faith may seek for understanding, with due regard for the philosophy and wisdom of these peoples."

Chapter 3

1. See Gustavo Gutiérrez, "L'írruption du pauvre dans la théologie de l'Amérique Latine," *Convergence* 1–2 (1981): 22.

2. See Gustavo Gutiérrez, *Beber en su propio pozo. En el itinerario espiritual de un pueblo* (CEP: Lima, 1983), 84, 59ff.; see also *Teología de la Liberación. Perspectivas*, 2nd ed. (Sígueme: Salamanca, 1972), 265ff.

3. About socioanalytical mediation, see Clodovis Boff, *Teologia e práctica. Teologia do politico e suas mediacoes* (Petrópolis: Vozes, 1978).

4. See PD 397 (see also EG 125). About the relationship between the wisdom and the scientific moments, see the critiques I made of Clodovis Boff's work, quoted in the previous note, in my *Teología de la liberación y doctrina social de la Iglesia* (Madrid: Cristiandad, 1987), chaps. 1 and 2.

5. The expression was coined by the Chilean theologian and pastoralist Joaquín Alliende; see "Diez tesis sobre pastoral popular," in AA. VV. *Religiosidad popular* (Salamanca: Sígueme, 1976), 119.

6. In other countries of the continent, you must keep in mind the important *afroamericano* contribution. Because Río de la Plata (Argentina, Bolivia, Paraguay, and Uruguay) was a poor region without important plantations, slaves were few and almost exclusively domestics, and after the "freedom

of the womb" (emancipation of children born to slave women, in force in Argentina since 1813), they easily mixed with the rest of the population.

7. A devotion brought in from Augsburg, Germany, by the present pope when he was a Jesuit priest and that spread widely in a few years, particularly in Buenos Aires and the greater metropolitan area.

8. Juan Luis Segundo speaks about this in "Les deux théologies de la libération en Amérique Latine," *Études* 361 (1984): 154–55.

9. These topics will be discussed further in chap. 5.

10. On the evolution of the social sciences in Latin America, see A. Methol Ferré, "El resurgimiento católico latinoamericano," in *Religión y Cultura* (Bogotá: CELAM, 1981), 63–124, and Pedro Morandé, *Cultura y modernización en América Latina* (Santiago de Chile: PUC, 1984).

11. Cf. Aldo J. Büntig, *El Catolicismo Popular en la Argentina, I: Cuaderno Sociológico* (Buenos Aires: Bonum, 1969) and *¿Magia, religión o cristianismo?* (Buenos Aires: Bonum, 1970). With theoretical perspectives and different authors, the results of an interdisciplinary investigation were published about "Popular Catholicism in Argentina" in six volumes, sociological, biblical, psychological, anthropological, historical, and pastoral.

12. Cf. Centro de Investigaciones y Orientación Social, "Religiosidad popular: reflexión y acción," in *La Religiosidad Popular en Santiago del Estero* (Santiago del Estero: Ediciones Universidad Católica de Santiago del Estero, 1983), 29–36, and the journal, *Cuadernos de Iglesia y Sociedad* (Buenos Aires). See also Gerardo Farrell and Juan Pedro Lumerman, *Religiosidad popular y fe* (Buenos Aires: Patria Grande, 1979).

13. Floreal Forni commented on this position in the Federación de Centros de Sociología de la Religión in "Reflexiones sociológicas sobre el tema de la religiosidad popular," in *La Religiosidad popular en Santiago del Estero* (Santiago del Estero: Ediciones Universidad Católica de Santiago del Estero, 1983), 52–53.

14. See R. Santillán Güemes, "Antropología, cultura y religiosidad popular," in *Reflexiones sociológicas sobre el tema*, 65–91, and *Cultura, creación del pueblo* (Buenos Aires: Guadalupe, 1985). Cf. also Ciro R. Lafon and Enrique Dussel, *El Catolicismo popular en la Argentina, IV: Cuaderno Antropológico* (Buenos Aires: Bonum, 1970). The works of Rodolfo Kush united anthropological field research with philosophical reflection: see, e.g., *Esbozo de una Antropología Filosófica Americana* (Buenos Aires: Castañeda, 1978).

15. About the Argentinian Church at this time, see L. Gera and G. Rodriguez Melgarejo, "Apuntes para una interpretación de la Iglesia Argentina," *Víspera* 15 (1970): 59–88. Popular ministry had its official endorsement in the "Documento de San Miguel" of the Episcopal Conference of Argentina (1969), particularly in section 6.

16. About the praxis of popular ministry in Buenos Aires, cf. G. Rodriguez Melgarejo, "Servicio al Pueblo de Dios desde un santuario," in *Iglesia y religiosidad popular en América Latina. Ponencias y documento final* (Bogotá: Secretaría General del CELAM, 1977), 325–43, and "Radiografía de un trabajo pastoral: San Cayetano (Liniers)," in Equipo SELADOC, *Religiosidad popular* (Salamanca: Sígueme, 1976), 303–16.

17. About the time of Menem, see G. Farrell et al., *Argentina, tiempo de cambios. Sociedad, Estado, Doctrina Social de la Iglesia* (Buenos Aires: San Pablo, 1996).

18. Cf. Grupo Gerardo Farrell, *Crisis y reconstrucción. Aportes desde el pensamiento social de la Iglesia. I. Dimensión política-económica y II: Dimensión social y ético cultural* (Buenos Aires: San Pablo, 2003).

19. See G. Gutiérrez, *La fuerza histórica de los pobres*, 2nd ed. (Lima: CEP, 1980), 377. On the various trends of liberation theology, see my *Teología de la liberación y praxis popular* and *Teología de la liberación y doctrina social de la Iglesia* (2nd eds. of both—Buenos Aires: Docencia, 2011).

20. See F. Boasso, *¿Qué es la Pastoral Popular?* (Buenos Aires: Patria Grande, 1974). Among the works of Lucio Gera, see "Pueblo, religion del pueblo e Iglesia," in *Iglesia y religiosidad popular en América Latina. Ponencias y documento final* (Bogotá: Secretaría General del CELAM, 1977), 258–83; "Cultura y dependencia a la luz de la reflexión teológica," *Stromata* 30 (1974): 169–224; "La Iglesia frente a la situación de dependencia," in *Teología, Pastoral y Dependencia* (Buenos Aires: Guadalupe, 1974), 11–64; "Conciencia histórica nacional," *Nexo* 4 (1984): 12–27; "Religión y cultura," *Nexo* 9 (1986): 51–72; L. Gera et al., *Comentario a la "Evangelii Nuntiandi* (Buenos Aires: Patria Grande, 1978).

21. For an example of this latter issue, see the research of E. Chamorro Greca, *Estudio sociológico sobre la imagen de Dios en el hombre medio de Córdoba* (Córdoba: Pontificia Universidad Católica Argentina, 1970) and G. Farrell and J. Lumerman, *Religiosidad popular y fe* (Buenos Aires: Patria Grande, 1979).

22. Something similar is attempted in philosophy; see, e.g., *Sabiduría popular, símbolo y filosofía. Diálogo internacional en torno de una propuesta latinoamericana*, comp. J. C. Scannone (Buenos Aires: Guadalupe, 1984), which gathers works presented by a group of Argentinian philosophers in Paris to European colleagues—among them, Lévinas—and the ensuing discussions. See also my *Nuevo punto de partida de la filosofía latinoamericana* (Buenos Aires: Guadalupe, 1990; 2nd ed., Buenos Aires: Docencia, 2011).

23. I apply a mature Thomistic understanding expressed in the *Summa Theologica*, first part, question 1, about the function of philosophy respective to a speculative theology, to the mediation of the human sciences in theology. See M. Corbin, *Le chemin de la théologie chez Thomas d'Aquin* (Paris: Beauchesne, 1974), particularly chap. 4.

24. See, e.g., P. Ribeiro De Oliveira, "¿Qué significa analíticamente 'pueblo'?" *Concilium* 196 (1984): 427–39, and L. Boff "Significado teológico de pueblo de Dios e iglesia popular," *Concilium* 196 (1984): 441–54. See also Equipo de Teólogos de la Clar, "Qué es el pueblo," *Pastoral popular* 30 (1979): 72–78.

25. See E. Laclau, *La razón populista* (Buenos Aires: Fondo de Cultura Económica, 2005).

26. See Leonardo Boff, *Iglesia, carisma y poder: ensayos de eclesiología militante* (Santander: Sal Terrae, 1982).

27. For an updated understanding of the analogy, see L. B. Puntel, *Analogie und Geschichtlichkeit. Philosophiegeschichtlichkritischer Versch über das Grundproblem der Metaphysik* (Freiburg: Herder, 1969); J. C. Scannone, *Religión y nuevo pensamiento* (Barcelona: Anthropos, 2005), chap. 7.

28. Another case of this interaction (in the understanding of liberation) is treated in my *Teología de la liberación y praxis popular* (Salamanca: Sígueme, 1976), chap. 2; likewise, I analyze *theoretically* the articulation between social analysis and theology in chap. 2 of my *Teología de la liberación y doctrina social de la Iglesia* (Madrid: Cristiandad, 1987).

Chapter 4

1. Such denomination does not assume that the relationship between wisdom (*sophía*) and philosophy (and between Christian wisdom and theology) is reduced to a "before" and an "after" as if the first one were only valid

insofar as it can ultimately be articulated reflectively and conceptually in the second.

2. See Karl Rahner, "Einleitende Überlegungen zum Verhältnis von Theologie und Volksreligion," in Karl Rahner et al., *Volksreligion—Religion des Volkes* (Stuttgart: Kohlhammer, 1979), 14.

3. I am speaking of a universal situated, different from the Hegelian abstract and concrete, in my *Nuevo punto de partida en la filosofía latinoamericana* (Buenos Aires: Guadalupe, 1990; 2nd ed., Buenos Aires: Docencia, 2011), and *Religión y nuevo pensamiento* (Barcelona: Anthropos; Mexico DF: UAM [Iztapalapa], 2005). I owe the concept to Mario Casalla; for my part, I interpret it as universal *analogical*.

4. Regarding the real symbol, see Karl Rahner, "Zur Theologie des Symbols," in *Schriften zur Theologie IV* (Einsiedeln: Benziger, 1960), 275–312.

5. I allude to Ricœur when I speak of a philosophy starting from the symbol (since the symbol is food for thought), to the distinction between hermeneutics of suspicion and recollection of the meaning and to the "metaphoric truth."

6. See my considerations about the value of the "anadialectic" method for a universally situated thought in my "Nuevo pensamiento, analogia y anadialéctica," *Stromata* 68 (2012): 33–52.

7. See J. L. Segundo, *Liberación de la teología* (Buenos Aires: Lohlé, 1975), 260. The relationship between wisdom and science (philosophical or theological) could be illuminated by the relationship of the world of life and sciences, according to the Husserl of *Krisis*.

8. I allude here to the distinction made by Bernard Lonergan among the intentional operations *insight* and *judgment* and among the respective functional specializations in his work *Method in Theology* (New York: Herder and Herder, 1972), and the use I will make of it later, in chap. 7.

9. See my considerations, particularly the philosophical ones, in my "El sujeto comunitario de la espiritualidad y mística populares," *Stromata* 70 (2014): 183–96. On this topic in William of Ockham and the *communitas collectiva* as subject according to Francis de Marchia, see D. Ansorge, "Eine 'arme Kirche'? Überlegungen zu einer kenotischen Ekklesiologie," in *Eine arme Kirche für die Armen. Theologische Bedeuntung und praktische Konsequenzen*, ed. J. Gallegos Sánchez and Markus Luber (Regensburg: Pustet, 2016), 57–94, particularly 75ff.

10. In Christology, this is the term for the community of proprieties between both natures of Christ; of course, I am using an analogy. The question of inculturated theology is connected to that of popular theology, about which I will speak in chap. 6.

11. *Revista Eclesiástica Brasileira* 158 (June 1980): 216–42.

12. See Joaquín Alliende, "Reflexiones sobre la religiosidad popular en América Latina," *Criterio* 1763 (1977): 228–33. I refer to the document "Iglesia and religiosidad popular en América Latina" in the book by the same name (Bogotá: CELAM, 1977), 283–317.

13. In meetings among European and Latin American thinkers, some of the former coincided in fact in the appreciations I make in this text, referred, in those cases, to the respective philosophies. See those of Jean Ladrière, made in a meeting of the School of Philosophy of Louvain-la-Neuve, and those of Peter Ulrich, in one from the Goethe Institute in Paris, respectively; Ladrière's foreword to my *Discernimiento crítico de la acción y pasión históricas* (Barcelona: Anthropos, 2009); and the interventions of Peter Ulrich in the dialogues as reproduced in J. C. Scannone, ed., *Sabiduría popular, símbolo y filosofía* (Buenos Aires: Guadalupe, 1984).

14. See what Julio R. Méndez says about Latin American "estimative logic" (*lógica cordial*) in his "Matrices culturales europeas en Latinoamérica," in *In ascolto dell'America. Popoli, culture, religione, strade per il future. Atti del Convegno Internazionale, 7–9 aprile 2014*, ed. A. Trevisiol (Rome: Pontificia Università Urbaniana, 2014), 69–91.

15. These reflections can be complemented with my article "The Symbolic Witnessing of the Tinkunaco Rite," in *Witnessing, Prophecy, Politics, and Wisdom*, ed. Maria Clara Lucchetti Bingemer and P. Casarella (Maryknoll, NY: Orbis Books, 2014), 122–29.

16. About this popular feast, cf. J. C. Vera Vallejo, *Las fiestas de San Nicolás en La Rioja*, 4th ed. (La Rioja: Talleres de la Imprenta del estado, 1970); J. Cáceres Freyre, *El encuentro o Tincunaco* (Buenos Aires: Instituto Nacional de Antropología, 1967); Bruno C. Jacovella, *Fiestas tradicionales argentinas* (Buenos Aires: Lajouane, 1953); J. A. Ortiz, *El Tinkunaco. La gran fiesta de La Rioja* (La Rioja [s-e] 2006). The Riojan writer Joaquín Víctor González describes it in his work *Mis montañas* (see the edition, with prologue and notes by Arturo Marasso [Buenos Aires: Ediciones Estrada, 1958]).

17. In the next chapter, see what Gaston Fessard and Alberto Methol Ferré explain about both dialectics, inspired by St. Paul.

18. See the historical data and legendary aspects in Luis Julián Plandolit Plandolit, *El apóstol de América. San Francisco Solano* (Madrid: Cisneros, 1963; with bibliography and sources); Nicolás Rivera, *La Rioja. Sus orígenes y tradición* (Buenos Aires: Imprenta López, 1959); Mariel Caldas, "El tinkunaco riojano: experiencia de religiosidad popular interpretada desde las categorías de fiesta y diálogo" (master's thesis in pastoral theology, UCA, School of Theology, 2011), https://repositorio.uca.edu.ar/handle/123456789/550. The indigenous rebellion (*diaguita*) and their conversion by St. Francis Solano are historical facts and took place on Easter in 1593.

19. See Paul Ricœur, *La métaphore vive* (Paris: Seuil, 1975), particularly the seventh and eighth essays, and chap. 13 of my *Nuevo punto de partida en la filosofía latinoamericana*.

20. See L. Liberti, *Mons E. Angelelli. Pastor que evangeliza promoviendo integralmente al hombre* (Buenos Aires: Guadalupe, 2006).

Chapter 5

1. The revisionist history current in the 1930s did a critical "revision" of the Argentinian history written according to the "liberal" trend of the nineteenth century (Bartolomé Mitre, Vicente Fidel López). So-called post-revisionism, an heir to the former, avoids its rather Manichean attitude, rescuing in more scientific terms what is valid in both.

2. This historical recognition connects with what Lucio Gera found in the villages and among the people of God through a synthetic and global wisdom, in his article "La Iglesia frente a la situación de dependencia," in L. Gera, A. Büntig, and O. Catena, *Teología, pastoral y dependencia* (Buenos Aires: Guadalupe, 1974), 9–64, esp. 19–20. Likewise, Joseph Comblin affirms that beyond scientific rationality there is a way of understanding the global reality that is within the reach of simple people of goodwill. Cf. J. Comblin, "Libertad y liberación. Conceptos teológicos," *Concilium* 46 (June 1974): 395.

3. About this double relationship (causal and hermeneutical) among events, see C. Mesters, *Por tràs das palabras* (Petrópolis: Vozes, 1974). The Blondelian interrelationship between the series of causes and the order of goals can be applied to them, according to *L'Action* (1893).

4. Cf. G. Fessard, "Esquisse du mystère de la société et de l'histoire," *Recherches de Science Religieuse* 35 (1948): 5–54 and 161–225, in particular from page 186; Fessard, *De l'actualité historique*, vol. 1 (Paris, 1960); A. Methol

Ferré, "Análisis de las raíces de la evangelización lationamericana," *Stromata* 33 (1977): 93–112.

5. The second one corresponds to one of the priorities of Pope Francis (see EG 226–30); see chap. 11.

6. See Darcy Ribeiro, "Los pueblos trasplantados III—Los rioplatenses," in *Las Américas y la civilización* 3 (Buenos Aires, 1969). I share Julio de Zan's criticisms of Ribeiro in his article "Para una filosofía de la cultura y una filosofía política nacional," in *Cultura popular y Filosofía de la liberación* (Buenos Aires: F. G. Cambeiro, 1975), 95ff. I call "creole" foundational, but not in opposition to other terminology such as mestizo, because it implies cultural miscegenation, which can have racial overtones.

7. Salta is in the Argentinian Northwest, where there is mestizaje with the Quechuas and Aymaras, as in a large part of Bolivia; Corrientes is in the northeast, with a Guarani mestizaje, like Paraguay; along the coast and in other regions (the center, Cuyo, in the border with Chile, or Patagonia in the South), European immigration prevailed, but it was not the only one (e.g., also Arab and Japanese).

8. "Cabecitas negras" was the pejorative name that those with Indian traits were given in the 1940s. In the Argentina of the first half of the twentieth century, gringos were Italians or English people (because they were blond) and the Spaniards were Galician.

9. Cf. Vincent Sierra, *Historia de la Argentina* (Buenos Aires: Unión de Editores Latinos, 1956), 14ff.; J. M. Rosa, *Historia Argentina I* (Buenos Aires, 1974), 109ff.

10. On this topic, see the pointed reflections of Miguel Ángel Fiorito and José Luis Lazzarini, "Originalidad de nuestra organización popular," in *Boletín de Espiritualidad* 57 (February 1975).

11. For José María Rosa, both the eastern upheaval (with Artigas) and the "crying out of the orilleros" (the poor residents of the outskirts of Buenos Aires) demonstrate the rising of the ideals of the May Revolution by the simple people, see his *Historia Argentina II* (Buenos Aires, 1974), 271 and 286 (*porteños* are the residents of the port, in this case Buenos Aires). In my opinion, Artigas does not have the ambiguities that plague other historical figures.

12. See the inaugural address of Congress of April 1813, in which Artigas affirmed before the assembly, "My authority flows from you and ceases before your sovereign presence"; "the sacred vow of your general will placed me as your leader." Cf. the collection of documents published by Óscar Bruschera

under the title *Artigas* (Montevideo: Biblioteca de Marcha, 1971), 93. In a circular letter to the people consulting them about the congress of Capilla Maciel (December 1813), he says, "There is nothing more sacred for me than the authority of the people....I will remove myself immediately if it is truly your will to not recognize me" (Bruschera, *Artigas,* 120). About will, authority, trust, the heart of the people, he speaks in various documents: see Bruschera, *Artigas,* 162, 167, 175. I consider this as a Hispanic-American interpretation of Rousseau's concept of "general will."

13. He affirms it in the "Introducción" (page 16) of the work quoted above.

14. See Bruschera, *Artigas,* 12. Such characteristics distinguish Artigas's proposals from the populist ones.

15. See her *Historia del peronismo* (Buenos Aires, 1973), 54.

16. I refer to his work, *¿Qué es la pastoral popular?* (Buenos Aires: Patria Grande, 1974).

17. According to the interpretation of Leopoldo Marechal in "Martín Fierro o el arte de ser argentinos y americanos," in Elbia Rosbaco de Marechal, *Mi vida con Leopoldo Marechal* (Buenos Aires: Paidós, 1973), 113–26.

18. See J. Hernández, "Cuatro palabras de conversación con los lectores," in C. A. Leumann's critical edition of *Martín Fierro* (Buenos Aires: Losada, 1958), 272. There is a classic anecdote of the shopkeeper who sent the following order to his wholesaler: "Twelve boxes of matches, a barrel of beer, twelve *Vueltas de Martín Fierro,* a hundred cans of sardines." "These are among the basic daily necessities," Miguel de Unamuno comments after quoting the story. Cf. "El gaucho Martín Fierro, poema popular gauchesco de D. José Hernández (argentino)," in J. Isaacson, *Martín Fierro. Centenario—Testimonios* (Buenos Aires: Ministerio de Cultura y Educación, 1972), 55.

19. According to Carlos Astrada's expression in his book *El mito gaucho* (Buenos Aires: Secretaría de Cultura de la Nación, 1964).

20. See ICN, 4, 23. This does not imply a "monolithic and close cultural unity" excluding a "pluralistic and understanding spirit" (ICN, 20). Nor does it mean that all Argentinians are Christian or that in order to be fully Argentinian one must be Christian, but simply to share the national human and cultural values that in fact have been decisively influenced by Christianity (and, through it, from the "Abrahamic" religions). I consider that the conception of the faith-culture relationship through the mediation of the life theme that works as the ethical heart of each culture frees us from the juxtaposition

of faith and culture, without allowing us to fall into the fundamentalism and clericalism of what Alfonso Álvarez Bolado calls "nacionalcatolicismo"; see his "Teología política de España," in *Dios y la Ciudad. Nuevos planteamientos en teología política* (Madrid: Cristiandad, 1975), 146–200.

21. His work *Der Gegensatz* was translated into Italian as *L'opposizione polare* (Rome: La Civiltà Cattolica-Corriere della Sera, 2014). See also both Enrique Dussel's and my attempts to elaborate an "anadialectic"; cf. my article "Nuevo pensamiento, analogía y anadialéctica," *Stromata* 68 (2012): 33–56.

22. I am referring to the classical plays by Calderón de la Barca and Lope de Vega.

23. This would explain why the universal ideal of justice is more alive in the Third World, in each people, in the poor and oppressed; see F. Boasso, *¿Qué es la pastoral popular?* (Buenos Aires: Patria Grande, 1974), 46.

24. See *Declaración del Episcopado Argentino* (about the adaptation of Medellín to our country, popularly known as Documento de San Miguel), VI (Buenos Aires: Pastoral Popular, 1969), 37. Values such as justice are found in different cultures. That is why I don't take it up here in abstract, but specify both historically from our Christian roots and by the determination given by the predominant place it occupies, articulated with other values that shape our cultural ethos (e.g., the specific relationship that justice has in this world of values with national unity, with a sense of God incarnated, with loyalty to the just politician, etc.).

25. This was the name given to mestizos of Black and indigenous origin.

26. See Article 6 of the "Reglamento Provisorio de la Provincia Oriental para el fomento de la campaña y seguridad de sus hacendados," dated September 10, 1815. The expression "peoples clothed in dignity" appears, e.g., in the letter of December 27, 1819, to the Congress of Tucumán; cf. O. Bruschera, *Artigas* (Montevideo: Biblioteca de Marcha, 1971), 180, also 85.

27. See his letter to the governor of Corrientes, May 3, 1815, in Bruschera, *Artigas*, 159.

28. The "Fuero de los gauchos" is dated Salta, September 12, 1820. See V. Badano, *Apuntes de Historia Argentina* (Instituto Nacional del Profesorado Secundario de Paraná, 1947).

29. As Leopoldo Marechal says in the work mentioned in note 17 of this chapter.

30. Cf. chap. 5 of my *Teología de la liberación y doctrina social de la Iglesia* (Madrid: Cristianidad, 1987; 2nd ed., Buenos Aires: Docencia, 2011), titled

"Poesía popular y teología; contribución del 'Martín Fierro' a una teología de la liberación."

31. The two parts of the poem are usually referred to as "Going" and "Returning," since together they depict a journey into the desert and a return from it.

32. In speaking of the encounter between faith and culture in Latin America, F. Boasso says, "The Church welcomes the Indian, whose culture has been destroyed in upper levels, in its structures; by baptism, it gives him a new name (a new being or a recovery of being) and enters and supports him in the new emerging culture: mestizaje" (cf. op. cit. 19). The sense of dignity and human, Christian fraternity acquired in baptism is testified to in the letters from the Indian towns of the Jesuit reductions to the king of Spain, who had resolved to withdraw the Jesuits and to give these peoples to the Portuguese. The town of San Luis writes to him: "because it is not good for us, all Christians and belonging to God, to fight one another. We have not done evil to the holy king; therefore, we don't need a war, but, if they come to seek and find us, we will avenge our poor life." That is: because they are brothers and sisters of the Spaniards, they do not want a war against them, but because they have as much dignity as they, if they want to surrender them to the Portuguese, they will defend themselves. See quotes of these letters in O. Yorio, "Reflexión crítica desde la teología," *Stromata* 29 (1973): 171ff., 165 (where the sources are indicated).

33. See E. Hoornaert, "A evangelização segundo a Tradição Guadalupana," *Revista Eclesiástica Brasileira* 34 (1974): 524–45. About the Virgin of the Valley and the Indians of Choya, see P. A. Larrouy, *Documentos relativos a Nuestra Señora del Valle y a Catamarca*, vol. 1 (Buenos Aires: Compañía Sud-Americana de Billetes de Banco, 1915), for instance 221, 232–33, 285, 306 (witnesses to 1764); see also P. Soprano, *La Virgen del Valle y la Conquista del antiguo Tucumán* (Buenos Aires: Impr. del "Courrier de La Plata," 1889), 220ff. About the Virgin of Luján and the Black slave Manuel, cf. J. Salvaire, *Historia de Nuestra Señora de Luján*, vol. 2 (Buenos Aires: Coni, 1885), appendix A, pp. 4 and 6; and J. A. Presas, *Nuestra Señora de Luján y Sumampa* (Buenos Aires: Ediciones Autores Asociados Morón, 1974), 126ff. and 183ff. See mention in the previous chapter of the Tinkunaco.

34. See J. D. Perón, *La Comunidad Organizada. Esbozo filosófico* (Buenos Aires: Pleamar, 1949). The graphic concept of "insectification"—a derogatory reference to individualism—serves in this work to designate a totalizing collectivity. The formulation "organized community" agrees with

various expressions in pontifical documents and is probably inspired by them: see, e.g., the address of Pius XII to the Roman nobility on January 19, 1944, in A. F. Utz et al., *Relations humaines et société contemporaine,* vol. 1 (Fribourg: St-Paul, 1956), 596.

35. About his global conception of history, he speaks, for instance in *La hora de los pueblos,* dated Madrid 1968 and in *Actualización política* of 1971. In general, about Latin American unity, see J. C. Scannone and D. García Delgado (compilers), *Ética, Desarrollo y Región. Hacia un regionalismo integral* (Buenos Aires: CICCUS, 2006).

36. About this cultural counterposition, see J. Seibold, "Civilización y barbarie en la historia de la ciencia argentina. Aportes hermeneúticos para una nueva comprensión de la historia de la ciencia argentina," *Stromata* 31 (1975): 261–97; the author—as well as myself in the text—allude to the classic book by Domingo F. Sarmiento *Facundo. Civilización y barbarie,* see *Obras,* vol. 7 (Buenos Aires, 1896).

37. According to Pedro Trigo, the same thing is happening today in the synthesis between the Latin American suburban popular culture and scientific-technological culture: see P. Trigo, *Relaciones humanizadoras. Un imaginario alternativo* (Santiago, Chile: Universidad Alberto Hurtado, 2013). Something similar is currently (2016) taking place in the neighborhoods of greater Buenos Aires.

38. This sense of the "already" but "not yet" corresponds to the biblical dialectic of hope and is concretized in the symbolic celebration of the "not yet" in the "already celebrated" in the feast, which measures time. The sense of "feast" is characteristic of our peoples' concept of time.

39. About the crisis of 2001 and the reaction to it, see Grupo Gerardo Farrell, *Crisis y reconstrucción. Aportes desde el pensamiento social de la Iglesia, I: Dimensión político-económica, II: Dimensión social y ético-cultural* (Buenos Aires: San Pablo, 2003).

40. This letter is dated December 20, 1834. It is characteristic of the federal national strategy designed by Rosas in this document, not only the sense of *time,* but also the prevalence of the *whole* over the *parts,* with due respect to these, see J. Irazusta, *Vida política de J. M. de Rosas a través de su correspondencia II.* According to Ernesto López Rosas, SJ, this letter was Bergoglio's inspiration when he states his four principles (EG 217–37); see chap. 11.

41. See G. Furlong, "La religiosidad de Martín Fierro," *Actualidad Pastoral* 68 (February 1974): 6–10.

42. See the interesting reflection of J. A. Carrizo about these "divine" glosses in *Cancionero Popular de La Rioja,* vol. 1 (Buenos Aires: Espasa-Calpe Argentina, 1942), 231–35. In volume 2 of the same work (pages 70ff.), you can find a gloss of the Our Father "in a human fashion." It was a Spanish and Hispanic American custom to write glosses on love poems and attribute them to God, as is done in the Song of Songs.

43. See his article "Reflexiones actuales sobre una advocación chilena," *Teología y Vida* 15 (1974): 245–57. What Alliende says there about Our Lady of Mount Carmel for Chile is applicable also to our own case, while keeping in mind that she is the patroness of the Army of the Andes, which liberated Chile and Peru and strengthened Argentinian independence. Also, for Eduardo Pironio, veneration of Mary represents for Latin Americans the paschal moment of the mystery of Christ: see E. Pironio, "Reflexiones sobre el hombre nuevo en América Latina," in *Teología y mundo contemporáneo,* ed. A. Vargas-Machuca (Madrid: Cristiandad, 1975), 323.

44. See the letter of Artigas to the Indian Andresito, dated March 13, 1815, in O. Bruschera, *Artigas* (Montevideo, 1971), 131; in the same letter, he refers to God with the biblical name "God of hosts" on page 130. In it, Artigas precedes the present rereadings of Exodus from a perspective of liberation. See a similar biblical interpretation by a Mexican leader, the Cura Morelos in A. Churruca, "El pensamiento de Morelos. Una ideología liberadora," *Christus* (Mexico) 477 (August 1975): 18ff.

45. Let us recall the reconciliation of Perón with his democratic adversaries upon his return from Spain (1973), symbolized in his embrace of the radical leader Ricardo Balbín.

46. See the homily at the cathedral of Santa Fe in *El Litoral,* July 7, 1974. Note that this moment gathered former political adversaries (and even enemies) beyond partisanship and ideologies. Another powerful moment of unity beyond political and social divisions was experienced in the reaction of the people and the leaders in the face of the military events of Holy Week 1987: there also national unity prevailed in defense of democracy over the sectarian interests and struggle. The editorial column of *Criterio* (no. 1974 [April 23, 1987]: 153) affirms these events: "The secret Argentina, so many times alluded to, has again expressed itself to the surprise of many, and perhaps of itself, as a basically healthy society or one which, conscious of its public ailments, does not want to go backwards."

47. About the profound sense of the bicentennial, cf. Cardinal J. M. Bergoglio, *Hacia un bicentenario en justicia y solidaridad, 2010–2016. Nosotros como ciudadanos, nosotros como pueblo* (Buenos Aires: Claretiana, 2010); J. C. Scannone et al., *¿Hacia dónde? Debates, consensos y estrategias para la Argentina Bicentenaria* (Buenos Aires: La Crujía, 2010).

48. Due to disagreements about the location for the ceremony, the outgoing president did not hand the insignia to her successor, who belonged to a different political party.

49. For this formulation I am inspired by Jean Ladrière, adding the term *passion*; see his work about my approach in "Filosofía de la acción histórica," *Stromata* 55 (1999): 319–24, and my work *Discernimiento filosófico de la acción y pasión históricas. Planteo para el mundo global desde América Latina* (Barcelona: Anthropos, 2009).

50. Op cit. 38. With the Argentinian episcopate, I distinguish the "Argentinian people" (or that of any specific nation) from the "people of God in Argentina" (that nation) although, in fact, they might coincide to a great extent. Note that the document cited here shows the influence of Lucio Gera and the theologians of the COEPAL.

51. *Lumen Gentium* 12 refers to the *sensus fidei* ("sense of the faith") of the entire people of God.

52. I allude to Lonergan's theory of method, as I applied it to this issue in the previous chapter and will again in chap. 7. In order to illustrate a different structuring or configuration of experience, expression, and theological reflection of faith itself, we can apply what has been said by Joseph de Guibert about the different structuring of the same elements of various spiritualities taking place in the Church; cf. *La espiritualidad de la Compañía de Jesús* (Santander: Sal Terrae, 1955).

53. The allusion to Hegel must not be interpreted in the Hegelian sense; rather, it places the concept at the service of wisdom without exhausting it. See the relationship between wisdom and science, symbol and concept that I discuss in "Sabiduría popular y pensamiento especulativo," in my *Sabiduría popular, símbolo y filosofía* (Buenos Aires: Guadalupe, 1984), 52–74.

54. *Mutatis mutandis,* I affirm the socioanalytical mediation in chaps. 1 and 2 of *Teología de la Liberación y doctrina social de la Iglesia* (Madrid: Cristiandad, 1987; 2nd ed., Buenos Aires: Docencia, 2011), applying to them what St. Thomas says about the philosophical mediation in *Summa Theologica,* I. q 1.

55. Regarding the mediation of social sciences, Ignacio Ellacuría says, "It does not imply denial of the philosophical contribution, but its qualification." Cf. I. Ellacuría "Tesis sobre la posibilidad, necesidad y sentido de una teología latinoamericana," in *Teología y mundo contemporáneo,* ed. A. Vargas-Machuaca (Madrid: Cristiandad, 1975), 338.

56. I extend to all the mediations of which I have spoken what the instruction *Libertatis Nuntius* says about extra-theological contributions to theology: "A critical examination of the analytical methods borrowed from other disciplines must be carried out in a distinct way by theologians. It is the light of faith which provides theology with its principles. That is why the use of philosophical positions or of human sciences by the theologian has a value which might be called instrumental, yet must undergo a critical study from a theological perspective. In other words, the ultimate and decisive criterion for truth can only be a criterion which is itself theological. It is only in the light of faith, and what faith teaches us about the truth of man and the ultimate meaning of his destiny, that one can judge the validity or degree of validity of what other disciplines propose, often rather conjecturally, as being the truth about man, his history and destiny " (LN 7.10).

57. The first edition was published by Guadalupe, Buenos Aires, in 1990; the second, by Docencia, Buenos Aires, in 2011, with a foreword by Dina Picotti.

Chapter 6

1. See K. Rahner, "Einleitende Überlegungen zum Verhältnis von Theologie und Volksreligion," in *Volksreligion-Religion des Volkes,* ed. Karl Rahner et al. (Stuttgart: Kohlhammer, 1979), 12. See also my book *Weisheit und Befreiung. Volkstheologie in Latinamerika* (Düsseldorf: Patmos, 1992).

2. See Gustavo Gutiérrez, *Teología de la Liberación: Perspectivas* (Salamanca: Sígueme, 1972), 38.

3. See, among others, Adolf Exeler and Norbert Mette, et al., *Theologie des Volkes* (Mainz: Grünewald, 1978); *Lumière et Vie* 140 (1978), issue devoted to the "théologies populaires"; and the debate between A. Fierro and J. J. Tamayo in *Iglesia viva* 89–90 (1980): 533–38, and 93 (1981): 85–91.

4. See *Summa Theologica,* first part, question 1, article 2, c and ad 2; article 4 ad 1. About the *manuductio,* article 5 ad 2, see Michel Corbin, *Le chemin*

de la théologie chez Thomas d'Aquin (Paris: Beauchesne, 1974), chap. 4. On the *revelabile,* see also Étienne Gilson, *Le thomisme* (Paris: Vrien, 1948), 8–41.

5. On religious language, see chap. 6 of my *Religión y nuevo pensamiento* (Barcelona: Anthropos; Iztapalapa, Mexico: UAM, 2005) (inspired for the most part by Ricœur); about theological language, see *Religión y nuevo pensamiento,* chap. 7.

6. Lonergan distinguishes the following differentiations of consciousness: that of *common sense,* the scientific (or theoretical), the *religious* (which in this text we call "life in the Spirit"), that of the *scholar* (typical of historical-interpretative sciences), and that of *modern philosophy* (the transcendental subject). See Bernard Lonergan, "Unità e pluralità. La coerenza della verità Cristiana," in *Problemi e prospettive di Teologia Dogmática,* ed. K. Neufeld (Brescia: Queriniana, 1983), 122–25.

7. Cf. J. Sobrino, "La 'autoridad doctrinal' del pueblo de Dios en América Latina," *Concilium* 200 (1985): 78; G. Gutiérrez, "Quehacer teológico y experiencia eclesial," *Concilium* 196 (1984): 403. On the collective subject in EG, see chap. 10.

8. See G. Gutiérrez, "L'irruption du pauvre dans la théologie de l'Amerique Latine," *Convergence* 1–2 (1981): 24.

9. See, respectively, C. Boff, *Teologia e Prática. Teologia do Politico e suas mediações* (Petropolis: Vozes, 1978), and J. B. Libânio, "Théologies populares: légitimité et existence," *Lumière et Vie* 140 (1978): 85–100. Casiano Floristán agrees with Libânio, "Povo de Deus et Teologia Cristã," *Revista Eclesiástica Brasileira* 45 (1985): 296–309.

10. See G. Gutiérrez, "L'irruption du pauvre dans la théologie de l'Amerique Latine," *Convergence* 1–2 (1982): 403.

11. See C. Boff, "Agente de Pastoral e Povo," *Revista Eclesiástica Brasileira* 40 (1980): 216–42. On the models for thinking of the relationship between both modes of knowledge, I allude in the text to C. Cullen, "Sabiduría popular y fenomenología," in *Sabiduría popular, símbolo y filosofía,* ed. J. C. Scannone (Buenos Aires: Guadalupe, 1984), 30–31. In that volume, see also my "Sabiduría popular y pensamiento especulativo," 51–74.

12. On the relationship between the people and the New Testament, see H. Frankemölle, "Zur 'Theologie des Volkes' im Neuen Testament. Eine Problemskizze," in *Theologie des Volkes,* ed. Adolf Exeler and Norbert Mette, et al. (Mainz: Grünewald, 1978), 86–119.

13. See K. Rahner, "Einletende Überlegungen zum Verhältnis von Theologie und Volksreligion" in *Volksreligion: Religion des Volkes,* ed. K. Rahner et al. (Stuttgart: Kohlhammer, 1979), 14.

14. See J. B. Metz, "Breve apología de la narración," *Concilium* 85 (1973): 222–36.

15. See J. Sobrino, "La 'autoridad doctrinal' del pueblo de Dios en América Latina," *Concilium* 200 (1985).

16. On the relationship between the symbolic and speculative and practical, see chap. 15 of my, *Nuevo punto de partida en la filosofía latinoamericana.*

17. See what Juan Luis Segundo says about this in his *Liberación de la teología* (Buenos Aires: Lohlé, 1975), 260.

PART III

1. I will indicate it in the course of the chapter of this last part; see also my article, "El papa Francisco: ¿teólogo del pueblo?" *Criterio* 2414 (May 2015): 44–47.

Chapter 7

1. I am referring to the title of the important book by E. Dussel, *Ética de liberación en la época de la globalización y la exclusión* (Madrid: Trotta, 1998).

2. About this topic, see J. Gallegos Sánchez and M. Luber, eds., *Eine arme Kirche für die Armen. Theologische Bedeutung und praktische Konsequenzen* (Regensburg: Pustet, 2015); there, see my article "'Aus der Peripherie heraus kann man die Wirklichkeit besser erfassen.' Die Armen und die Gesellschaft in *Evangelii Gaudium*," 43–56.

3. See C. J. Pinto de Oliveira, "*Gaudium et Spes*: ¿nuevo paradigma de ética fundamental y social?" in *La constitución* Gaudium et Spes. *A 30 años de su promulgación* ed. J. C. Maccarone et al. (Buenos Aires: San Pablo, 1995), 51–108, esp. 57ff.

4. Cf. W. Marx, *Heidegger und die Tradition* (Stuttgart: Kohlhammer, 1961); M. M. Olivetti, "El problema de la comunidad ética," in *Sabiduría popular, símbolo y filosofía,* ed. J. C. Scannone (Buenos Aires: Guadalupe, 1984), 209–22.

5. See Pinto de Oliveira, "*Gaudium et Spes*," 71ff.

6. See note 3 of this chapter, my "La recepción del método de *Gaudium et Spes* en América Latina," 19–49.

7. See B. Lonergan, *Method in Theology* (New York: Herder and Herder, 1972).

8. See the application of the theory of Lonergan's method to the question of method in the theology of liberation in my book *Teología de la liberación y doctrina social de la Iglesia* (Madrid: Cristiandad, 1987; 2nd ed., Buenos Aires: Docencia, 2011, with a foreword by Marcelo Trejo), chaps. 1 and 2.

9. See B. Lonergan, "Natural Right and Historical Mindness," in *A Third Collection: Papers by Bernard J. F. Lonergan, S.J.*, ed. F. Crowe (New York: Paulist Press, 1985), 169–83, esp. 175ff.; see also my "Afectividad y método. La conversión afectiva en la teoría del método de B. Lonergan," *Stromata* 65 (2009): 173–86.

10. Among other places, see the interview with Antonio Spadaro in 2013, *Busquemos ser una Iglesia que encuentra caminos nuevos* (Bilbao: Mensajero, 2013).

11. I allude here to Mauricio Beuchot's *Tratado de hermenéutica analógica: hacia un nuevo modelo de interpretación*, 5th ed. (Mexico: UNAM, 2009); I present an updated understanding of this analogy in my *Religión y nuevo pensamiento* (Barcelona: Rubí, 2005), chap. 7.

12. About this history, see P. Trigo, "Una Iglesia pobre para los pobres. ¿A dónde nos lleva el sueño del papa Francisco?" *Revista Lationamericana de Teología* 30 (2013): 247–62.

13. See P. Corbelli, "La Iglesia de los pobres en el Concilio Vaticano II," *Umbrales* 2010–2011, http://umbrales.edu.uy/articulos/pobres.php.

14. See Benedict XVI, "Inaugural Address" of the Fifth General Conference of the Bishops of Latin American and Caribbean, Aparecida (Brazil), May 13 to 31, 2007, *Documento conclusivo: discípulos y misioneros de Jesucristo, para que nuestros pueblos en Él tengan vida* (Buenos Aires: Conferencia Episcopal Argentina, 2007), 281–99, esp. 287. See http://w2.vatican.va/content/benedict-xvi/en/speeches/2007/may/documents/hf_ben-xvi_spe_20070513_conference-aparecida.html for the entire document in English.

15. See V. Codina, "Los '¡No' del papa Francisco," *Religión Digital*, http://amerindiaenlared.org/noticia/413/los-no-del-papa-francisco/.

16. Michael Novak himself recognizes it in his article "A proposito di etica e capitalism. *Evangelii Gaudium* secondo me," *I Martedi* 329 (September–

October 2014): 30–35. See also D. Alonso de las Heras, "Evangelizzazione ed economia: denuncia e proposta," in Evangelii gaudium: *il testo ci interroga. Chiavi di lettura, testimonianze e prospettive,* ed. H. M. Yañez (Rome: Gregorian and Biblical Press: 2014); R. González Fabre, "Significado económico en *Evangelii gaudium,*" in *Francisco: la alegría que brota del pueblo. Una reflexión compartida de* Evangelii Gaudium, ed. J. Benedetti (Buenos Aires: Santa María, 2016), 287–332.

17. See P. Ricœur, "Civilisation universelle et cultures nationales," in *Histoire et Vérité* (Seuil: Paris, 1966).

18. See R. Guardini, "Das Ende der Neuzeit. Ein Versuch zur Orientierung," in *Da Ende der Neuzeit. Die Macht* (Ostilfdern: Grünewald, 2006).

19. I am referring to P. Ulrich, *Transformation der ökonomischen Vernunft.Fortschrittsperspektiven der modernen Industriegesellschaft* (Bern: Haupt, 1993). On donation in phenomenology, see, particularly, the trilogy of J. L. Marion, *Réduction et donation* (Paris: PUF, 1989); *Étant donné* (Paris: PUF, 1997); *De surcroît* (Paris: PUF, 2001).

20. See LS 149, note 117, quoting my article "La irrupción del pobre y la lógica de la gratuidad," in *Irrupción del pobre y quehacer filosófico. Hacia una nueva racionalidad,* ed. J. C. Scannone and M. Periné (Buenos Aires: Bonum. 1993), 213–39, esp. 225–30.

21. See P. Trigo, *La cultura del barrio* (Caracas: Universidad Católica Andrés Bello-Centro Gumilla, 2004).

22. Cf. E. A. Mance, *La revolución de las redes. La colaboración solidaria como una alternativa poscapitalista a la globalización actual* (Mexico: El Autor, 2006); D. García Delgado, "Las contradicciones culturales de los proyectos de modernización en los 80," *Le monde diplomatique* (edición latinoamericana) 4 (1989): 15–16n27, 17–18n28. See my "El comunitarianismo como alternativa viable," in L. Mendes de Almeida, et al., *El futuro de la reflexión teológica en América Latina* (Bogotá: CELAM, 1996), 185–241.

23. See Pope Francis, "Address to the Participants in the World Meeting of Popular Movements," October 28, 2014, http://www.vatican.va/content/francesco/en/speeches/2014/october/documents/papa-francesco_20141028_incontro-mondiale-movimenti-popolari.html. Regarding this meeting, see M. Czerny and P. Foglizzo, "The Strength of the Excluded: World Meeting of Popular Movements at the Vatican," http://www.thinkingfaith.org/articles/strength-excluded-world-meeting-popular-movements-vatican.

24. Pope Francis, "Address to the Participants in the World Meeting of Popular Movements."

25. Pope Francis, "Address to the Participants in the World Meeting of Popular Movements."

26. Pope Francis, "Address to the Participants in the World Meeting of Popular Movements."

27. Pope Francis, "Address to the Participants in the World Meeting of Popular Movements," October 28, 2014.

28. See Pope Francis, Speech to the Second World Meeting of Popular Movements, Santa Cruz de la Sierra, Bolivia, July 9, 2015, http://www.vatican.va/content/francesco/en/speeches/2015/july/documents/papa-francesco_20150709_bolivia-movimenti-popolari.html.

Chapter 8

1. This chapter corresponds to the second part of the article whose first part is chap. 1: "Papa Francesco e la teologia del popolo," *La Civiltà Cattolica* 3930 (March 15, 2014): 579–90.

2. In his first encyclical, *Laudato Si'*, the convergences are not so clear; however, in no. 149, note 117, he quotes one of my works located within the corresponding philosophical trend.

3. Bergoglio himself refers to his theological study for his admiration in reference that "the faithful people are infallible" in their belief, and he formulated it thus as his own reminder: "Whenever you want to know what the Church believes, go the magisterium ... but whenever you want to know how the church believes, go to the faithful people." See J. M. Bergoglio, *Meditaciones para religiosos* (Diego de Torres: San Miguel 1982; new ed., Bilbao: Mensajero, 2014), 46–47.; cf. EG 124.

4. I remember the doctoral thesis of Carlos María Galli, directed by Gera—unfortunately still unpublished in its totality—that is titled *El Pueblo de Dios y los pueblos del mundo. Catolicidad, encarnación e intercambio en la eclesiología actual* (1993). One of the chapters was published as ¨La encarnación del pueblo de Dios en la Iglesia y en la eclesiología latinoamericana," *Sedoi* 125 (1994).

5. See J. M. Bergoglio, opening address to the International Congress of Theology, "Evangelización de la cultura e inculturación del evangelio," *Stromata*

61 (1985): 161–65n3–4; the reference to Pedro Arrupe's intervention of the Synod of 1974 is found on p. 164.

6. In the Fourteenth Provincial Congregation (of the Jesuit Argentinian Province, February 18, 1974) he speaks, as provincial, of three of these criteria, without doing so explicitly from the superiority of the reality over the idea. (See the work quoted above, in note 2 of this chapter, *Meditaciones para religiosos*, 49–50.) He offers the presentation and development of the four in his conference as archbishop of Buenos Aires on the occasion of the Thirteenth Archdiocesan Day of Social Ministry (2010): "Hacia un bicentenario en justicia y solidaridad 2010–2016. Nosotros, como ciudadanos, nosotros, como pueblo," esp. in section 4. The whole document illustrates his concept of people: www.arzbaires.org.ar/inicio/homilias/homilias2010.htm#XIV_Jornada_Arquidiocesana_de_Pastoral_Social. I will develop this topic later, in chap. 11.

7. See E. Barba, *Correspondencia entre Rosas, Quiroga y López* (Buenos Aires: Hyspamérica, 1984), 94.

8. See R. Guardini, *Der Gegensatz. Versuche zu einer Philosophie des Lebendig-Konkreten* (Mainz: Grünewald, 1955).

9. Cf. G. Farrell et al., *Argentina: alternativas frente a la globalización* (Buenos Aires: San Pablo, 1999); A. Methol Ferré and A. Metalli, *El papa y el filósofo* (Buenos Aires: Biblos, 2013).

10. See the address of the pope in his meeting with CELAM (July 28, 2013) in Msgr. V. M. Fernández et al., *De la Misión Continental (Aparecida 2001) a la Misión Universal (JMJ Río 2013)* (Buenos Aires: Docencia, 2013), 287.

11. I refer to converging expressions of European phenomenologists of religion such as Bernhard Welte (see *Das Licht del Nichts. Von der Möglichkeit neuer religiösen Erfahrung* [Düsseldorf: Patmos, 1980], 54ff.) and Jean-Luc Marion (see his article "Métaphysique et Phénoménologie: une relève pour la théologie," *Bulletin de Littérature Ecclesiastique* 94 [1993]: 189–206, particularly 203). In the previous chapter, I alluded to the "dark night of culture," according to Chiara Lubich.

12. See P. Ricœur, "Le modèle du texte: l'action sensée considérée comme un texte" and "Expliquer et comprendre. Sur quelques connexions remarquables entre la théorie du texte, la théorie de l'action et la théorie de l'histoire," in *Du texte à l'action. Essais d'herméneutique II* (Paris: Seuil, 1986), 183–211 and 161–82, respectively.

Chapter 9

1. See J. M. Bergoglio, "Discurso Inaugural," in AA. VV., *Evangelización de la cultura e inculturación del Evangelio* (Buenos Aires: Guadalupe, 1986), 15–19.

2. See my "Papa Francesco e la teología del Popolo," *La Civiltà Cattolica* 3930 (March 15, 2014): 571–90, which is largely reproduced in the first chapter of this book.

3. See Jorge Seibold, *La mística popular* (Mexico, DF: Buena Prensa, 2006).

Chapter 10

1. This chapter was originally published as "Il soggetto comunitario della spiritualità e della mistica popolari," in *La Civiltà Cattolica* 3950 (January 17, 2015): 126–41.

2. See Karl Rahner, ed., *Befreiende Theologie* and *Volksreligion—Religion des Volkes* (Stuttgart: Kohlhammer, 1977 and 1979, respectively).

3. In addition to chap. 1 of this work, see my *Evangelización, cultura y teología* (Buenos Aires: Guadalupe, 1990; 2nd ed., Buenos Aires: Docencia, 2011); S. Politi, *Teología del pueblo. Una propuesta argentina a la teología latinoamericana 1967–1975* (Buenos Aires: Castañeda, 1992); M. González, *Reflexión teológica en Argentina (1962–2010). Aportes para un mapeo de sus relaciones y desafíos hacia el futuro* (Buenos Aires: Docencia, 2010).

4. In the Puebla Document, see esp. those sections. See also J. Alliende, "Diez tesis sobre pastoral popular," in *Religiosidad popular* (Salamanca: Sígueme, 1976), 119.

5. See G. Gutiérrez, *Beber en su propio pozo. En el itinerario espiritual de un pueblo* (Lima: CEP, 1983) and J. R. Seibold, *Mística popular* (Mexico, DF: Buena Prensa, 2006).

6. See G. Gutiérrez, *Beber en su propio pozo*, 101.

7. E. C. Bianchi, *Pobres en este mundo, ricos en la fe. La fe de los pobres de América latina según Rafael Tello* (Buenos Aires: Ágape, 2012), esp. chap. 3.

8. See P. Coda, "Trinidad y antropología," in A. Bertolini et al., *Antropología trinitaria para nuestros pueblos* (Bogotá: CELAM, 2014), 23–50; G. M. Zanghì, *Leggendo un Carisma. Chiara Lubich e la Cultura* (Rome: Città Nuova, 2013).

9. This concept comes from the Jesuit theologian Francisco Suárez of the Salamanca School and has been taken up once again by the theology of the people. See my "Lo social y lo político según Francisco Suárez," *Stromata* 54 (1998): 85–118.

10. In EG, he speaks of each particular church as "primary subject of evangelization."

11. As I commented in previous chapters, when Fr. Jorge Mario Bergoglio was the rector of the Faculty of Philosophy and Theology of San Miguel in Argentina, he organized an international congress of theology on these two topics (1985), whose proceedings were published in *Stromata* 61 (1985), nos. 3–4; see there his opening keynote address about the topic of the congress, on 161–65.

12. See how Carlos Galli comments on this biblical expression in the speculative part of his unpublished doctoral dissertation, directed by Lucio Gera: "El pueblo de Dios y los pueblos del mundo. Catolicidad, encarnación e intercambio en la eclesiología actual" (1993). In the New Testament, the Greek word *laós* is used to speak about the people of God and *éthnos* to refer to nations.

13. See E. C. Bianchi, *Pobres en este mundo, ricos en la fe. La fe de los pobres de América Latina según Rafael Tello* (Buenos Aires: Ágape, 2012), chap. 5, section 6, where he quotes the *Summa Theologica*, II–II, q. 2, art. 2.

14. Whelan refers to Lonergan's theology of history in chaps. 7 and 20 of B. J. F. Lonergan, *Insight: A Study on Human Understanding* (London: Longmans, Green, 1957). See G. Whelan, "*Evangelii Gaudium* come 'teologia contestuale': aiutare la Chiesa ad 'alzarsi al livello dei suoi tempi,'" in Evangelii gaudium*: il testo ci interroga. Chiavi di lettura, testimonianze e prospettive*, ed. H. M. Yañez (Rome: Gregorian and Biblical Press, 2014), 23–28.

15. See P. Ricœur, "La raison pratique," in *Rationality Today—La rationalité aujourd'hui*, ed. Théodore F. Geraets (Ottawa: University of Ottawa Press, 1979), 238ff.

16. The Greek words *noûs* and *pneûma* are both translated as "spirit," but with the two different meanings that are respectively indicated in the text.

17. See J. L. Marion, "El tercero o el relevo del dual," *Stromata* 62 (2006): 93–120. See also my "La comunión de nosotros y el tercero. Comentario a la conferencia de Jean-Luc Marion," *Stromata* 62 (2006): 121–28, and "El reconocimiento mutuo y el tercero," *Stromata* 64 (2008): 207–18.

18. See J. L. Marion, *Le phénomène érotique. Six méditations* (Paris: Grasset, 2003).

19. C. G. Fessard, *Le mystère de la société. Recherches sur le sens de l'histoire* (Namur: Culture et Vérité, 1997).

20. See J. C. Scannone, ed., *Sabiduría popular, símbolo y filosofía. Diálogo internacional en torno de una interpretación latinoamericana* (Buenos Aires: Guadalupe, 1984).

21. On the original Latin American racial and cultural mixing, see PD 408; on the present mixing of cultural visions, see my "Algunos caracteres socioculturales de la situación lationamericana actual como desafío para la teología," in C. Avenatti de Palumbo (coordinator), *Miradas desde el Bicentenarion. Imágenes, figuras y poéticas* (Buenos Aires: Educa, 2011), 111–19.

Chapter 11

1. In this chapter, I develop what was simply stated in chap. 8.

2. Particularly of his work *Der Gegensatz. Versuche zu einer Philosophie des Lebendig Konkreten* (Mainz: Grünewald, 1955).

3. In this, he coincides with the Argentinian theology of the people or of culture. See my *Le pape du peuple. Bergoglio raconté par sonconfrère théologien, jésuite et argentin. Entretiens avec Bernadette Sauvaget* (Paris: Cerf, 2015).

4. I am comparing the communicative understanding of power in Arendt with that of the Spanish Jesuit theologian Francisco Suárez in my previously cited "Lo social y lo político según Francisco Suárez. Hacia una relectura latinoamericana actual de la filosofía política de Suárez," *Stromata* 54 (1998): 85–118.

5. See M. Toso, *Il Vangelo della gioia. Implicanzi pastorali, pedagogique e progettuali per l'impegno sociale de cattolici* (Rome: Societá Cooperativa Sociale Frate Jacopa, 2014).

6. See J. M. Bergoglio, *Noi come cittadini. Noi come popolo. Verso un bicentenario in giustizia e solidarietà 2010–2016* (Vatican City: Librería Editrice Vaticana; Milan: Jaca Book, 2013), 6 and 59 (henceforth, NCNP).

7. I am alluding to X. Zubiri's *Inteligencia sentiente. Inteligencia y realidad* (Madrid: Alianza, 1980).

8. See the text of the letter in E. Barba, *Correspondencia entre Rosas, Quiroga y López* (Buenos Aires: Hyspamérica, 1984), 94. I refer to the oral testimony I received from Fr. López Rosas.

9. See J. M. Bergoglio, *Meditaciones para religiosos* (San Miguel: Diego de Torres, 1982; new ed., Bilbao: Mensajero, 2014), 49ff., where he quotes three of the principles, but that of the superiority of reality over idea.

10. This can be related to the priority of unity over conflict. See Francis, *Non fatevi rubare la Speranza* (Vatican City: Librería Editrice Vaticana; Milan: Mondadori, 2013), 142 and 144–49; it had been published in CIS (Rome) 20 (1990): nn. 63–64, 121–42. On page 161 of *Non fatevi rubare la Speranza,* he alludes to the four principles.

11. Quoted above in this chapter (NCNP).

12. See F. Rosenzweig, "Das neue Denken. Einige nachträgliche Bemerkungen sum *Stern der Eslösung*" (1925) in *Der Mensch und sein Werk. Gesammelte Schriften III: Zweistromland. Kleine Schrifen zu Glauben und Denken* (The Hague: Martinus Nijhoff, 1983).

13. In EG, note 182, he quotes R. Guardini, *Das Ende der Neuzeit,* 9th ed. (Würzburg: Werkbund 1965), 30–31. Translated as *The End of the Modern World* (Wilmington, DE: ISI Books, 2013).

14. It is interesting to pose a comparison with Paul Ricœur, who, in *Finitude et culpabilité,* vol. 1: *L'homme faillible* (Paris: Aubier, 1960), opposes infinitude (plenitude) of happiness to finitude (limitation) of character.

15. These are two of the key concepts in the Aparecida Document.

16. See R. Girard, *Des choses cachées depuis la fondation du monde* (Paris: Grasset, 1978).

17. See NCNP, 161.

18. My italics.

19. For example, in Central Europe during the twentieth century, profound conflicts of capital and labor were resolved at the national dimension, at the superior level of the social market economy, and at the social state of law.

20. This is why he gives so much importance to knowing "how to listen" to others. See Pope Francis/J. M. Bergoglio, *La misericordia è una carezza. Vivere il giubileo nella realtà di ogni giorno,* ed. Antonio Spadaro (Milan: Rizzoli, 2015), 216ff.

21. On this contribution of contemporaneous philosophies of language, see my article "Una teologia serena, fatta in ginocchio," *La Civiltà Cattolica* 3935 (June 7, 2014): 421–32.

22. See my "Justicia, conocimiento y espiritualidad," *Stromata* 70 (2014): 23–28.

23. In the context of EG 125, Francis refers explicitly to the "affective connaturality given by love," alluding with the word "connaturality" to St. Thomas, who applies it precisely to the theme of wisdom.

24. This epitaph appears in *Imago primi saeculi Societatis Iesu* (1640). The Latin original says, "Non coerceri maximo, contineri tamen a minumo, divinum est." See the brief commentary by Pascual Cebollada at www.espiritualidadignaciana.org/index.php?op.

25. *Non fatevi rubare la Speranza.* In both texts, he refers to the existential reflections of Fr. Ismael Quiles, SJ. For my part, I believe that this text, rather than Quiles's, points to the experience of Blondel, who also draws from the Ignatian Spiritual Exercises; see my "La filosofia dell'azione di Blondel e l'agire di papa Francesco," *La Civiltà Cattolica* 3969 (November 14, 2015): 216–33. In my opinion, Blondel's influence reached Bergoglio through Fessard and his dialectic of the Exercises.

26. See *Non fatevi rubare la Speranza,* 151–53.

27. See D. Fares, "Prefazione. L'arte di guardare il mondo," in the Italian translation of Guardini's *Der Gegensatz,* published in the collection "La biblioteca di papa Francesco" (work quoted above in note 2 of this chapter), V.

28. See my "Interpretación de la actual realidad histórica; semillas de future," in J. C. Scannone et al., *El surgimiento de un nuevo paradigma. Una mirada interdisciplinar desde América Latina* (Buenos Aires: CICCUS, 2015), 23–46; there (pp. 40ff.), I call Pope Francis "a new sign of the times in the flesh."